Structure: The Use Case Set

SharedClearVision
Prepare a statement of purpose for the sys... ... ... clearly describes the objectives of the system and supports the mission of the organization. Freely distribute it to everyone involved with the project.

VisibleBoundary
Establish a visible boundary between the system and its environment by enumerating both the equipment and people that interact with the system.

ClearCastOfCharacters
Identify the actors the system must interact with and the role each plays with respect to the system. Clearly describe each.

UserValuedTransactions
Identify the valuable services that the system delivers to the actors to satisfy their business purposes.

EverUnfoldingStory
Organize the use case set as a hierarchical story that can be either unfolded to get more detail or folded up to hide detail and show more context.

Structure: The Use Case

CompleteSingleGoal
Write each use case to address one complete and well-defined goal. That goal may be at any level in the **EveryUnfoldingStory**.

VerbPhraseName
Name the use case with an active verb phrase that represents the goal of the primary actor.

ScenarioPlusFragments
Write the success story line as a simple scenario without any consideration for possible failures. Below it, place story fragments that show what alternatives may occur.

ExhaustiveAlternatives
Capture all alternatives and failures that must be handled in the use case.

Adornments
Create additional fields in the use case template that are outside the scenario text, to hold the supplementary information that is useful to associate with the use case.

PreciseAndReadable
Write the use case to be readable enough so that the stakeholders bother to read and evaluate it, and precise enough so that the developers understand what they are building.

Structure: The Scenario

DetectableConditions
Include only detectable conditions. Merge conditions that have the same net effect on the system.

LeveledSteps
Keep scenarios to three to nine steps. Ideally, the steps are all at similar levels and at a level of abstraction just below the use case goal.

Structure: The Step

ActorIntentAccomplished
Write each step to show clearly which actor is performing the action, and what the actor gets accomplished.

ForwardProgress
Eliminate or merge steps that do not advance the actor. Simplify passages that distract the reader from this progress.

TechnologyNeutral
Write each step in a technology-neutral manner.

Patterns for Effective Use Cases

The Agile Software Development Series

Alistair Cockburn and Jim Highsmith, Series Editors
For more information check out http://www.awprofessional.com/

Agile software development centers on four values identified in the Agile Alliance's Manifesto:

- Individuals and interactions over processes and tools

- Working software over comprehensive documentation

- Customer collaboration over contract negotiation

- Responding to change over following a plan

The development of Agile software requires innovation and responsiveness, based on generating and sharing knowledge within a development team and with the customer. Agile software developers draw on the strengths of customers, users, and developers, finding just enough process to balance quality and agility.

The books in **The Agile Software Development Series** focus on sharing the experiences of such Agile developers. Individual books address individual techniques (such as Use Cases), group techniques (such as collaborative decision making), and proven solutions to different problems from a variety of organizational cultures. The result is a core of Agile best practices that will enrich your experience and improve your work.

Titles in the Series:

Alistair Cockburn, *Surviving Object-Oriented Projects*, ISBN 0-201-49834-0

Alistair Cockburn, *Writing Effective Use Cases*, ISBN 0-201-70225-8

Lars Mathiassen, Jan Pries-Heje, and Ojelanki Ngwenyama, *Improving Software Organizations: From Principles to Practice*, ISBN 0-201-75820-2

Alistair Cockburn, *Agile Software Development*, ISBN 0-201-69969-9

Jim Highsmith, *Agile Software Development Ecosystems*, ISBN 0-201-76043-6

Steve Adolph, Paul Bramble, Alistair Cockburn, and Andy Pols, *Patterns for Effective Use Cases*, ISBN 0-201-72184-8

Patterns for Effective Use Cases

Steve Adolph and Paul Bramble

With Contributions by Alistair Cockburn and Andy Pols

✦✦ Addison-Wesley

Boston • San Francisco • New York • Toronto • Montreal
London • Munich • Paris • Madrid
Capetown • Sydney • Tokyo • Singapore • Mexico City

The publisher offers discounts on this book when ordered in quantity for bulk purchases and special sales. For more information, please contact:

U.S. Corporate and Government Sales
(800) 382-3419
corpsales@pearsontechgroup.com

For sales outside of the U.S., please contact:

International Sales
(317) 581-3793
international@pearsontechgroup.com

Visit Addison-Wesley on the Web: www.awprofessional.com

Library of Congress Cataloging-in-Publication Data

Patterns for effective use cases / Steve Adolph . . . [et al.].
    p. cm.
Includes bibliographical references and index.
ISBN 0-201-72184-8
   1. Software patterns. 2. Application software—Development. 3. Use cases (Systems engineering) I. Adolph, U.S.

QA76.76.P37 P38 2003
005.1—dc21   2002074419

ISBN 0-201-72184-8
Text printed on recycled paper
1 2 3 4 5 6 7 8 9 10—CRS—0605040302
First printing, August 2002

Photo credits appear on page 219.

To my best friend and wife Fariba. For all your support and patience, thank you.

—Steve

To Christine, Elizabeth, Michael, and Rebecca, for all your love and support, and to Mom and Dad for teaching me many things, including how to write.

—Paul

To all the people at the original use case patterns workshop for generating ideas, and to Fariba, Deanna, and Christine for graciously hosting our mini-PLUC workshops.

—Alistair

To Steve, Paul, and Alistair for their patience.

—Andy

Contents

Foreword by Craig Larman   *xiii*
Preface   *xv*
Acknowledgments   *xxi*

Chapter 1   *What Is a Quality Use Case?*   **1**

1.1 Why Use Cases at All?. *1*
1.2 What's So Hard about Telling Good Stories? *2*
1.3 Why a Use Case Pattern Language? *5*
1.4 What Are Patterns? *6*
1.5 How Should I Use This Pattern Language? *9*
1.6 What Is the Use Case Pattern Form? *10*
      Stepping through a Sample Pattern. *11*
1.7 Organization of the Pattern Language. *19*
      Development Patterns. *19*
      Structural Patterns. *21*
1.8 Supplement: A Brief Tutorial on Writing Use Cases. *23*

Chapter 2   *The Team*   **29**

2.1 Team Organizational Issues. *30*
2.2 SmallWritingTeam *31*
      Examples *33*

2.3 ParticipatingAudience *35*
    Examples *37*
2.4 BalancedTeam *39*
    Examples *41*
2.5 Trade-offs and Collaborations *43*

Chapter 3   *The Process*   **45**

3.1 BreadthBeforeDepth *48*
    Examples *51*
    BreadthBeforeDepth and UML, by Dan Rawsthorne *51*
3.2 SpiralDevelopment *52*
    Examples *54*
    SpiralDevelopment and UML Models, by Dan Rawsthorne *57*
3.3 MultipleForms *58*
    Examples *60*
3.4 TwoTierReview *64*
    Examples *66*
3.5 QuittingTime *68*
    Examples *71*
3.6 WritersLicense *73*
    Examples *75*
3.7 Trade-offs and Collaborations *75*

Chapter 4   *The Use Case Set*   **77**

4.1 SharedClearVision *80*
    Examples *82*
4.2 VisibleBoundary *86*
    Examples *88*
    VisibleBoundary and UML Models, by Dan Rawsthorne *89*
4.3 ClearCastOfCharacters *90*
    Examples *92*
4.4 UserValuedTransactions *95*
    Examples *98*
4.5 EverUnfoldingStory *102*
    Examples *104*
    EverUnfoldingStory and UML Models, by Dan Rawsthorne *111*
4.6 Trade-offs and Collaborations *113*

Chapter 5   *The Use Case*   **115**

5.1 CompleteSingleGoal 118
    Examples *121*
5.2 VerbPhraseName. **122**
    Examples *123*
5.3 ScenarioPlusFragments **125**
    Examples *128*
5.4 ExhaustiveAlternatives **129**
    Examples *131*
5.5 Adornments. **133**
    Examples *135*
5.6 PreciseAndReadable . . . . , , , , , , , ...**138**
    Examples . . . . , ... *140*
5.7 Trade-offs and Collaborations **142**

Chapter 6   *Scenarios and Steps*   **145**

6.1 DetectableConditions **148**
    Examples *150*
6.2 LeveledSteps **153**
    Examples *154*
6.3 ActorIntentAccomplished **158**
    Examples *159*
6.4 ForwardProgress **162**
    Examples *163*
6.5 TechnologyNeutral **167**
    Examples *169*
6.6 Trade-offs and Collaborations **171**

Chapter 7   *Use Case Relationships*   **173**

7.1 CommonSubBehavior **176**
    Examples *178*
    CommonSubBehavior and UML, by Dan Rawsthorne *180*
7.2 InterruptsAsExtensions **182**
    Examples *184*
    InterruptsAsExtensions and UML, by Dan Rawsthorne *186*
    Extensions and UML Extension Points *187*

7.3 PromotedAlternative *190*
　　Examples 191
　　PromotedAlternative and UML, by Dan Rawsthorne. 195
7.4 Trade-offs and Collaborations. *196*
7.5 CapturedAbstraction—A Pattern for Applying UML Generalization,
　　by Dan Rawsthorne *198*
　　Examples 199
　　CapturedAbstraction and UML 200

Chapter 8 *Editing Existing Use Cases* **201**

8.1 RedistributeTheWealth *204*
　　Examples 206
8.2 MergeDroplets *209*
　　Examples 211
8.3 CleanHouse *213*
　　Examples 215
8.4 Trade-offs and Collaborations. *215*

References   *217*
Photo Credits   *219*
Index   *223*

Foreword

Since 1994, the Standish Group has published annual "Chaos" reports on project failure and success factors, analyzing tens of thousands of projects. In the failure column, over 30 percent of the pain factors were strongly related to requirements issues. And the 2000 National Software Quality Experiment (run by the U.S. Department of Defense) identified that the highest factor in defects, 41 percent, was related to lack of definition and traceability regarding requirements. In the "Chaos TEN" list of critical success factors identified by the Chaos studies, *high user involvement* and *clear basic requirements* are two of the key ingredients.

Clearly, doing a better job with requirements is needed. But—and this is a common trap—the classic "waterfall" or sequential life-cycle advice of attempting to specify fully and stabilize the requirements in the first phase of a project is not usually the answer. The evidence: Research into the high degree of requirements change on software projects (upwards of 50 percent change) and the high level of project challenge and failure associated with attempts to "nail the requirements" in step one. Research now shows that part of the answer is adopting an iterative life cycle, in which the requirements are incrementally and adaptively defined and refined, in parallel with short time-boxed implementation iterations. The iterations drive requirements clarification through quick feedback and adaptation cycles, based on building key parts of the system quickly, before all the requirements are "defined."

Yet even more can be done to improve requirements definition and increase user involvement. Part of that is to use a language of requirements that appeals to the average participant, that emphasizes fulfilling the real goals of the user, and that pulls related requirements together, describing them in a cohesive context. This is the language of *use cases,* first described by Dr. Ivar Jacobson in 1986.

Although use cases are popular, they have also acquired the appellation "abuse cases" by some methodology wonks, because of the myriad examples of their poor creation and misuse. Therefore, I am delighted to see learning aids that help us write quality use cases, such as the influential *Writing Effective Use Cases* (Cockburn 2001) and now this excellent—and complementary to Cockburn—text on use case guidelines and patterns by Steve Adolph and Paul Bramble. The pattern form is an excellent mechanism to learn and share best practices, and we will all benefit from studying and applying their advice. In the early 1990s, I was sitting in my office at a college in Vancouver, British Columbia, when in walked Steve, to share the room. We immediately struck up a friendship. I was impressed by his passion for building—and the methods of building—excellent software. I first met Paul in the mid-1990s when I was serving at his company in Phoenix, Arizona, and shared his interest in patterns as a vehicle to capture and educate on best practices. Knowing their mutual interests, I suggested they connect at OOPSLA 98 in Vancouver, which they did. It's great to see skilled colleagues, who have practiced, thought, and taught long and hard on a subject, share their insights so that we can all benefit.

—Craig Larman
Dallas, Texas
May 2002
www.craiglarman.com

Preface

Use cases are popular for modeling, yet people often struggle when writing them. They understand the basic concepts of use cases, but find that actually writing useful ones turns out to be harder than they expect. One factor contributing to this difficulty is that we lack objective criteria to help judge the quality of use cases. Many people find it difficult to articulate the characteristics of an effective use case.

This book examines the problems people encounter while writing use cases. It describes simple, elegant, and proven solutions to the specific problems of writing use cases on real projects. We have identified approximately three dozen patterns that professionals can use to evaluate their use cases. We have based these patterns on the observable signs of quality that successful projects tend to exhibit. Our goals are to provide a vocabulary for discussing and sharing these properties with other people, to offer advice for writing and organizing use cases effectively, and to give some "diagnostics" for evaluating use cases. We want these patterns to become second nature. Our hope is to find people saying, "Do we have a **SharedClearVision**?" (p. 80) or "Does this use case have a **CompleteSingleGoal**?" (p. 118) when discussing their use cases.

Audience

This book is intended for anyone who deals with use cases and wishes to learn more about them. It assumes that you have a working knowledge of use cases, and have some experience writing them. It is the follow-up to Alistair Cockburn's *Writing Effective Use Cases*. If you are unfamiliar or inexperienced with use cases, then we recommend that you read Alistair's book first.

Use cases are helpful for designing business processes, whether based on software or not. We do not intend for this book to be yet another software development book, written in "geek-speak" that is indiscernible to all but the most technically gifted. Yet, we understand that use cases are predominantly a software development tool, and we, being software developers, cannot help but focus on this area. We hope that this book helps all the participants of a project understand the software development community; we have tried to illustrate this topic in a usable manner for all who work with use cases.

Organization

This book is organized as a catalog of approximately three dozen patterns offering criteria for evaluating the quality of use cases. Each pattern describes a specific guideline or "sign of quality" that you can use to judge the caliber of a use case in a particular area. Because each organization has its own culture and its own way of doing things, use cases that work well for one organization may completely miss the mark in another. Patterns document generalized solutions and as such provide a simple, yet effective, mechanism for describing the characteristics of quality use cases. Patterns can transcend organizational differences, allowing people to tailor the solution to their specific needs.

We document our patterns using the style of Christopher Alexander, in which we define the problem, the context in which it occurs, and a solution. We find this format to be very readable, and it is more appropriate for our topic and a diverse audience. Pattern names appear in bold type. For example, **ActorIntentAccomplished** (p. 158) and **EverUnfoldingStory** (p. 102) are both patterns described in this book. We include the page number in parentheses after the pattern name to help you locate its description.

The patterns are organized into categories. For example, Chapter 2 describes organizational patterns, Chapter 3 describes process patterns, and Chapter 4 describes the use case set patterns.

Each pattern has one or more examples demonstrating either the benefit of implementing the solution recommended by the pattern or the consequences of what happens when you don't. We based as many of these examples on live projects as we could; however, we sanitized them, to protect the companies and people involved (quite rightly), and we streamlined them for readability. Moreover, we simplified many of them because real use cases are often long and can be quite complicated, especially the ones demonstrating bad practices. We hope that you find these examples useful. You may apply some of our other patterns to these samples, and find ways to improve them.

We illustrate our patterns with a story that runs throughout the book, following a group of developers from a national travel agency as they write some use cases for their new product, the "Wings Over the World" travel reservation system. This story portrays an environment in which many of the problems described in the book can occur and therefore provides a background for discussing the patterns. The story also helps us give examples that succinctly demonstrate a pattern that may be difficult or impossible to illustrate with real examples. While the Wings Over the World examples may be contrived, they are based on our experiences, and many of the people, conversations, examples, and even the red-eye flight are composites of real events, real conversations, and real use cases.

How to Use This Book

Reading a pattern catalog cover to cover is usually not most people's idea of fun. Your first reading of this book can be either to familiarize yourself with the patterns or to serve as a tutorial for what makes a quality use case. Either way, read Chapter 1 first, which gives you the background for use cases, patterns, and the pattern categories.

If your objective is just to become familiar with the patterns, simply read the introduction of each subsequent chapter, and then read the problem, context, and solution of each pattern. If you find a pattern interesting, or particularly germane to your specific situation, then read it more closely. Don't feel that you need to understand fully one pattern before you examine another. Once you have this knowledge, you can use the book as a reference. Store it on your shelf within easy reach, so that you can look up a pattern later when you are having a problem writing a use case, or when you are reading one and something just looks wrong.

This book can also be used as a tutorial to understand the signs of quality for a well-written use case. After reading Chapter 1, skim through each chapter and read the Wings Over the World example to get a feel for the environment that gives rise to many of the problems addressed by these patterns. Read the chapter introduction to understand the pattern category and get a brief overview of each of the patterns in that chapter. Skim the patterns themselves, read the problem statement, and the solution. Take a look at the examples and make sure you understand how the pattern improves the quality of the use case or the process to create the use case.

A great approach to learning these patterns is to hold "brown-bag" or "lunch-and-learn" sessions, which many people use to learn patterns. To do this, have someone present one or two patterns at a lunchtime seminar every week. Next, discuss the pattern, its intention, and its trade-offs. Then look at the examples, and talk about how they compare with your organization's use cases.

What about UML?

The Unified Modeling Language (UML) is the software industry's latest attempt to sign a modeling language nonproliferation treaty with itself. When most people think of use cases and UML they simply think of diagramming tools. Others think of UML as defining semantics for constructs such as includes or extends. Some are UML enthusiasts, and others are not. One thing on which we all agree is that rigidly following UML semantics does not guarantee quality use cases. Many people who have never even heard of UML write great use cases. However, UML is an important influence on use cases and therefore we have included guidelines for the effective use of UML with the relevant patterns.

Why Don't We Use a Single Use Case Template for the Examples?

With the exception of the Wings Over the World use cases, most of the use cases presented throughout this book are sanitized versions of real production use cases. Many of these use cases appear different because they are the work of different writers. We chose not to create a uniform template to present all the examples because we did not want to advocate a specific use case template. There are enough around now, and just as we did not want to imply there is only one true way to write a use case, we also did not want to imply there is only one true use case template.

We chose to use different styles for our use case diagrams for the same reason, employing a variety of different drawing and Computed-Aided Software Engineering (CASE) tools to generate them.

The Agile Software Development Series

This book is one in a collection of books, the Agile Software Development Series, that highlights light, human-powered software development techniques. Some books discuss a single technique, some a single role on the project, and some discuss team collaboration issues.

The book series is based on two common principles:

1. Different projects have different needs. Systems have different characteristics and are built by teams of various sizes, containing people having diverse values and priorities. It cannot be possible to describe the one, best way of producing software.
2. Focusing on skills, communication, and community allows the project to be more effective and more agile than focusing on processes and plans.

Accordingly, the book series runs along three main tracks:

1. How one person can improve his or her effectiveness on projects through particular techniques;
2. How a group of people can improve their combined effectiveness through various group techniques; and
3. How particular examples of successful methodologies can serve as models for your own adaptations.

- *Agile Software Development* elaborates the ideas of software development as a cooperative game, of methodology as coordination of culture, and of methodology families. It separates the different aspects of methodologies: techniques from activities, work products and standards.

- *Agile Software Development Ecosystems* discusses problems in software development, principles that unite in common across the diverse experts in the Agile Alliance, a group of people who wrote the *Manifesto for Agile Software Development* (www.manifesto.com), and common agile practices.

- *Writing Effective Use Cases* is a technique guide, describing the nuts and bolts of use case writing. Although you can use the techniques on almost any project, the templates and writing standards must be selected according to the needs of each individual project.

- *Patterns for Effective Use Cases* is a handbook for writing high-quality use cases, providing a set of patterns for gauging the quality of use cases, and offering suggestions for improvement when your use cases fail to meet them. You can apply the concepts from this follow-up to *Writing Effective Use Cases* to all types of use cases, regardless of your organization's style.

- Among the other books in the series, *Improving Software Organizations* and *Surviving Object-Oriented Projects* (SOOP) are in the line of group techniques, and *Crystal Clear* (CC) is in the line of sample methodologies.

Pattern Language Heritage

Paul Bramble began researching the concept of use case patterns in the summer of 1997, after receiving numerous suggestions from his colleague Linda Rising (author of *The Pattern Handbook* [Rising 1998] and *The Pattern Almanac* [Rising 2000]). He had been defining a generic use case development process for their company when he realized that use cases are highly dependent on the personalities of the group using them. Recognizing that this research required the input of multiple people and experiences, he co-organized a workshop on use case patterns with Alistair Cockburn at OOPSLA 98 in Vancouver, British Columbia. Eleven participants attended the workshop, and four of them (Paul, Alistair, Andy Pols, and Steve Adolph) agreed to continue the research. It took them well over two years to define their use case pattern language, requiring several meetings in the western United States and Canada, as well as two ChiliPLoP conferences to workshop several of their patterns.

We know that there are many more potential patterns out there that people use every day—whether they are conscious of it or not—to create high quality use cases. We sincerely hope this book helps to inspire debate and motivate others to capture these patterns.

Acknowledgments

This book has been a long time in the making. It has seen many rewrites and has been influenced by many people. We would like to thank our families, who had to put up with our zany brainstorming and arm-wrestling writing sessions, especially our wives Fariba and Christine, who proofread and edited this text countless times. Also, Elizabeth, Michael, and Rebecca for being patient with their daddy as he wrote on "their" computer.

Alistair Cockburn, Andy Pols, Steve, and Paul jointly put the structure of the pattern language in place in a series of work sessions we loosely termed Bear Plop, Horse Plop, and Bird Plop. Through those sessions, we identified the overall pattern language structure and the initial names, forces, and resolutions for the patterns. Alistair and Andy provided important feedback about the pattern language, as the two of us continued to develop the material for this book.

We are indebted to Linda Rising, who not only reviewed the manuscript, but also offered invaluable help on structuring our patterns and was a great source of encouragement. Linda planted the original seeds for this book, and served as unofficial pattern consultant.

The genesis of this work was the Use Case Pattern Workshop at OOPSLA 98. Our thanks to co-leader Greg Gibson and those who contributed to the founding of this research: John Artim, Ted Lefkovitz, Dr. Ben Lieberman, Susan Lilly, Rick Ratliff, Dan Rawsthorne, and Dr. Liping Zhao. The group did an excellent job identifying the various forces involved in writing and using use cases. We were particularly influenced by Rick's Sans GUI and Breadth First patterns, even though we didn't use these patterns directly in this book.

Early versions of this pattern language were workshopped at ChiliPLoP, and we thank Neil Harrison and David Delano for shepherding us during this part of its development. Neil contributed his Liberating Form pattern, which while not used in this language certainly helped us to understand clearly the benefit of use cases. Kim Lee also made contributions during the ChiliPLoP workshop, and we are indebted to her for her elegant Borodin Quartet pattern. While the pattern is not part of our language, it helped influence our development patterns. We also want to thank Jim Coplien for his encouragement and guidance.

A special thanks goes to Dan Rawsthorne, who was part of the original OOPSLA sessions and who joined us at the ChiliPLoP sessions. He contributed the sections explaining the application of the patterns to UML, helping us wrap up a lot of loose ends.

Reviewers play an important role in the development of any book, and we had good ones: Linda Rising, Dan Rawsthorne, Pete McBreen, Rusty Walters, and Don Olson. Thanks for the good reviews and the constructive advice!

We are also indebted to the following people:

◆ Craig Larman, for introducing Steve Adolph and Paul Bramble to each other.

◆ Joshua Kerievsky, for turning a two-hour flight delay into a wonderful opportunity to understand the Alexandrian pattern form.

◆ David Roberts, for suggesting a Graduate Alternatives pattern which became our **PromotedAlternative** (p. 190) pattern.

◆ Colleagues and friends Gary Wong and Arsham (Ash) Hamidi, who took time to review early drafts.

◆ The team at Addison-Wesley for their help and patience.

◆ My colleagues at Emperative for their support and their much-appreciated help with proofreading.

◆ Lastly, the people who have influenced our careers, including Dr. Donald Miller and Terry Packer, who helped us believe in ourselves, provided a fertile learning environment, and gave us the freedom to follow our passion.

Steve, Andy, Alistair, and Paul in Colorado.

Chapter 1

What Is a Quality Use Case?

> *The hardest single part of building a software system is deciding precisely what to build.*
> —Frederick Brooks, "No Silver Bullet: Essence and Accidents
>   of Software Engineering"

1.1 Why Use Cases at All?

"I understand the requirements, but what does it actually do?" is a question often asked by systems analysts, business analysts, product managers, and programmers when confronted by two hundred pages of traditional IEEE-standard-style "The system shall . . ." functional requirements. After reading these convoluted documents, many of us have often gone back to the customers and pleaded, "What do you want this system to do? Tell me a story about how you are going to use this system."

People like stories, and from one point of view, use cases are simply stories about how people (or other things) use a system to perform some task. In this sense, use cases are nothing new; we have always had ways of telling stories about systems. We have used everything from flowcharts to message traces, to storyboards, to just plain prose. So what are the advantages of use cases?

- ◆ First, use cases give us a semiformal framework for structuring the stories. Ivar Jacobson gave us the concepts of actors and use cases and rules for how actors and use cases communicate. It wasn't enough just to tell a story. The story had to have a purpose or, in Jacobson's words, "yield a result of measurable value to an individual actor of the system" (Jacobson 1995, p. 105).

Just as excessive structure and formality can make requirements unusable, so can the complete lack of structure. If everyone is free to tell stories about the system in any manner they choose, how can you determine if the requirements are correct? How do you find redundant stories? How do you spot holes in the stories? Some structure is necessary; otherwise, people's creativity will work at cross-purposes.

It is this semiformal structuring that liberates the creativity of people. Rigid formal requirement models can be stifling, and are unusable by most people because they have not been expertly trained in the appropriate modeling technique. This semiformal structuring makes it relatively easy for the end user of a system to read the document with very little training. End users may then actually read the requirements document, and be better able to substantiate the system proposal while it is still in the writing stage.

♦ Second, use cases describe the system requirements for the error situations, in every use case and at every level of description. Since much or most of the system complexity lies in handling error situations, describing such requirements means that the associated difficulties are detected and discussed early, rather than late, in the development cycle.

♦ Third, although use cases are essentially a functional decomposition technique, they have become a popular element of object-oriented software development. Several people, including Jacobson (1992) and Larman (2002) describe methodologies for realizing the objects necessary to implement the behavior described by the use case. One can write a set of use cases describing the system's functional behavior and then use these techniques to design the objects necessary to implement that behavior.

♦ Finally, use cases provide good scaffolding on which to hang other project information. The project manager can build estimates and release schedules around them. Data and business rule specifiers can associate their requirements to the use cases in which they are needed. User interface designers can design and link their designs to the relevant use cases. Testers can construct test scenarios from the success and failure conditions described in the use cases. Many modern software development processes are built around use cases.

1.2 What's So Hard about Telling Good Stories?

Writing use cases was supposed to be easy. One reason for their popularity is that a well-written use case is relatively easy to read. People may suppose that easy-to-read also means easy-to-write, but that is a mistake. It can be terribly hard to write easy-to-read stories. Use cases are stories, prose essays, and so bring along all the associated difficulties of story writing in general. As Rusty Walters remarked in *Writing Effective Use Cases* (Cockburn 2001, p. 205), "I did not understand this as the fundamental problem for [the first] four years."

The following example illustrates some very common mistakes encountered by teachers of use case writing. This use case fragment describes the actions a student performs when registering for her courses. It is not a horrible use case—we have all written some like this—but it is a long way from being a good use case.

Use Case 1.1   Use Case Horror: Example of a Poorly Written Use Case

Register for Course (Main Scenario, Poorly Written Version)

1   Display a blank schedule.
2.   Display a list of all classes in the following way: The left window lists all the courses in the system in alphabetical order. The lower window displays the times the highlighted course is available. The third window shows all the courses currently in the schedule.
3.   Do
4.   Student clicks on a course.
5.   Update the lower window to show the times the course is available.
6.   Student clicks on a course time and then clicks on the "Add Course" button.
7.   Check if the Student has the necessary prerequisites and that the course offering is open.
8.   If the course is open and the Student has the necessary prerequisites, add the Student to the course. Display the updated schedule showing the new course. If no, put up a message, "You are missing the prerequisites. Choose another course."
9.   Mark the course offering as "enrolled" in the schedule.
10.   End do when the Student clicks on "Save Schedule."
11.   Save the schedule and return to the main selection screen.

The problems with this fragment include:

◆ *Too much user interface detail.* In many poorly written use cases, we often see references to mouse clicks, list boxes, and window design. In the normal course of events, the use case is written as a set of *requirements* that the system must satisfy. The user interface design details are not usually requirements; they are usually design choices. Those design choices are made later, after the use cases have been written and reviewed. The initial design choices are often changed during development, still satisfying the overall requirements. Use case experts universally warn against including the user interface design inside use cases. Doing so is costly because it adds writing and reviewing time, and it makes the requirements document longer—and more likely not to be read carefully. Furthermore, it makes the requirements set "brittle," in the sense that small design decisions will invalidate or force an expensive revision of the requirements document. This is the single most critical mistake to avoid. The **Adornments** (p. 133) and **TechnologyNeutral** (p. 167) patterns describe how to steer clear of excessive detail.

♦ *Too many use cases at low goal levels.* Computer programmers, who often are "stuck" with the job of writing the requirements document, have a tendency to produce numerous low-level use cases on the level of "Authorize user". These writers are very interested in describing individual system functions and features, largely because those are the functions they will have to implement. However, requirements documents written at such a level are very long, and difficult for end users to read. These documents do not show well what the system will contribute to the lives of the end consumers of the system. The **CompleteSingleGoal** (p. 118) pattern describes how properly to structure use cases to avoid this problem.

♦ *Using a use case for non-behavioral information.* Sometimes writers are told, "Use cases are great. Write everything in use cases." But a use case is not good for everything; it is really only good for describing behavior. Everything that the system must *do* should really go into a use case, but everything else should really go into some other format. Some writers will produce immensely detailed use cases describing the completion of a user interface form, with each field in the form getting one or two lines of description. A much better approach is to create an **Adornment** by simply attaching the form to the back of the use case and writing in the appropriate step: "User provides the information on form XYZ (see attachment)." This shortens both the writing and the reading, without sacrificing detail. Performance requirements, complex business rules, data structures, and product line descriptions are all valuable, but better captured with other requirements tools such as tables, formulas, or state machines—or placed in another section of the requirements document.

♦ *Too long.* The above three common errors produce use cases that are long and hard to read. A well-written use case is short, usually only three to nine steps long. (Oddly, many people feel embarrassed with such a short start to their use case. They should not fear, however, as there are usually more than enough extension conditions to make the use case worth writing and reading.) The pattern **LeveledSteps** (p. 153) describes how to write balanced, reasonably sized use cases.

♦ *Not a complete goal accomplishment.* While shorter is better, some use case writers do not capture the complete behavior for goal accomplishment, but only describe a fragment of the necessary behavior. This causes trouble during implementation, since the use cases do not connect to each other, and the programmers have to guess how to sew them together. A related mistake is not considering all the possible failure conditions or alternative behaviors. Once again, the programmers will discover these in their programming, and will either have to guess at what to program or bring the project to a halt while someone investigates what the system should do. The patterns **CompleteSingleGoal** (p. 118) and **ExhaustiveAlternatives** (p. 129) provide advice on associating goals with use cases and including all necessary failure conditions.

◆ *Sentence fragments.* A relatively minor, but still noticeable, mistake is writing in sentence fragments, as done in the poorly written example of Use Case 1a. One could argue that such minor writing errors don't matter, but on all but the smallest projects there are many use case writers and readers. Omitting the actors' names in the action steps easily causes confusion over the course of the project, a damage far greater than the cost of simply remembering to write full sentences at the beginning. The pattern **ActorIntentAccomplished** (p. 158) describes how to write scenarios with clear, unambiguous steps.

1.3 Why a Use Case Pattern Language?

There are no absolute criteria we can use to differentiate between good and poor quality use cases. Authors and teachers have always had a difficult time saying *why* the good ones were good and what was wrong with the bad ones. To see the difference between good and bad, and the difficulty in identifying what makes the difference, try your hand at comparing this fragment against the poorly written example in Use Case 1.1.

Use Case 1.2   Main Scenario for a Well-Written Use Case

Register for Course
1. Student requests a new schedule.
2. The system prepares a blank schedule form and pulls in a list of open and available courses from the Course Catalog System.
3. Student selects primary and alternate courses from the available offerings.
4. For each course, the system verifies that the Student has the necessary prerequisites and adds the Student to the course, marking the Student as "enrolled" in that course in the schedule.
5. When the Student indicates the schedule is complete, the system saves the schedule.

Notice that the well-written use case is much shorter, contains fewer details, and is easier to read than the first one. Yet we cannot simply say, "Write concise, less detailed use cases that are easy to read." Some problems are long and incredibly complex, involving many details, and as a result yield long, detailed, and somewhat difficult to read use cases, no matter how well written.

To make matters worse, each development organization has its own culture, its own people, and its own way of doing things. What works for one organization may not work for another. This disparity makes it impossible to define a "one-size-fits-all" process for creating high-quality use cases.

We want to capture guidelines that can help us write good use cases and evaluate existing ones. We must find some way to describe these terms so that they are meaningful in different organizations and development cultures.

To counter the common problems in writing use cases and push the result toward well-written use cases, we have constructed and cataloged in this handbook a small set of patterns that gives us a vocabulary for describing the characteristics of a good-quality use case. Put another way, these are characteristics that signify that quality is present in the writing. Some of these patterns apply to a single sentence in the use case, some apply to a single scenario, and some apply to the set of extensions or to the use case itself. More patterns are needed to discuss multiple use cases and more still to discuss the entire use case set, even the place of a use case in the requirements document. We find that simply describing the use case itself is insufficient, and discussions quickly move from the use cases themselves to the teams writing them and the processes they use for constructing and reviewing the use cases.

The patterns in this language describe the signs of quality about the use cases and the writing process. These signs of quality serve several purposes. They provide a vocabulary for writing use cases, giving people the words they need to express what they want to see, or change, in a set of use cases. While we do not expect these patterns to help the starting writer produce excellent use cases, they can be invaluable for the more experienced writer, offering time-tested advice for improving their use cases. These patterns are best considered as a diagnostic tool, and should be of great use in reviewing the use case drafts to improve their quality. The absence of any sign indicates that something important is missing, because a good set of use cases exhibits all of these patterns.

1.4 What Are Patterns?

We based our pattern style on Christopher Alexander's work (1977, 1979) on *pattern languages*. His patterns capture just the information we need, and in a highly readable form. Each pattern indicates *what is present in a good example,* what sorts of thoughts or trade-offs push the writer toward and away from a good result, our recommendation for dealing with them, and examples of these ideas in action.

Alexander, a building architect, recognized common structures in cities, communities, and buildings that he considered to be "alive." His research resulted in the creation of what he called a language, one he believed would enable people to design almost any kind of building and community, a language based on the way that people resolved those forces that show up over and over again, in building situations all over the world. He called these recurring themes *patterns.*

Alexander wrote: "Each pattern describes a problem which occurs over and over again in our environment, and then describes the core of the solution to that problem in such a way that you could use this solution a million times over without doing it the same way twice" (Alexander 1977, p. x). Alexander intended that patterns answer questions such as "Where should I place a terrace?" "How should I design the front entrance?" or even "How should I organize my community?"

Alexander wrote a five-hundred-page book to describe what a pattern is. The one-sentence version might be this: "A pattern is a three-part rule that expresses a certain relationship between a certain context, a problem, and a solution" (Alexander 1979, p. 247). Like a rule, a pattern has a problem, and then proposes a solution to the problem. The context helps us understand when the solution to the problem is appropriate.

Alexander's patterns never really caught on in the architectural community, but they became the rage in the software development community around 1995, with the publication of the book *Design Patterns: Elements of Reusable Object Oriented Software* (Gamma et al. 1995). This book used patterns to capture good solutions to common problems programmers experienced when designing software. Of course, like any worthwhile idea in technology, shortly thereafter, pattern-hype grew out of control, propelling patterns as the next magic bullet for all software development.

It is time to get patterns back to their appropriate place: as signs of quality, and as strategies. When used as a sign of quality, a pattern expresses what is present in a well-formed example (of whatever is being discussed). For instance, when lighting a room, Alexander's *Light on Two Sides of Every Room* states that people are instinctively drawn to rooms that have natural lighting on two or more walls (Alexander 1977). An example in this book, for use cases, is **VerbPhraseName** (p. 122), where the name of a use case is a verb phrase describing the intention of the primary actor. When used to capture a strategy, a pattern names a way to deal with conflicting pressures. An example in software design from *Design Patterns* is *Visitor,* which describes how to traverse complex data structures without changing the class of the object being traversed (Gamma 1995). An example from software project management is Cockburn's

Gold Rush: When you don't have time to capture requirements completely and then design the program carefully, do them in parallel, carefully monitoring communication and rework issues (Cockburn 1998).

Patterns as signs of quality are aids for diagnosing, revising, and improving a group's work. Patterns as strategies help people thread their way through complex situations. These two contributions of the pattern form should not be lost amid the hype over the term.

Although we like the form of Alexander's pattern writing, it is our experience that people can become confused by the word *pattern*. That word often brings to the listener's mind repeating visual designs on ties, carpets, and wallpaper. Even today, some people who are familiar with the concept of software patterns think of them as plug-and-play solutions. They fail to realize that a pattern is often part of a larger, more comprehensive language. In neither case do readers get a clear indication of what they might encounter in the book, nor do they get the connection to quality that we are after.

Despite these reservations about the word *patterns,* we chose to write our handbook using the pattern form rather than as simple heuristics or rules. A guideline or rule says only "do this," without exploring the alternatives and their ramifications, while the pattern form supports that discussion. Equally important, a pattern introduces phrases in a vocabulary, phrases that allow people to shorten long discussions. Often, that phrase is all that is left of the pattern in a person's mind—which is quite fine. People who have read *Design Patterns* simply say "Visitor" and understand the trade-offs and issues the pattern entails. We hope the readers of this book will be able to simply say, **"CompleteSingleGoal"** (p. 118), **"ExhaustiveAlternatives"** (p. 129), or **"TwoTierReview"** (p. 64) and similarly understand the corrections and discussions involved.

There is one final relationship between the entries in this handbook and Christopher Alexander's original pattern language: the individual entries do not stand alone, but lead to each other. We keep finding a remarkable similarity between Alexander's discussion of the relationship between cities, single buildings, and building components and our own discussions of sets of use cases, single use cases, and the components of use cases. We discovered, for example, that considering only the entries below the level of a single use case, we were still missing critical signs of use case quality. We needed to consider the larger level of discussion to find the missing entry (for example, this is how we identified **UserValuedTransactions** [p. 95]). While this similarity between our work and Alexander's is not at all critical to the use of this handbook, we trust that aficionados of Christopher Alexander's pattern languages will enjoy the similarities.

1.5 *How Should I Use This Pattern Language?*

Patterns can be very beneficial to a project when used correctly. However, it's not always easy to use them in the right way, especially when you don't understand them. Here are some common misconceptions about patterns.

- *Patterns offer a complete methodology in and of themselves.* Patterns are supplements that fill in the gaps of our knowledge with solutions to specific problems; they do not give us the complete picture. However, some people mistakenly believe that patterns tell them everything they need to know about a subject. For example, some instructors go so far as to base their object-oriented design courses on the book *Design Patterns,* instead of a formally defined methodology. However, these patterns offer solutions to real problems encountered in object-oriented development, and as such are more diagnostic in nature—that is, try this solution when you have that problem (Coplien 1998).

- *Using patterns guarantees success.* In his book *Patterns of Software,* Richard Gabriel (1996) recounts how Christopher Alexander discovered that several architectural projects using his pattern language failed to produce the better, "living" buildings he envisioned. Instead, the resulting buildings were no different nor better than other buildings, even though the architects believed that they were radically different. Alexander was convinced "that they failed because the geometry of the buildings was not as different from the standard modern geometry as it needed to be to generate the quality" (Gabriel 1996, p. 59). In other words, in these cases, using his patterns made little if any visible difference. He felt much of the blame lay in the process. The people controlling the process—the lenders, the zoning commissioner, and others—were not using the pattern language, yet they wielded a lot of control over the project. Gabriel goes on to claim that these findings hold for software development: "The structure of the system follows the structure of the organization that put it together, and to some extent, its quality follows the nature of the process used to produce it" (Gabriel 1996, p. 59).

- *Patterns offer new solutions to old problems.* As Linda Rising (1998, p. 10) says, "Patterns are not theoretical constructs created in an ivory tower, they are artifacts that have been discovered in more than one existing system." Patterns are essentially a documentation mechanism that captures general, tried-and-true solutions to common, recurring problems. Accordingly, patterns rarely present new ideas or leading-edge research, but rather document solutions that have proved to be effective in many different situations and environments. In fact, experienced people reading a pattern language for the first time should be struck by the feeling that they have seen some of these solutions before.

◆ *Patterns are applicable in all situations.* A pattern is a solution to a problem within a context (Coplien 1996). The key word here is context, the idea being that a pattern applies only within a well-defined area. The patterns in this book present solutions that carefully balance several competing forces within the problem space. Sometimes, however, a particular force becomes more important and takes on special meaning. For example, an organization writing use cases using sensitive company information might want to hide some details, or even actors, from their customers. Or a company describing a system that relies on several well-defined and complicated business rules that everyone involved in the project needs to understand might want to include these rules in their use cases. In this case, it might be more important for the company to publish their business rules in their use cases rather than make their use cases simple and easily understood. In both instances, these organizations need to balance the forces involved, to determine the advantages of following a specific guideline. In these situations, our recommendations are not necessarily the best, and you may need to tailor them to better fit your needs or even ignore them altogether.

So don't think of this pattern language as a complete methodology for writing use cases. Instead, treat it as a set of guidelines to help you fill in the gaps in your knowledge, evaluate the quality of your use cases, or augment your particular use case writing process. Take each of our guidelines with a grain of salt. Evaluate them, and determine if they apply to your use cases and your situation. They will apply in most instances, because they describe common techniques for everyday situations. But the world won't come to an end if you decide not to follow a particular guideline if you feel you have a good reason for avoiding it. Disasters are more likely to occur if you avoid using a guideline you should clearly follow, or try to force one to work when the situation clearly indicates otherwise.

1.6 What Is the Use Case Pattern Form?

Pattern aficionados like to refer to the template they use to write patterns as a "form." Like all standards, everyone seems to have their own, and of course we're no different. Each one of our patterns is presented using a template or form that is based on Christopher Alexander's form presented in *A Pattern Language* (Alexander 1977). This form is frequently referred to as the *Alexandrian* form.

Our form includes the following sections:

◆ The Pattern Name
◆ A Picture

- ◆ The Context
- ◆ The Problem Statement
- ◆ A Metaphoric Story
- ◆ The Forces Affecting the Problem
- ◆ The Solution
- ◆ Examples

Stepping through a Sample Pattern

The best illustration is the real thing. Consider the pattern **UserValuedTransactions** (p. 95) shown here as Figure 1.1.

UserValuedTransactions ———————————— Pattern Name

You have established a **SharedClearVision** (p. 80) of the project ——— Context
and have defined a **ClearCastOfCharacters** (p. 90) who need services
from the system.

A system is deficient if it cannot deliver services that are valuable ——— Problem
to its users and if it does not support the goals and objectives spec- Statement
ified by the system vision.

A few years ago one of the authors bumped into a colleague who
was working for a start-up firm that was building a radio advertising
distribution network. The idea was simple: Advertisers were using
couriers to distribute tapes of their ads to radio stations, but even
with overnight delivery, it could be two to three days before a new
ad was actually playing over the radio. The colleague's company had ——— Metaphoric
built a continent-wide private network to distribute advertising Story
spots to radio stations nearly instantaneously. Furthermore, with the
company's proprietary protocols and compression hardware, they
could guarantee quality of service to their clients.

It seemed like a license to print money. Offer a service that is
cheaper, faster, and more reliable than what is currently available
and the world will beat a path to your door. This was a case right out
of Marketing 101. But the market never developed. Eventually the
company succumbed to the inevitable, and it was taken over.

A while later this story was mentioned to a radio DJ at a local station. "Doesn't surprise me that they failed," he said. "Radio is a local
media. Almost no one does national campaigns."

(continued)

Figure 1.1 A sample pattern (continued)

A well-written set of use cases clearly and accurately describes the ———— **Forces**
essential actions that a system provides. This information allows customers to preview a system before it is built and determine whether
it offers the kind of services that they find valuable.

*A set of use cases should capture the fundamental value-added ser-
vices that users and stakeholders need from the system.* An organization commissions the development of a system because that
system will return some benefit. Use cases allow the organization's
project team to inspect a system before it is built, so that they can
verify that it is what they want, request changes, or decide that it
doesn't meet their needs. Use cases should describe the kinds of things
that users find valuable, so they can present the system in its best
light. A system that does not deliver needed valuable services to its
actors is deficient, can lose money, and will sully the reputation of
the development organization.

*It is relatively easy to identify low-level transactions, but it can be
difficult to identify useful services.* It is usually easier to describe the
individual routine transactions that a system may provide than it is
to discover what the user really wants to do with the system. Doing
it the easy way often leads to "CRUD" (Create, Read, Update, and
Delete). It is not unusual to see use cases with names like *Create Employee Record, Read Employee Record,* or *Delete Employee Record.*
While such use cases may be technically correct, they do not capture
what is valuable to the user. Is creating an employee record important, or does the user really want to *Hire Employee*?

*Use cases need to be relatively stable because they form "anchor
points" for the rest of the product development process.* Constant
changes to use cases can ripple through the rest of the development
process, creating havoc for the developers and significantly increasing the cost. To keep this cost low, we want to write each case at a
level high enough to insulate it from inconsequential changes. Otherwise, the writers will constantly be updating their use cases every
time someone changes some trivial detail. Worse, the readers will
have trouble understanding the use cases, because their meaning
will be constantly changing.

Readers want to see easily how the system will meet its goals (see
SharedClearVision). Just as a picture is worth a thousand words, a
use case is worth a thousand pages of system specifications. But even
pictures can be hard to understand when they are too complex or
abstract. Concise use cases that stick to the point are easier to read
than long, flowery ones.

(continued)

Figure 1.1 A sample pattern (continued)

People tend to work at a level that is either too high or too low.
People tend to use excessive detail when describing things they understand or find interesting. Conversely, they tend to gloss over details they don't understand or find boring. Use cases should be
somewhere in the middle, containing enough information to describe system behavior adequately, without describing it in great detail ("what" versus "how"). If we write them at too high a level, then
they will not be useful to the system developers, because they do not
describe the system in enough detail. However, if use cases contain
too much detail, then it is difficult for non-programmers to understand the system from their very high level. In the words of Ian Graham (1997), use cases should contain only necessary but essential
information.

Therefore:

> **Identify the valuable services that the system delivers to the** ——————— Solution
> **actors to satisfy their business purposes.**

Ideally, a set of use cases should contain all of the information
necessary to depict a system but no more. Each use case should describe some unique, essential service that is valuable to at least one
user or stakeholder.

Use the **ClearCastOfCharacters** and **SharedClearVision** to identify
those services that the system should provide. Define as many valuable services as you can for each actor in your cast of characters. Each
service must help at least one actor reach a goal. Being unable to
identify any service for an actor may indicate that the actor might
not represent a valid system user; you may need to remove that actor from the cast. Conversely, if you identify a service that doesn't
map to an actor in your cast, it may indicate that you have not identified all of the actors.

For each service that you identify, ask "What value does this service provide to the users or stakeholders?" Get rid of those services
that fail to add value to the system. You don't want to waste valuable time writing use cases or implementing code for a feature that
no one will use or cares about.

Users and stakeholders prefer to see the bottom line rather than
an itemized list of CRUD-style services, so examine each service and
determine whether each one stands by itself or is part of a larger,
more valuable service. Fold those services that cannot stand by themselves into more comprehensive ones that address one key objective,

(continued)

Figure 1.1 *A sample pattern (continued)*

and then eliminate duplicates. A client booking an airline reservation is interested in getting a good flight at a good price. The client doesn't care how many times the system updates its databases or files as the travel agent books a seat.

Write use cases around these goals. While you want to minimize the number of use cases in your collection, each use case should be a cohesive unit that describes one and only one key concept between an actor and the system, a **CompleteSingleGoal** (p. 118). Describe this collection in sufficient detail to adequately convey its purpose, yet make the use case at a high enough level so as to be insulated from simple changes.

This singleness of purpose does not prevent a use case from addressing more than one goal, as long as the use case is cohesive and achieves a unified purpose. For example, a high-level use case can reference several subordinate use cases in an **EverUnfoldingStory** (p. 102), but these use cases must work together to accomplish a common purpose.

Figure 1.1 *A sample pattern*

As this example shows, a pattern contains several sections, including the ones described next.

The Name

Each of our patterns begins with a name in bold text, usually a noun phrase that emphasizes a common characteristic of the solution being proposed. A good name sets the tone for the pattern and should evoke a picture of its solution in your mind. The name becomes part of our vocabulary for discussing the signs of quality that good use cases possess, or those that are missing from a poor use case. For example, a colleague can criticize a use case model because the services offered are too low level and therefore offer no **UserValuedTransactions** value to the users:

> JAN: Look, Bob, this is not going to help me. Use cases called Display Form and Read File don't tell me anything about what this system actually does. These are not **UserValuedTransactions**.

> BOB: So what are some **UserValuedTransactions** for our users?

> JAN: How about *Apply for Mortgage,* and *File Supporting Documentation*?

The name of our example, **UserValuedTransactions**, hopefully brings an image to mind of a service that is valuable to someone, the kind of service for which someone will say, "Yes, this helps me do my job," or "This is something for which I would pay real money."

Patterns frequently refer to other patterns by name. **UserValuedTransactions** makes several references to **SharedClearVision** (p. 80), **ClearCastOfCharacters** (p. 90), **CompleteSingleGoal** (p. 118), and **EverUnfoldingStory** (p. 102) during the course of its discussion.

A Picture

Each pattern contains a picture that is intended to provide a visual metaphor for the pattern. While not shown in this example, the visual metaphor for **UserValued-Transactions** is a line of people waiting to place a bet with a bookie. Their willingness to stand in line to pay money illustrates that they believe this action to be worthwhile. The fact that other people may feel otherwise about this service does not detract from the image because any one person is likely to value only a portion of the services that a system offers. Illustrations provide a nice touch to the pattern as well as underscore the pattern's intent. (We obtained most of our photos from the Library of Congress American Memory Collection, because we feel that they provide a pleasant, unified visual theme.)

The Context

A problem doesn't occur in a vacuum. Certain conditions must hold for a problem to be consequential. This section provides the context that makes the problem relevant. It describes the boundaries that constrain the pattern and the arena in which its solution is pertinent. It also describes how this pattern relates to other patterns in the language (Alexander 1977) and specifies which, if any, patterns are prerequisites to this one.

The context for **UserValuedTransactions** is:

You have established a **SharedClearVision** (p. 80) of the project and have defined a **ClearCastOfCharacters** (p. 90) who need services from the system.

This statement tells us that we need to know who the actors are before we can find out what they need the system to do for them. It is pointless to start describing the services that a system is supposed to provide if we don't know who needs them. Before you can identify any **UserValuedTransactions**, you must understand the project's **SharedClearVision** and know who will be using the system—that is, its **ClearCast-OfCharacters**. If you do not know these, then you cannot possibly determine which services are valuable.

The Problem Statement

Each of our patterns describes a problem that people often experience when writing use cases. Our problem statements consist of one or two sentences in bold type that describe what can happen when a use case fails to meet a certain standard. The statement also reflects the risks associated with not following that standard.

The problem statement for **UserValuedTransactions** is expressed this way:

> **A system is deficient if it cannot deliver services that are valuable to its users and it does not support the goals and objectives specified by the system vision.**

This problem statement informs you that you need to write use cases that meet the user's real needs if you wish to sell them your system. While this assertion appears to state the obvious, we shall soon see that several factors exist that cause people to write use cases that fail to address the user's need.

We could have written the problem statement as "How do you find the fundamental services a system offers?" except that expressing the problem as a question does not really convey the problem's consequences. It does not tell us why the pattern is significant, nor does it describe the consequences of ignoring it. Therefore, we write our problem statements to describe what would happen if your use case model did not follow this guideline.

The Metaphoric Story

Some patterns describe simple problems, while others address complex, hard-to-understand issues. Yet simple and complex are relative terms that depend on the reader's experience. We include either a metaphoric story or a lightweight case study to make the pattern easier to understand and to provide you with an intuitive feel for the problem and its solution. These stories usually have nothing to do with use cases, or even software development, but serve to illustrate the pattern in a practical, easy-to-understand manner. Although analogies are not normally part of the Alexandrian form, we believe they provide a good synopsis of the pattern's intent.

In the example in Figure 1.1, the metaphoric story describes a company that developed a product that very few customers found valuable. It emphasizes the problem statement by demonstrating what can happen to a product when its intended users don't find it to be particularly useful.

The Forces Affecting the Problem

This section outlines the various factors that affect the problem, and the trade-offs between them that complicate and constrain the solution. Pattern writers refer to these trade-offs as "forces" because they will push or pull you in different and sometimes competing directions as you attempt to solve a problem. In our forces section, we describe the important trade-offs that you as the use case writer must resolve for the specific situation that you are facing. Each force is written in a specific format. The first statement, written in italics, summarizes the force. The remainder of the paragraph(s) describes the force and its trade-offs in more detail.

So what are the forces that we are trying to balance when finding **UserValued-Transactions** (p. 95)? Briefly, they are:

- *A set of use cases should capture the fundamental value-added services the users and stakeholders need from the system.*
- *It is relatively easy to identify low-level transactions, but it can be difficult to identify useful services.*
- *Use cases need to be relatively stable because they form "anchor points" for the rest of the product development process.*
- *Readers want to see easily how the system will meet its goals (see* **SharedClear-Vision***).*
- *People tend to work at a level that is either too high or too low.*

The first force in this example states the obvious fact that we want to know what basic services the system offers to its users. Yet this information is important because it helps us grapple with the next force, which if not countered, can lead to us writing ridiculously small use cases. Without other guidance, people will always take the path of least resistance, and it is usually very easy to describe low-level system services.

At first glance it might seem absurd that someone would intentionally write use cases that describe how a system offers useless services to its users (perhaps the antithesis of a use case is a useless case). But this is where the forces come into play. These are the competing trade-offs that complicate the problem, which if taken too far can lead to suboptimal solutions. The purpose of a pattern is to provide instructions to bring these forces into an optimal balance for your particular situation. The forces are the things that if taken too far will make us do something absurd, like writing use cases that are useless to the users.

Why do we go to these lengths to explain the problem in this manner? Because we want you to grasp the richness of the problem and gain an in-depth understanding of the trade-offs that push most people to the solution. Few problems have a one-size-fits-all solution, and the better your understanding of the problem's trade-offs, the better you can adapt the solution to your specific situation, or determine that the solution is not appropriate for your needs.

The Solution

This section of the pattern presents a common, well-tried solution that balances the competing forces and reflects the characteristics of well-written use cases. The essence of the solution is written in bold text and follows a "Therefore" in the pattern. The bold text summarizes the solution that attempts to bring the forces into balance. A discussion follows the solution, explaining it further and identifying other patterns that complete this one.

The essential solution for our **UserValuedTransactions** pattern is this:

Therefore:

Identify the valuable services that the system delivers to the actors to satisfy their business purposes.

This solution aims to solve the problem within the constraints imposed by the forces. "Identify the valuable services . . ." limits the goal set to use cases that benefit the users instead of smaller, implementation-oriented use cases that are not particularly valuable to the user. ". . . that the system delivers to the actors to satisfy their business purposes" implies that we should focus on the actors and define transactions that are meaningful to them, rather than system or implementation details.

The solution may often seem familiar, or even obvious, but that is what patterns are all about. A pattern should not be some grand revelation but rather a piece of advice that your grandmother could have told you (assuming Grandma wrote use cases, but then, hey, Dilbert's mom is apparently a telecommunications engineer). Our patterns capture the tried and true experience of those who have had success writing use cases. Our contribution is that we have given a name to that knowledge, and packaged it with other like pieces of knowledge and experience.

The Examples

Each pattern has one or more examples demonstrating either the benefit of implementing the solution recommended by the pattern or the consequences of what happens when you don't. We based many of these examples on live projects, but we sanitized and simplified many of them because real use cases are often long and can be quite complicated, especially the ones demonstrating bad practices. Many of our examples follow a group of developers from a national travel agency as they write some use cases for their new product, the Wings Over the World travel reservation system. We based these examples on our experiences and many of them are composites of real people, events, conversations, and use cases.

1.7 *Organization of the Pattern Language*

Our pattern language consists of thirty-one patterns, organized into two broad categories: development patterns and structural patterns. Development patterns describe the characteristics of proven use case writing practices, and offer criteria for measuring the quality of the writing process. Structural patterns describe the basic components of use cases, explain how they should be organized, and offer criteria for judging their use. These two broad categories are further broken down into sub-categories of related patterns.

There are three subcategories of development patterns:

- Team organization—patterns for judging and improving the quality of how the use case team is organized
- Process—patterns for judging and improving the quality of the methodology the team follows to create use cases
- Editing—patterns for judging and improving the quality of the individual use cases as the underlying requirements change and the writer's knowledge grows

There are four subcategories of structural patterns:

- Use case sets—patterns for judging and improving the quality of a collection of use cases
- Use cases—patterns for judging and improving the quality of an individual use case
- Scenarios and steps—patterns for judging and improving the quality of use case scenarios, and the steps within those scenarios
- Use case relationships—patterns for judging and improving the quality of the structuring relationships between the use cases in a collection

Each chapter in the remainder of the book addresses one subcategory.

Development Patterns

Individuality and organizational cultures make it difficult to define a universal process for writing use cases. Instead, you have to do what "feels right" for your organization. But "feels right" is hard to quantify, as it depends on a host of variable factors. Although it is not the purpose of this book to recommend a specific use case writing process, we have identified several good characteristics of effective use case development. The development patterns in our language offer guidelines in several areas to help you improve your own process. These patterns cover three topics: (1) the composition of the teams writing use cases, (2) the techniques for creating a set of use cases, and (3) techniques for editing existing use cases into better ones.

The Team

Group dynamics is an important but often overlooked aspect of use case development. The personal interactions between the writers can affect the resulting use cases as much as the techniques that are used to identify and write them. This section of our book investigates the people issues associated with use case development, and outlines several techniques for optimizing writing teams, enabling them to produce better use cases.

Writing **PreciseAndReadable** (p. 138) use cases requires both a **BalancedTeam** (p. 39) (balanced skills and personalities) and a **ParticipatingAudience** (p. 35). The sponsors, developers, usage experts, and domain experts all contribute to the work and review it. However, too many writers soon spoil the plot, and so a **SmallWritingTeam** (p. 31) should be used for any one writing task.

The Process

Following a good process is critical to writing quality use cases. This process doesn't have to be elegant or "high powered," but it does need to cover all the bases. For developing use cases, good process means balancing discovery versus writing, and content versus need. You don't want to write use cases so quickly that you overwhelm the writers as they struggle to learn the system, nor do you want to be constantly rewriting or discarding your previous work. At the same time, you need to progress at a reasonably quick pace, so that your developers can begin building the system. You only want enough content to describe your system adequately; you don't want to waste time writing any more than that. This section of the book investigates process issues and offers some advice for improving yours.

Although we do not advocate any specific process for creating use cases, we find that effective groups work **BreadthBeforeDepth** (p. 48), naming many use cases before partially expanding some, and completing the main success scenario before investigating failure handling, achieving a **SpiralDevelopment** (p. 52) of the use case set.

The **SmallWritingTeam** (p. 31) integrates its work with a **TwoTierReview** (p. 64), where an inner circle of colleagues representing different specialties first reviews and adjusts the work before passing it to a large group with representatives from all stakeholders, including customers.

The effective team understands when it is **QuittingTime** (p. 68). Rather than getting bogged down in long arguments about cosmetic issues, team members allow a certain amount of **WritersLicense** (p. 73), recognizing that trying to enforce identical writing habits or petty standards soon stops adding economic value to the endeavor.

Not every project team needs the same volume of detail to accomplish its mission, and so we see the need for **MultipleForms** (p. 58) of use cases. Indeed, these forms may each find its appropriate moment on the same project!

Editing

Use cases can become prematurely outdated because the underlying requirements are highly unstable and subject to change. Use cases are highly dynamic, and will undergo metamorphosis as your understanding of the system evolves. Behavior that made sense at the start of the writing process may no longer make sense as you discover more about the system through research and talking to customers, resulting in a collection of obsolete or fragmented use cases. This section describes several common techniques for improving the quality of use cases.

During the writing process, team members will periodically find themselves with either large, complex, and hard-to-read use cases or lots of small, insignificant ones. They should **RedistributeTheWealth** (p. 204) of the large ones to smaller ones, and **MergeDroplets** (p. 209), folding the too-small ones into others. They may eventually discover that some are simply irrelevant; to deal with those, they can **CleanHouse** (p. 213).

Structural Patterns

We have identified four basic levels of use case structure: (1) sets of use cases, (2) use cases, (3) scenarios and steps, and (4) relationships. Use case sets describe the behavior of a system and consist of individual use cases, each of which describes some useful service an individual actor needs. Each use case is a collection of scenarios that, when taken together, describe all the different ways an actor can either reach or fail to reach a specific goal. Individual scenarios consist of steps, each describing an action that an actor or the system must take to move the primary actor closer to his or her (or its) goal.

Use cases often interact with other use cases in the same set. We have identified patterns for structuring some of these relationships. These relationship patterns describe techniques for handling repetitive or excessively complex behavior.

Use Case Sets

Use case sets are collections of use cases and related information, organized in a usable manner as a use case model. A set contains system-level information about a product, including its actors, its boundaries, and the relationships between its members. This level is primarily organizational, as it describes key characteristics of the collection rather than specific behavior. People working at this level often refer to individual use cases by name and ignore their contents.

The most important thing about use cases as a set is that they should reflect a **SharedClearVision** (p. 80) for a system with a clear and **VisibleBoundary** (p. 86). The use cases are collectively structured with higher-level use cases referencing lower-level use cases in an **EverUnfoldingStory** (p. 102) that shows a **ClearCastOf-Characters** (p. 90) interacting with the system to achieve their goals. While the goals that get described sit at various levels, the crucial and interesting ones describe **UserValuedTransactions** (p. 95), in which the primary actor accomplishes a goal that he views as a primary service of the system under discussion.

Use Cases

An individual use case illustrates how actors can use a system to meet a particular goal, showing all of the appropriate paths that they might take to get there, as well as those situations that could cause them to fail. This level is still organizational in nature, providing order and structure so that the reader is able easily to identify and follow the different paths through the use case as they trace the actor's progress toward his goal. It also serves as a focal point for related material.

Each use case contains a collection of successful and unsuccessful scenarios that describe the various situations that an actor is likely to encounter when attempting to achieve his goal. The failure cases are especially important, because they describe the various error conditions that can happen and the actions necessary to resolve them.

A single use case describes the pursuit of a **CompleteSingleGoal** (p. 118), and should have a descriptive **VerbPhraseName** (p. 122) that gives the reader an idea of its purpose. Each use case structures the multiple ways it can achieve or abandon its goal as a **ScenarioPlusFragments** (p. 125), with a collection of scenario fragments describing what happens under differing conditions. A complete use case considers **ExhaustiveAlternatives** (p. 129), so that the developers are not surprised with an unexpected situation late in development.

In order to satisfy the sponsor, the users, the developers, and the writers strive to make the use case **PreciseAndReadable** (p. 138), one of the arts of use case writing, and an achievable goal. One aspect of this is to remove performance requirements, data formats, and ideas for the user interface from the use case text, and document them separately as **Adornments** (p. 133). This practice keeps the use case robust with respect to shifting technologies and user interface designs, yet clean of unnecessary, confusing clutter.

Scenarios and Steps

Scenarios describe a single and complete sequence of events within a use case that an actor follows as she attempts to achieve a particular goal, and results in either success or failure. While scenarios describe behavior, they are still somewhat organizational in nature because they provide structure to a series of steps, which combine to form a coherent and purposeful description. This provides the reader with a systematic view of a particular action sequence.

Each scenario fragment after the main success scenario describes the behavior of the actors under some **DetectableConditions** (p. 148) (detectable to the system under discussion). Part of the readability of attractive use cases is **LeveledSteps** (p. 151), keeping all the steps at about the same level of detail.

Steps describe single actions within a scenario and detail the interchange between the system and actor as they act out a use case. Each step, depending on its goal level, adds some amount of clarity to its scenario, and represents a singular action that either the system or the actor takes as they interact.

Each step should make distinct **ForwardProgress** (p. 162) toward the goal. Since the user interface details and other design decisions appear as **Adornments** (p. 133), you can write each step in a **TechnologyNeutral** (p. 167) manner, to the greatest extent possible. Last, each step should make the **ActorIntentAccomplished** (p. 158), so that the readers always can tell who is doing what.

Relationships

Use cases occasionally share some common behavior, and when they do, it is efficient to reuse existing text rather than repeat the same sequence of events each time they are needed. Ivar Jacobson defined the concepts of *includes, generalizes,* and *extends* to handle these situations. Unfortunately, everyone seems to have his or her own ideas as to what these terms mean. This section describes how people successfully use these concepts to improve their use cases.

People have developed a variety of overly complex mechanisms for using the *includes, extends,* and *generalizes* relationships. Some of these mechanisms work well; others just make a confusing situation worse. Simplicity seems to be the best course. The simplest and most natural relationship is to move the **CommonSub-Behavior** (p. 176) to a sub–use case referenced by the others via the *includes* relationship when a common set of actions recurs in several use cases. When a single event can interrupt the flow of a use case multiple times, then the writers should document those **InterruptsAsExtensions** (p. 182). If a given alternative begins to dominate the use case, then you should consider a **PromotedAlternative** (p. 190), promoting that alternative to an extension use case. While we have not seen enough examples of generalization to create a pattern, our colleague Dan Rawsthorne has contributed the pattern **CapturedAbstraction** (p. 198) which suggests when to use generalization.

1.8 Supplement: A Brief Tutorial on Writing Use Cases

Anything that has behavior is an *actor*. This convention allows us to refer equally easily to people, computer programs, and companies, without worrying about which category of actor is playing the role at that moment. A use case, then, describes the way in which a particular system under discussion (SuD), an actor in its own right, inter-acts with other actors.

To describe the many complicated interactions that a system will have over its lifetime, we link any one use case with the goal of an actor who wants something from the SuD at that moment, and describe all the ways that the system may come to deliver or abandon the goal of that "primary actor."

Then we structure the writing in an interesting way: First of all, we describe how the actors behave in a simple situation in which the goal gets achieved. After that, we name all the conditions under which the behavior is different, and describe the differ-ent behavior that ensues, always bearing in mind that sometimes the goal will suc-ceed and sometimes it will fail. These are called *extensions* or *alternate courses* of behavior within the use case.

We can see now that the use cases discussed so far were just fragments, since they described only the simple case of goal success (what some people call the "happy day" scenario). The complete use case is too long to put in here, but looks essentially like Use Case 1.3.

Use Case 1.3 *Register for Courses:* Use Case with Extensions

Register for Courses (Use Case with Extensions)

Primary actor: Student

System under Discussion: Course Enrollment System

Level: User Goal

1. Student requests to construct a schedule.
2. The system prepares a blank schedule form.
3. The system pulls in a list of open and available courses from the Course Catalog System.
4. Student selects up to 4 primary course offerings and 2 alternate course offer-ings from the available offerings.
5. For each course, the system verifies that the Student has the necessary prereq-uisites and adds the Student to the course, marking the Student as "enrolled" in that course in the schedule.
6. When the Student indicates the schedule is complete, the system saves the schedule.

Extensions:

1a. Student already has a schedule:

   System brings up the current version of the Student's schedule for editing in-stead of creating a new one.

1b. Current semester is closed and next semester is not yet open:

   System lets Student look at existing schedules, but not create new ones.

3a. Course Catalog System does not respond:
     The system notifies the Student and terminates the use case.
4a. Course full or Student has not fulfilled all prerequisites:
     System disables selection of that course and notifies the Student.

People sometimes find that a briefer way of writing is desirable (for example, for very small projects, and projects in which the use cases are merely being used to estimate work effort, not specify the system). In other situations, a more exact way of writing is needed (such as military contract outsourcing, large distributed projects, and life-critical systems). It is important to recognize that there is no one, best format for use cases, but that the amount of detail to put into a use case depends on the project and the team at hand, and the purpose of use case writing.

While it is all very well to say that a use case describes the behavior involved in trying to achieve a goal, the difficulty is that goals exist at many levels. Any one goal is achieved by achieving subgoals. For example, I might have a goal to send my children to school in a rich section of the city. To achieve that goal, I have to earn enough money to buy a house in that school district. To do that, I need to close some big business deals, so my next subgoal is to win some particular contract. To do that, I may decide my next subgoal is to win over a particular decision maker, and so I take him to lunch for a discussion.

Each of these goals can be described using a use case, although I have not yet specified a particular SuD for them. Continuing the subgoals, I find I need cash to take him to lunch, and so I go to a local cash-dispensing machine, where my goal is to get some cash. My first subgoal, now directly related to the cash machine as an SuD, is to identify myself, to which end I have subgoals to insert my card into the machine, type in my identification number, and hit the Enter key. (People who know Alistair have already learned that he can make almost any goal involve going to an ATM to get cash!)

All in all, I could write any of the following use cases within the framework of the information given so far: *Find Enter Key, Authorize User, Insert ATM Card, Get Cash, Win Contract, Buy a Too-Expensive House, Get Kids into Good School.*

This capacity of use cases to describe goals at all levels is wonderful but confusing to use case writers. Different writers describe different levels of goals, some staying high *(Get Cash),* and some staying at terribly low levels *(Authorize User, Insert ATM Card).* For most systems, it is critical to identify the goal level in which the system contributes direct, take-home value to the primary actor (see the entry **UserValued-Transactions** (p. 95). This level we refer to as *user goal.* Then we write additional use cases for goals at higher and lower levels as needed. These we refer to as *summary* and *subfunction,* respectively. Figure 1.2, adapted from *Writing Effective Use Cases*

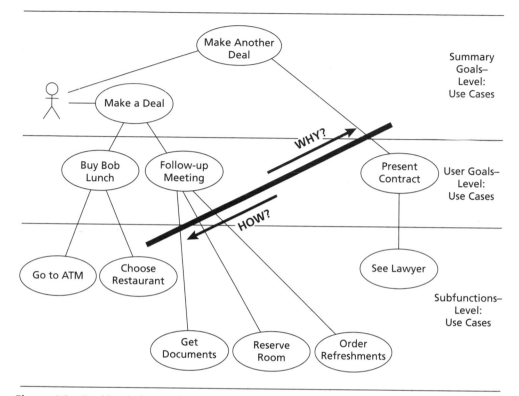

Figure 1.2 *Goal levels for sending your kids to a better school*

(Cockburn 2001), illustrates goal levels by describing some of the deals necessary to get the kids into a better school.

Use cases are read and used by two very different groups of people: (1) end users or business experts, who often are not versed in the technical and implementation difficulties; and (2) programmers, who need very precise answers to their questions in order to make the computer program work properly. It is not obvious that any form of writing can satisfy both groups of people, but use cases have shown themselves as fitting this narrow range. The art of use case writing is to get the precision in writing without overwhelming the non-programmer business reader.

To create use cases that are correct and precise but still readable, the writing team *must* include:

◆ At least one person with a background in programming, to get the required accuracy and precision of description

- At least one person with deep knowledge of the business rules that the system must enforce
- At least one person with intimate knowledge of how the system will actually be used

In other words, producing a set of use cases is not a job for one person, or even one group of people with the same job description. It is a team effort, requiring people with different backgrounds and even different personalities. When this team does its job well, the result is readable *and* precise.

This book is not an introduction to use cases. Rather, it is a handbook about how to write meaningful, high-quality use cases. Therefore, we have provided only a brief summary of use cases in this chapter. If you want to learn more about use cases in general, we recommend Alistair Cockburn's *Writing Effective Use Cases* (2001). More discussion of use cases is available at the Web site *www.usecases.org*. You may refer to these sources for introductory, template, and tools-descriptive material, and continue reading this book to improve your ability to detect and discuss the signs of quality in your use case writing.

Chapter 2

The Team

◆ **All Hands on Deck!**

It's 5:00 p.m. on a sunny West Coast afternoon. You're just closing the last of your files and powering down your workstation when your boss calls you over to her office and tells you, "Good news! We won the Wings Over the World contract."

This is great news. Wings Over the World is a national travel agency that is modernizing its aging software infrastructure. This project is potentially worth millions to your company, and you are the principal consultant on the bid. You might finally make full partner now.

The boss shakes your hand. "You did great! They really liked your presentation, and they want you to take point on this one."

Your boss continues, "They're really excited about this use case stuff you told them about, and they want to make this a real 'all-hands effort.'" You hear the sharp *sproing* of a red flag snapping up. "They really want to fast-track this, so they've lined up about a dozen people for their use case team, and they want you to be part of it." Before you can open your mouth, your boss cautions you, "Oh, by the way, most of their travel agents haven't completely bought into the new system concept yet, and they don't want us disturbing them. So you are to work only with their business analysts and programmers in their IT group while gathering the requirements."

Now you hear a rapid succession of *sproings* as more red flags snap up. Things are not looking good: You have a large and probably unfocused team. The team is developer heavy with few domain experts and no actual users. Finally, you have little or no access to users and other important stakeholders, so you can only guess at what they really want. Use cases were never intended to solve these problems.

2.1 Team Organizational Issues

Human behavior is an important yet often overlooked aspect of use case development. The personal interactions between the writers can affect the resulting use cases as much as the techniques used to identify and write them.

Unfortunately, many development organizations seem oblivious to the importance that team composition has on creating good use cases. Instead, they treat the effort as a necessary evil that anyone, experienced or otherwise, can do. Management may not understand or support the use case concept, or developers themselves might consider writing use cases to be busy work—an unnecessary prerequisite to the "real work" of writing code. Even when an organization embraces use cases enthusiastically, it can fail to dedicate the resources necessary to do a good job or fail to control the number of people involved.

Team size is the most critical factor influencing the quality of the use cases. Not only is it inefficient to have numerous people defining the system, but also the compromises made to align numerous and competing system visions may lead to unsatisfactory results. Each use case writing team should be a **SmallWritingTeam** (p. 31), where the number of writers on any use case is limited to two or three people, to avoid inefficiencies or design by committee.

While you want to keep the use case writing team small, you still want to involve as many stakeholders in the writing process as possible, to ensure that the use cases meet all of your stakeholders' needs. However, talking with external customers can present an enormous challenge to a project. Some companies don't want outsiders to access their rank-and-file employees, and even internal organizational boundaries can get in the way, to the detriment of the final product. **ParticipatingAudience** (p. 35) resolves the competing issues of managing team size while involving all of the target audience in the use case development process.

Team composition is another factor influencing the quality of use cases. An unbalanced team, consisting of similar, like-minded individuals, will examine a system from only one point of view, frequently that of the software developers rather than that of the users. Unbalanced teams are often inefficient and can wander in search of an elusive goal. Including a domain expert or expert user can keep the team on track, but it can also inhibit a team from original thinking when the expert is overpoweringly dominant. Effective teams are **BalancedTeams** (p. 39), containing a complementary mixture of skills, expertise, and even personalities, where each participant provides a distinct view of the system being modeled.

A skilled team of men and women workers complete assembly on the interior of a fuselage section for a new B-17F (Flying Fortress) bomber, Seattle, Washington

2.2 SmallWritingTeam

You have a **SharedClearVision** (p. 80) for a system and are organizing teams to write use cases.

> Using too many people to write a use case is inefficient, and the compromises made to align the many different points of view may result in a less than satisfactory system.

Musicians have a saying, "Two guitarists, three songs," implying that any time two guitarists play guitars together, they somehow end up simultaneously playing three different songs. Musicians have a reputation for being self-absorbed, and often bicker over whose song to play, or how to play it. The more members in the group, the more likely these disagreements, as the musicians compete to "do their thing." Many groups limit band size to avoid these problems.

You can experience similar problems when writing use cases, because everyone writing them wants to contribute their two cents' worth and be heard.

Use cases require the views and expertise of diverse groups. A set of use cases must capture the domain knowledge and experience of the people who will use the system, yet be precise enough for the development team to use as an input for system design. Large systems can be especially difficult to describe, because they can support many different kinds of users performing many different kinds of activities. In some situations, the number of people needed to contribute information and review the use cases can grow as large as 50 people.

Getting a large group of people together is difficult. The more people that must meet, the more difficult it is to find an agreeable meeting time. People who work on other projects or work in other geographic locations can't just pop down the hall for a quick discussion. Meeting with external customers often presents the biggest challenge, because their company may discourage such meetings or forbid them outright.

In theory, the more people you have working on use cases, the faster you can finish writing them. Throwing a lot of people at a problem is a common reaction to meeting tight schedule pressure. It is especially tempting with use cases because many people think that writing them is easy, and that anyone can do them. This approach might work when there is more work than people, but can make things much worse when a team is already adequately staffed.

Teams that are too large become inefficient. Teams having too many members tend to bog down over minor matters. Overstaffing a team can waste its members' time by minimizing their participation and giving them too little to do. As a result, the team either loses interest and slacks off, or members tend to overproduce, creating an artifact with too much detail and redundant or unnecessary information.

Large teams can lead to design by committee and feature bloat. Large teams are especially vulnerable to design by committee, where the project assumes a life of its own. "Groupthink" prevails, causing the team to lose focus and stray from the vision, resulting in a model bearing little resemblance to the intended system. Members add all kinds of unnecessary features, resulting in a model that fulfills all of the team members' desires without satisfying anyone.

Therefore:

> Restrict the number of people refining any one work product to just two or three people. Use a **TwoTierReview** (p. 64) process to include more people.

The fewer the number of people who are responsible for the creation of use cases, the better. It is easier for a small team to meet, communicate, and reach a consensus. A team of two or three people is small enough to keep out of each other's way, yet broad enough to write meaningful use cases. You can use several **SmallWritingTeams**; however, you should appoint one person as the use case architect and give him or her the responsibility for maintaining a consistent vision through all the use cases.

At the same time, try to represent different viewpoints on each team. Create **BalancedTeams** (p. 39), using people with different backgrounds, skills, and personalities so that the teams don't fall into the rut of looking at the use cases the same way. Diversity is especially important for projects aimed at a widespread audience, because it is likely that the various users will use the product in many different ways.

You can maximize participation, while avoiding large teams, by using **ParticipatingAudience** (p. 35) and **TwoTierReviews** to involve more people in the process. These two patterns describe methods for consulting many different people without cluttering the use case writing process. These practices allow different interest groups to focus on the details they consider important, while shielding them from details raised by other stakeholders with different interests.

Examples

Facilitating Large Groups: No Design without Representation

In his article "Use Case Blue," Andy Kraus (1996) describes the effort involved in facilitating a large group that was collecting use cases. He recounts six weeks of sessions, using an average of 15 to 20 participants, eliciting requirements for replacing the Automated Regional Justice Information System (ARJIS). It required the services of various people from 23 police departments and 16 individual contributors. While smaller teams might have been more desirable, business conditions and the complexity of the system forced them to use the large-group approach. During the course of their endeavor, they held meetings with 8 to 25 people in attendance. While fewer people would have been more manageable, Andy claims, "Only by having representation of the diverse ARJIS membership in the room at the same time could we flush out nuances to the requirements caused by the differing philosophies and operating procedures among the members." But such an effort took its toll, as Andy also claimed that they encountered all of the problems that they were told to expect from having such a large group. For example, "Without knowing in advance what the real system actors were, it was impossible for us to predict which users would need to come to which sessions." They solved the problem by holding a kickoff planning session to derive a schedule for future sessions.

This project was successful, but required a lot of effort to manage. However, some groups find that this type of approach requires too much energy to be effective.

Large Groups and Frequent Checkpoints

We know an expert in the field who was involved in a similar situation with a company that had arranged for an expert facilitator and 14 people (10 field representatives and 4 business analysts) to write use cases for an extended period of time, eventually yielding around three dozen use cases. Things started out slowly, as the group had to listen to people express their opinions one at a time.

Fortunately, the group had the flexibility to adjust their procedure as needed. They devised a branch-and-join process, using their group meetings for brainstorming sessions and administrative issues. They divided into small groups, based on who was best qualified to work on what use case. If only one person was qualified for a particular topic, he got someone to help. Once a group finished a draft of a use case, they passed it around for review, with the others penciling their comments on the same sheet. These reviews were especially effective because they localized all of the reviewers' comments to one sheet of paper, keeping the reviewers aware of the previous reviewer's thoughts, and making it easier to organize and apply their suggestions to the use cases once the review was complete.

The facilitator was somewhat uncomfortable with this distributed approach. However, the group consistently elected to do the work in small teams, as they found it much easier and far more efficient. Moreover, they greatly increased their throughput and decreased the duration of the effort by working on seven use cases at a time rather than one.

Armistice Day gathering in Lititz, Pennsylvania. The audience bow their heads in tribute to boys in the service.

2.3 ParticipatingAudience

You are a **SmallWritingTeam** (p. 31) creating use cases.

You cannot satisfy stakeholders' needs without their input and feedback.

Buying stock in a company makes you a part owner, and entitles you to attend stockholder meetings and to vote on company issues. The company's board of directors is legally required to represent their shareholders' best interest, which can be difficult because companies may have millions of stockholders. It is impossible for the board to listen to everyone. To alleviate this problem, companies allow their stockholders to vote by proxy, where the stockholders can assign their right to vote to someone else. This way, one person can represent hundreds or even thousands of people at the meeting, keeping it small. However, stockholders who disagree with the direction the company is going can attend the meeting and voice their sentiments.

Writing use cases is similar because it is not always possible or practical to involve everyone you need every step of the way. Stakeholder input is invaluable because your goal is to develop a system that pleases your stakeholders, and they often know far more about their needs than you can possibly ever know. To model the system effectively, you must discover what they need, know, and want, and allow them to have a voice in the process. The true art is to know when and how to do this without having to involve them in every step along the way.

Many different groups have a vested interest in a set of use cases. Developers are not the only people depending on a set of use cases. Large development organizations consist of many different groups with various responsibilities, styles, and needs. Each of these groups relies on the same use cases to complete their portion of the product development process. Each one of these groups has its own use for the use cases and looks at the use cases differently.

If the customers don't like it, they won't buy it. Ultimately, customers are the final authority on your product, because they are the ones who have to pay for it. While you may think that your product is fabulous, they may hate it. They don't care how hard it was for you to build, or how much time you spent building it. They just care that it does what they want. If your product doesn't meet their needs, then it is a failure.

It is usually impractical to include your entire target audience in the use case development process. Several factors make it difficult to talk to everyone interested in your product. Large projects require the services of far more people than you can consult. Often, stakeholders reside in different geographical areas, making them extremely difficult to locate or talk with. Other companies may not like you talking with their employees, or your own company may want to keep your project under wraps for competitive reasons. In the case of off-the-shelf products, you don't really know who your stakeholders are, and can only guess.

Development organizations don't adequately represent end users. A common problem in software development is that the developers often assume that the users share their perspective of the system. Unfortunately, developers are often isolated from their customers, and don't really understand their needs. As a result, the systems that they develop are often hard for everyday users to use because they target the wrong audience. For example, a group of high-powered developers might prefer to use an interface requiring regular expressions as input. However, most people find regular expressions to be too abstract, and they would become extremely frustrated after trying to use this interface. Even other highly skilled users might not appreciate the more difficult interface, because they want an easy-to-use product that doesn't require much thought or a steep learning curve.

Therefore:

> **Actively involve your customers and internal stakeholders in the use case development process when possible.**

Include your customers in the use case development process from the start. If you are developing use cases as an individual effort, consult with your customers often and seek their input. If working as a team, then try to include a customer representative as a team member when you don't have a clear understanding of the product. His or her presence provides you with a wonderful opportunity to learn firsthand what it is that the customer really wants.

This kind of relationship makes it easier for you to keep your customers aware of any potential issues that may arise, and obtain their assistance immediately, rather than proceed through a time-consuming formal process. Most important, cooperation can foster a spirit of understanding as well as give customers a sense of ownership in the use cases, improving the chances that they will accept the final product.

While customers are the most important stakeholders, they are not the only ones. Internal groups such as quality assurance and documentation often depend on your use cases, and it is important that you consult with them as well. Treat all stakeholders as customers, and consider including internal stakeholders on your use case development teams when they can provide valuable insight into the product.

Try to represent the users' viewpoint when they are unavailable. Sometimes the users are inaccessible. Many organizations will not allow outside companies access to their employees, and even internal departmental boundaries can limit access. The reasons may be valid or frivolous, but don't fret or give up when you can't talk directly to the users. Instead, use other techniques to elicit this information. The book *Software for Use* (Constantine and Lockwood 1999) describes many practical techniques for obtaining user information without directly contacting users. These techniques include utilizing user surrogates such as domain experts and trainers, consulting with members of nonuser groups such as marketing or technical support, or relying on indirect sources such as manuals, records, or even questionnaires. While not as straightforward as direct user participation, these techniques offer a valid alternative.

Reviews, especially well structured **TwoTierReviews** (p. 64) that make good use of the customers' time, provide a good vehicle for sharing use cases with customers, and can even allow you access to those customers and users that you can't see otherwise.

Examples

Soliciting customer input has been a key part of requirements elicitation for years. Yet surprisingly, some teams don't do it. We know of one team that focused entirely on some complex requirement specifications, didn't talk to the end users, and ended up writing over 500 use cases before they threw in the towel. The project was shelved.

The Job Flow Engine

We find it amazing that people don't take the time to investigate the users' side of a project, because this technique is so helpful. One of the authors was part of a small project team developing a job flow engine to control the execution of some specialized programs across a set of distributed workstations. The team interviewed many potential users, discovered what they needed, and documented as use cases their various processes, both manual and automated. The resulting product was successful because it provided exactly the needed services, and allowed the users to automate correctly some complicated time-consuming processes. Without the use cases, the result wouldn't have been nearly so positive.

Making Movies

It should come as no surprise that soliciting customer input is a common practice in many industries, and was well established long before the first modern computer.

Customer consultation has been part of the movie-making process for decades. In the 1930s, MGM sponsored the Marx Brothers on cross-country vaudeville tours prior to filming *A Night at the Opera* (1935) and *A Day at the Races* (1937), so that they could use the audience as proving grounds for much of their material. If a joke bombed, they either changed it until it worked or they dropped it. They fine-tuned those lines that were somewhat funny, and kept those skits that brought down the house. Consequently, these two films rank among their all-time best. However, MGM stopped sponsoring these tours after *A Day at the Races,* and the quality of the brothers' subsequent films dropped significantly (Marx 1972, pp. 174–75).

To the Moon

In some instances, the **SmallWritingTeam** (p. 31) absolutely depends upon the **ParticipatingAudience**. For example, consider a trip to the moon. The *Apollo Saturn V* spacecraft contained over two million separate working systems, yet severe weight and fuel constraints prevented NASA from sending more than three people on the spacecraft. Obviously, there was no way that three people could comprehend that many systems, let alone be proficient enough to troubleshoot them when problems arose. To get around this problem, NASA assembled a large group of experts, simulators, computers, and communications equipment to assist the flight from the ground. Likewise, some use cases can be so complex that they cannot be written without vital participation from the audience.

Tightrope performers at a 4-H Club fair, Cimarron, Kansas

2.4 *BalancedTeam*

You are organizing **SmallWritingTeams** (p. 31) to write use cases.

Using teams of similar, like-minded individuals to develop use cases can result in a set of limited, narrowly ranged use cases that do not satisfy everyone's needs.

A musical quartet consists of four people singing or playing different parts that blend together to create a unified sound. You would defeat the purpose of a quartet if you chose four singers to sing the same part. Instead, you would want singers with different ranges who could harmonize together, because it is this arrangement that gives a quartet its distinct and rich sound.

Writing meaningful use cases requires the creative input of several people having different viewpoints; otherwise, the results tend to be flat and narrowly focused. A homogeneous team often fails to appreciate the other stakeholders' needs, and produces inadequate use cases as a result.

Groups of individuals sharing a common technical background tend to focus on the same limited issues. This tendency is not surprising, as each member is trained to consider the same issues and use the same techniques to solve a problem. While their approach provides satisfactory solutions, it doesn't encourage the out-of-the-box thinking needed at this stage of product development. Although the members of this group are usually more specialized than most of their clientele, they often fail to think about the system from their users' viewpoint, which can be dangerous for a number of reasons.

Each profession uses its own specialized vocabulary, which people outside of that profession do not understand. Documents full of one profession's jargon can be very confusing for people with other backgrounds. Even if outsiders understand the generalities of this terminology, they usually fail to grasp its subtle implications and can overlook or misinterpret its key points.

Teams need different expertise at different moments. Teams often need subject matter experts at the start of a new project. Later, as the team members become more familiar with the subject, they need experts less, but they may need to know more about other technical areas as the project evolves to address the needs of new and different users.

Good teams are balanced so that each team member's specialties compensate for some other team member's weakness. Teams often fail without this balance. For example, athletic teams are highly specialized. Consider a championship baseball team, which usually includes great pitchers, solid hitters, and players with good defensive skills. Very few, if any, of the pitchers are expected to be good hitters, as their job is to challenge the opposing team's players and prevent them from hitting the ball. It is the job of the other eight players on the field to back up the pitcher by making good defensive plays and to score runs. Teams that are strong in all three of these areas routinely beat mediocre teams with one or two exceptional players.

Similarly, a team comprising members with complementary skills is better suited for defining use cases that will support many different user types, because they are more likely to address more issues. This balance is especially critical in today's world with its explosive technical growth, where no one individual can even begin to keep up with all the latest technologies. Software development improves as we improve people's personal skills and improve the team's collaboration.

Therefore:

> Staff the team with people from different specialties to champion the interests of the stakeholders in the development process. Make sure the team contains both developers *and* end users.

Ignore the tendency to use only your best programmers or software engineers for writing all of the use cases. While domain experts and expert users can be essential for the more critical use cases, be careful about putting them on a team that they will dominate. Instead, use a healthy mix of articulate people with varying backgrounds and viewpoints. If you are writing use cases for several different organizations, try to represent the more important ones on some of your teams, especially when most of your potential system's users are nontechnical, and use **ParticipatingAudience** (p. 35) to fill in the gaps. If your product has significant legal issues, consider involving someone from your legal department, and so forth. Try to include people who think in low-level details as well as those who function at the big-picture level. Look for abstract thinkers and problem solvers, artists and technicians. The team must be diverse enough to provide combined field, corporate, and technical viewpoints.

Try to include people who are good at maintaining focus. They will know when to quit, to prevent feature creep and help the **SmallWritingTeam** avoid diving into bottomless pits. Otherwise, the more detail oriented people will inevitably write low-level use cases that attempt to resolve the system's technical issues rather than describe its behavior and how people will likely use it.

Examples

Lack of Diversity

Many organizations fail to achieve a satisfactory level of diversity because they simply assign software developers to write use cases. Unfortunately, this approach often yields use cases that are too detail oriented, or ones that describe solutions rather than behavior.

One of the authors participated in a group that was writing essential use cases (high-level use cases capturing the essence of a system's behavior) describing a voice messaging dictionary system. Within a matter of minutes, the team began identifying low-level use cases describing the interactions between the dictionary's database attributes. When told that these issues were too technical in nature to be considered "essential," the team disagreed, stating that this information was indeed high level. These people weren't novices: all of them were experienced and knowledgeable use case writers, but they couldn't help themselves. They were problem solvers by nature, and honestly believed that they were operating at an abstract level.

The point is, highly specialized teams tend to produce use cases like Use Case 2.1.

Use Case 2.1   Use Case Horror: *Provision a Cross-Connect* (Engineering-Centric Version)

Provision a Cross-Connect (Engineering-Centric Version)
Primary Actor: Network Administrator: Person provisioning **Network Elements**.
Secondary Actor: **Network Element** Device being provisioned.
Level: User Goal
Preconditions: Network Element is accessible and user has a valid account on it.
Success Guarantee: Cross-connect is "active."
Main Success Scenario:
1. The use case begins when the **Network Administrator** activates account on **Network Element**_(ACT-USER:TID:USERID:::PASSWORD).
2. The **Network Element** establishes a session.
3. The **Network Administrator** enters_ENT-STSnC:TID:FROMAID::::IS; (or ENT-T3:TID:AID::::IS; if it is on a DS3) to establish the source STS.
4. The **Network Element** establishes the "From AID" STS.
5. The **Network Administrator** enters ENT-STSnC:TID:TOAID::::IS; (or ENT-T3:TID:AID::::IS; if it is on a DS3) to establish the sink STS.
6. The **Network Element** establishes the "To AID" STS.
7. The **Network Administrator** enters _ENT-CRS-STSnC:TID::FROMAID,TOAID:::; to establish the cross-connection.

8. The system establishes the cross-connection.
9. The user logs off of the **Network Element** (CANC-USER:TID:userid:;)
10. The use case terminates when the **Network Element** terminates the session.

However, this use case is confusing because it contains fragments of TL1 code, which is a special language for interacting with telecommunication equipment. Most software developers would find this use case perfectly acceptable, especially if they knew TL1, because it would tell them how to provision the device. Unfortunately, it leaves those stakeholders who don't understand TL1 in the dark. Worse, the use case is only valid for TL1 implementations, and isn't general enough if you suddenly have to use other protocols. The version in Use Case 2.2 is much more general and easier to understand.

Use Case 2.2   *Provision a Cross-Connect* (User-Friendly Version)

Provision a Cross-Connect
Primary Actor: Network Administrator: Person provisioning **Network Elements**.
Secondary Actor: Network Element Device being provisioned.
Level: User Goal
Preconditions: Network Element is accessible and user has a valid account on it.
Success Guarantee: Cross-connect is provisioned and viable.
Main Success Scenario:
1. The use case begins when the **Network Administrator** logs on to the **Network Element**.
2. The **Network Element** verifies the user and begins a session.
3. The **Network Administrator** determines the size of the cross-connection, and sets up the endpoints accordingly.
4. The **Network Element** establishes the endpoints.
5. The **Network Administrator** defines the cross-connection.
6. The **Network Element** establishes the cross-connection.
7. The user logs off of the **Network Element**.
8. The use case terminates when the **Network Element** terminates the session.

This version is better because it is easier to read and supports multiple protocols. You could still include the TL1 samples for the implementers, but as **Adornments** (p. 133) (see Chapter 5) at the end of the use case, or in a separate document.

2.5 *Trade-offs and Collaborations*

Using small, balanced writing teams and controlling audience participation is an easy way to improve the quality of your use cases. While not difficult, organizing such teams does require forethought, and it requires balancing several competing forces involving team size, audience involvement, and skills. There is no one perfect mix that always works; it is up to each development organization to balance these patterns to determine what team arrangements will work best with their particular circumstances.

We cannot say enough about the importance of involving your customers in the use case development process. One of the most significant benefits of use cases is that they model how the system delivers measurable value to its users. Being unable to talk to the customer, whatever the reason, increases your risk, so you should find some other way to gather this information. Larry Constantine (Constantine and Lockwood 1999) offers excellent advice on dealing with these kinds of circumstances in his book *Software for Use*.

Though the three patterns we just described complement each other well, they do create some tension with **ParticipatingAudience** (p. 35) and **BalancedTeam** (p. 39) trying to enlarge the group and **SmallWritingTeam** (p. 31) trying to shrink it. However, the intention behind **SmallWritingTeam** is to keep the process manageable. **ParticipatingAudience** provides a mechanism for many other people to contribute to the use case process without overwhelming it, and therefore it avoids the problems of excessively large teams. **ParticipatingAudience** also helps a group become a **BalancedTeam** by involving people with different backgrounds and viewpoints to influence the use cases without increasing the development team's size. The diversity these two patterns provide helps steer the teams toward using a common vocabulary, rather than a discipline-specific one.

To illustrate these points, consider what kinds of teams would be best suited for writing use cases for a project involving pharmaceutical manufacturing. These kinds of systems must meet exacting standards for purity and precision, as well as rigorous legal and accounting requirements. A pharmaceutical company manufacturing controlled substances must be able to account for 100 percent of the controlled substances they use, or they face unwanted visits from the Drug Enforcement Administration.

First, you would want to set up **SmallWritingTeams**, because you want the writers to exercise tight control over their use cases, and write with a high degree of precision. But you also need a high degree of **ParticipatingAudience**, probably more than usual, to verify that the resulting product meets all required standards and complies with the law. In this case, **BalancedTeam** has the greatest impact on the results because of the complexity of the problem and the number of technologies involved.

Most likely, you would want to staff your teams with combinations of software developers, pharmacists, biochemists, and even lawyers, depending on the needs of the various use cases.

The biggest benefit of using **BalancedTeam** in this instance is that it forces the writers to use a common, understandable terminology in their use cases. Commonality is especially important in this situation because each of the disciplines involved in developing this product has its own exclusive and highly specialized vocabulary. **ParticipatingAudience** helps counterbalance this problem to some degree, but even then, one audience will likely have trouble with another's terminology. Software developers talk about stacks, queues, XML, Bridges and Visitors, while the biochemists describe chemical reactions such as "dehydrohalogenation" and use complicated chemical formulas. Lawyers also have a reputation for obtuse writing; imagine reading use cases like "the Line Supervisor actor shall henceforth be known as the party of the third part . . .".

It's important, but team organization is only a small part of the picture. A team also needs to follow a good process to be able to identify and write quality use cases, which is the subject of the next chapter.

Chapter 3

The Process

It's Monday morning and you've had a great weekend with the family. On Friday after-noon your boss told you that you would lead the use case effort for your new client, the national travel agency, Wings Over the World. Now you're having your first phone conversation with Karen, Wings' Chief Information Officer, since doing your original presentation.

You: I just got the news on Friday that we're going ahead with this. Can you tell me what you have done since my presentation three weeks ago?

Karen: Well, I was really impressed with your explanation of how use cases will help us out on this project. We've always had a lot of problems gathering our functional requirements, and this sounds like just the ticket for us. I wanted to get my people started quickly, so I brought in an instructor for a couple of days to teach a use case course. All I can say is, people are really excited by this. Anyway, the instructor gave them a great template that covers everything you can think of in a use case, from soup to nuts. I've got everyone on the team now working on the use cases, and they're just turning these things out a mile a minute.

Once again you hear that familiar sproing *sound of red flags popping up. Templates are wonderful, you think, but can they ever be misused and abused. After a short pause, Karen confirms they are having problems.*

Karen: I have a big favor to ask you. I know you're not scheduled to be here until next week, but is it possible that you could come sooner?

More sproings.

Karen: The way you explained the use cases, and the way our course instructor explained them, we thought they would be easy to write. But obviously we're doing something wrong, because we're running into some problems. We're really anxious to get you in here to help us out.

You: What kind of problems?

Karen: Well, you know it's no secret that we've had methodology problems on past projects. There are a lot of cowboys here. Anyway, Ahmed, our architect on this project, is really insistent that we do things right this time, and that means we go by the book and follow the use case template that our instructor gave us. Well, people are having all kinds of problems filling in the preconditions, post-conditions, triggers, goal statements, and all that. While most of us are really happy to be trying out these use cases, some of the old hands are getting a bit frustrated. I was hoping you could maybe go over all the fields in the template?

You don't know whether to laugh or cry. But right now you know that the last thing you want to do is sound condescending.

You: It's a bit early in the process to be writing detailed use cases; we should just try to get the big picture first, then refine the use cases.

Karen: Well, Ahmed said we needed detailed specs, otherwise there was just too much that would be left to the programmers. But I think I have to agree with you on this one, because Ralph and Sitra got into a big fight last week.

You: A fight? Over what? I thought they worked well together.

Karen: Not really a fight, more of a programmer's territorial dispute. Ralph is our billing expert and Sitra is our RAPIER expert. Ralph wrote a billing use case that overlaps and in some situations contradicts Sitra's use case for the RAPIER interface. Both of them have spent about two solid weeks writing their use cases, and neither wants to throw their work away.

You: What about the agent reps, what do they think about all this so far?

Karen: I'm a little bit worried about their buy-in to this project because all they've done is complain. They've always complained that our specs are too complex or that they can't find what they're looking for. Well, all right, we're trying to go the distance for them by writing use cases, and they're still complaining. Not only that, but some of the travel agents' reps are even refusing to show up for our JAD sessions and reviews. They keep saying there are too many reviews and that they've got better things to do than correct our spelling.

You: If I can swing it I'll try to hop tonight's red-eye and be there tomorrow, and we can sort this out.

Karen: I really appreciate your dedication. I knew there was a reason we selected you. Oh, and one last thing . . .

You: What is it?

Karen: Well, when do we know we're done? Ahmed is really insisting that we go by the book, and Ralph is really getting impatient and saying we should just get on with the job.

After you hang up, you immediately call Travel and have them book your tickets for tonight's red-eye. You decide you better get there now and get this project back on track before these guys dig themselves any deeper into the hole they have started.

Wouldn't it be wonderful if there was one well-defined process for writing use cases? Then we could all learn the one universal methodology and know that everyone else clearly understands our ideas. Unfortunately, writing good use cases is highly personalized; everyone has his or her own style, and every organization has its own way of doing things, based on its culture and business needs. After all, it is these differences that give a business its competitive advantage. What is good for one group is not necessarily good for another.

While there is no one-size-fits-all process for creating use cases, we have captured common elements of good processes in the process patterns. It is important to note that these patterns do not constitute a process; that is, they don't follow one after the other. Rather, they make statements that are true about the process. For example, **TwoTier-Review** (p. 64) describes inner reviews followed by an outer review. This pattern will be found in organizations using slightly different processes for writing their use cases.

An effective process creates use cases in a **BreadthBeforeDepth** (p. 48) manner, identifying potential use cases before describing them, adding details in a controlled manner, and achieving a **SpiralDevelopment** (p. 52) of the use case set. One of the biggest mistakes that people make while developing use cases is writing them sequentially. They start developing one use case, taking whatever time they need to write it, and don't start on the next one until the first one is finished. This approach has two drawbacks: (1) it is easy to get bogged down on difficult use cases at the expense of the remaining ones; and (2) facts uncovered during the development of later use cases often necessitate a rewrite of the earlier ones, wasting the original effort.

When it comes to use cases, different groups within a development organization should have the freedom to choose the format and level of detail that best meet their needs, instead of being required to use some "official" style. An effective process allows the writers to choose from **MultipleForms** (p. 58) and determine the appropriate level of detail. The group should use the same format for all the use cases in the same project to avoid confusion, but it is their decision to make, based on the project's complexity and the audience's need.

Reviews are a time-proven way of identifying errors and inadequacies; however, a traditional review process can often be ineffective for use cases because they can require a large, diverse group of reviewers with competing needs. To get around this problem, **TwoTierReview** describes how to stage reviews, in which those closest to the use cases review their correctness and completeness before turning them over to the larger group to review from a system standpoint.

One of the most difficult questions involving use case development is when to stop. The effective team knows when it is **QuittingTime** (p. 68). Rather than getting bogged down in long arguments about cosmetic issues, they allow a certain amount of **WritersLicense** (p. 73), recognizing that trying to enforce identical writing habits on everyone doesn't add economic value to the endeavor.

*Blasting crew going into an
ore vein with a horizontal drill.
Mahoning pit, Hibbing, Minnesota.*

3.1 *BreadthBeforeDepth* *

You are starting to write use cases with a **SharedClearVision** (p. 80) and a **Clear-CastOfCharacters** (p. 90).

> **You will not make timely progress or create coherent use case sets if you waste energy writing detailed use cases sequentially.**

It's hard to imagine building a house without an architect's sketch or drawing that shows us the big picture of how the completed house will look, and how it will relate to and influence its surroundings. The architect may also provide interior sketches to help us visualize the inside of the house. From these sketches an architect will begin to create the detailed plans for the house.

But homes have not always been designed in such a breadth-first manner. Back in the "good old days," there was no big picture, and people living on the frontier literally built their houses one room at a time. Materials were scarce, and settlers didn't have the time to build large homes, so they just made do. Later, as they prospered and their families grew, they added more rooms onto the house, again one at a time. The results of this process are interesting: If you visit one of these homes today, you will notice unusual features such as exterior walls on the inside, or bedrooms you can only enter through other bedrooms. The tour guides at Abraham Lincoln's house in Springfield, Illinois, will tell you that the second floor "floats"; it is not anchored to any supporting walls because someone added it on later.

*This pattern was influenced by Rick Ratliff's **Breadth First** pattern from the OOPSLA 98 Use Case Patterns workshop.

You can write better use cases if you have a good idea of what they will look like when you are finished. Unfortunately, you usually don't know that much about a system when you start. Developing use cases is a process in which you are continually learning and reevaluating your model. Fortunately, there are some things that you can do to help guide you along the way, and provide order to your process.

Requirements gathering is a process of discovery. It starts with a vague notion of the desired system, which makes it impossible to get the details correct the first time around. In most cases the people who commission the software system do not know exactly what they want and are unable to articulate their needs. The use case writing process is an iterative one in which you must define, analyze, and refine your underlying requirements in order to resolve conflicts and remove ambiguities from your model. The writing team will naturally write more suitable use cases once they better understand the system.

People are drawn into writing the details early. It is always difficult to begin a new project, and thinking about the whole, poorly understood system can be overwhelming. Trying to ramp up quickly is hard, and getting your head around a complex system is much akin to boiling the ocean. Developers often feel uncomfortable about spending the time necessary to comprehend a whole system, as they feel that they are wasting too much time, and should be producing something tangible instead. When people are not sure how to proceed, they have a tendency to dive into the nitty-gritty details and start specifying detailed requirements about the small parts of the system that they understand, even if those parts are not very important to the big picture. Unfortunately, project managers encourage this tendency because they measure progress based on concrete deliverables, and complete use cases fit the bill perfectly.

People lose energy or get bogged down in too much detail. A typical use case may have up to four general elements: actors and goals, main success scenario, failure conditions, and failure handling. It is easy to get drawn into pursuing too much detail when you are writing the narrative of the use case, as it is tempting to examine the alternatives. But whenever people follow a step with too many details—for example, its failure conditions and failure handling—they tend to lose their focus and energy describing all the possible extension conditions.

It is advantageous to get an overview early. If you start with an outline and then write just the essence of each use case, you give each stakeholder the opportunity to offer correction and insight early in the process. This approach also permits the work to be prioritized and split across multiple groups and releases, increasing parallelism and improving productivity.

The more detailed your early endeavors, the more you will have to change them as you learn more about the system. Most projects are short on time and energy, so continually changing the same use case is discouraging and stressful. The participants may start questioning their involvement and lose confidence in their use cases altogether.

Therefore:

> Conserve your energy by developing an overview of your use cases first, then progressively add detail, working across a group of related use cases.

Start writing your use cases by outlining them before adding detail. Identify candidate use cases by associating a meaningful goal for each actor, defining a use case for every combination (**UserValuedTransactions** [p. 95]). Using the goal, derive a **VerbPhraseName** (p. 122) for each use case. Once you feel that you have defined a fairly complete set of use cases, work through your set, refining it, combining equivalent use cases and eliminating unnecessary ones (see **MergeDroplets** [p. 209]), **RedistributeTheWealth** [p. 204]), and **CleanHouse** [p. 213]). The resulting set of system goals provides a fundamental, shared understanding for the stakeholders and helps reduce the amount of refactoring required later on.

Once your overview is complete, develop the outlined use cases in an incremental manner, increasing the precision as you learn more about the system. Avoid the tendencies to complete an entire use case all at once or to write them one at a time. Instead, develop your use cases in a series of **SpiralDevelopment** (p. 52) cycles, incrementally adding detail and reviewing the effect the new detail has on the model, until you determine that it is **QuittingTime** (p. 68). Expand your use cases into **ScenarioPlusFragments** (p. 125) by describing the main success scenario of each use case, naming the various conditions that can occur, and then fleshing out some of the more important ones. Again, be ruthless about eliminating nonessential pieces from the collection. Add more detail to the fragments, creating a list of **ExhaustiveAlternatives** (p. 129) in the next cycle.

Templates are an essential use case development tool that provide organization and a common look and feel to the use cases. They are especially valuable when doing incremental development, because templates can serve as placeholders that allow the writers to organize their use cases while they are still missing large pieces. Simple or lower priority use cases don't always require the same amount of information as the more critical ones, so you can use **MultipleForms** (p. 58) to document each use case with an appropriate level of detail and precision.

Sometimes you do need to finish some use cases before others. In that case, take an incremental approach based on project priority. Identify the most important use cases, such as those that define the project, or those that need to be done first, based on business or technical issues. Prioritize these as you start writing, and work on them in groups for the aforementioned reasons. You may work on other use cases as well, but not at the expense of the most important ones.

BreadthBeforeDepth provides order to the use case writing process. The overview lets you see the big picture without getting bogged down in details. Working at a high level makes it easier to sketch in the system and its boundaries, as well as verify that your use cases provide complete coverage of all of the system's functionality. This high-level view also allows you to start project planning, and it enables you to prioritize your work and develop the most important use cases first—and do the less important ones later.

Working across a group of related use cases makes it easier to realign the use cases and eliminate the ones you determine to be unnecessary before expending much effort on them. Frederick Brooks's classic quote, "Be prepared to throw one away . . . because you will" (1995), is appropriate for writing use cases. Often a team learns more about a system's requirements as the project progresses, and the writers may have to dramatically alter or even throw away earlier work. The sooner you can identify unnecessary use cases, the better.

Examples

This pattern is closely related to the following one, **SpiralDevelopment** (p. 52). Therefore, we will defer offering an example until we have discussed it.

◆ **BreadthBeforeDepth and UML, by Dan Rawsthorne**

The UML's Use Case Model is an overview/summary of the functionality of the system. It does a very good job of documenting this functionality at the lowest possible level of precision—listing simply the **VerbPhraseName** (p. 122) of the use cases. Therefore, using a diagram during requirements gathering prevents use case writers from diving into the details too early.

In particular, drawing actors and use case ovals on a whiteboard is a good way to briefly outline a system's functionality. These use cases often naturally group themselves based on functional goals or actors, and enable the developers to spot any glaring holes or omissions in the functionality. By transferring this whiteboard drawing to paper, one has a permanent record of the conversation and a starting point for further discussion of overall functionality of the system.

It is tempting to put too much information on the diagram. Try to avoid this, as it quickly devolves into a quest for form over substance—and that can't be good! At early stages of development it is probably enough just to show the actors and use cases, and be very sparing with the use case relationships. My own inclination is to initially restrict myself to *includes* relationships as I refactor common functionality out of my use cases. As time goes on, I can add relationships as I need to, based on the **CommonSubBehavior** (p. 176), **InterruptsAsExtensions** (p. 182), **PromotedAlternative** (p. 190), and **CapturedAbstraction** (p. 198) patterns.

Spiral fire escape, St. Louis, Missouri

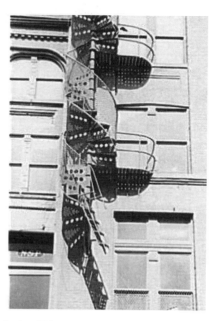

3.2 *SpiralDevelopment*

You are writing use cases in a **BreadthBeforeDepth** (p. 48) manner.

> Developing use cases in a single pass is difficult and can make it expensive to incorporate new information into them. Even worse, it can delay the discovery of risk factors.

"Hindsight is 20/20," "I wish I knew then what I know now," and "If only I could turn the clock back" are all-too-common expressions that people use when they realize that they could have done better if they had had more information available to them earlier.

Writing use cases iteratively gives us a type of hindsight in that we can easily go back and scrap or redo them if we discover that they are not working out. We may lose some of our work, but much less than we would have lost had we simply written complete use cases one at a time. More important, we can identify and confront potential problems sooner using the iterative approach.

It can take a long time to understand a system's behavior. Learning is a linear process, and the more complicated the topic, the longer it takes to understand it. Students may like to "cram" before exams, but this technique only temporarily plants facts into their heads without giving them an understanding of the subject matter. Gaining a thorough understanding of a complex topic requires examining it piece by piece, using trial and error to learn its intricacies.

Delays are expensive. Requirements gathering is critical to a product's success, but it is only one part of the overall project. Many projects have tight deadlines, with many people depending on your use cases. So you need to finish your use cases as soon as possible so that others can ramp up to full speed.

The requirements are likely to change as a result of our examining them. Requirements are frequently volatile and likely to change as we learn more about them. There almost seems to be a Heisenberg Uncertainty Principle that applies to requirements: Analyzing a requirement tends to change the requirement. A requirement that once seemed cast in concrete crumbles upon further analysis. As you examine one requirement, you are likely to uncover information about others, and often discover that several requirements are wrong or missing. Another challenge is separating wants from needs. Things will eventually stabilize, but only after much analysis and rework.

The cost of requirements mistakes is high. An argument that is sometimes used to justify the waterfall software development life cycle is the downstream cost of fixing a requirements mistake. Such a mistake caught during the requirements analysis phase may cost only a nominal dollar to fix; the same mistake caught in the design phase, $2. The cost quickly escalates the later the mistake is discovered: implementation, $4; test, $20; deployment, $68 (Boehm 1981). No wonder there is a desire to get the requirements right the first time, up front.

If you dive in too quickly, you will overwhelm others. Use case development is usually a learning process for everyone involved. People require time to learn, and while you may understand the system, if you go too quickly, you may leave everyone else behind. It is important to finish your use cases in a timely manner, but it is more important that the whole organization has a chance to learn the system well, as they will be carrying most of the development load.

Therefore:

> Develop use cases in an iterative, breadth-first manner, with each iteration progressively increasing the precision and accuracy of the use case set.

Working along **BreadthBeforeDepth**, pause when you have listed the actors and their goals, and work with that list for a while. Use the list to set up the project plan, estimate work, prioritize the use cases' value—even to help set up the development teams.

Continuing with **BreadthBeforeDepth**, choose a working subset of the use cases to expand, and pause again when you have a set of main success scenarios, to review the purpose of the system. Take the opportunity at this moment to review the use cases. See whether you need to **MergeDroplets** (p. 209) or **CleanHouse** (p. 213), or in any other way improve the structure. You may find yourself revising the list of actors and goals at this point.

You will probably find yourself revising your list of use cases one more time when you start working out the extension-handling behavior for your use cases. It often happens that new use cases turn up at this point. For example, when writing use cases for a simple ATM system, people usually don't think about what happens when there is a communications break between the ATM and its host computer. While writing down the details for handling that situation, it slowly occurs to people that when communications come back up, the ATM will have some specific work to do. Handling that system condition will force the team to create a new use case such as *Reestablish Communications,* which did not exist before.

SpiralDevelopment interacts with **BreadthBeforeDepth**. Imagine working to build all the use cases **BreadthBeforeDepth**, without any plan to revise the use cases along the way. Experience shows us, however, that as people add to the use case, they uncover new situations for which they have to write use cases, detect new similarities across use cases, and find new and better ways to structure the use case set. **Spiral-Development** advises the team that they will have to pause and regroup their work, and it indicates where to pause to review their work.

Key to the successful use of iterative development, of which **SpiralDevelopment** is an example, are knowing how to manage your energy in reviewing, and when it is time to stop. Use a **TwoTier Review** (p. 64), and stop as soon as you are sure that your use cases are good enough to meet your stakeholders' needs, so that you can avoid the law of diminishing returns. **QuittingTime** (p. 68) provides a set of criteria that you can use to determine that point.

Examples

Wings Over the World

The expression "Can't see the forest for the trees" describes one of the mistakes made by the use case team in this installment of the Wings Over the World story. Many use case teams divide the system up and assign portions to different use case writers. Each use case writer goes off and independently begins to write detailed use cases. Even though requirements may be vague, ambiguous, inconsistent, missing, or just plain wrong, the use case writers attempt to write very detailed use cases. Detail becomes a substitute for accuracy, and disagreements often break out between the writers as they try to resolve their differences. In this installment of the Wings Over the World story, a source of friction between Sitra and Ralph is that Sitra's work makes Ralph's work obsolete. Worse, Ralph has invested weeks of effort into writing his use case, and is not very happy about having to scrap that work.

Never underestimate the benefits of the big picture and incrementally developing and readjusting your use cases. When someone invests a lot of effort into creating a use case (or any other project artifact for that matter) he is reluctant to discard it, even when it really is unnecessary or incorrect. If Wings Over the World had followed the solution recommended by **BreadthBeforeDepth**, what would their work products look like?

First, they could start with something simple, such as an actor list that just enumerates the actors and the names of use cases they use. For example, a fragment of the Wings Over the World actor list may look something like Table 3.1.

Table 3.1 *Sample Actor List for Wings Over the World*

Actor	Use Case
Agent	*Reserve Flight*
	Book Flight
	Cancel Flight Reservation
	Request Upgrade
	Open Passenger Profile
	Close Passenger Profile
Airline	*Cancel Flight*
	Discount Flight

An actor list is not very precise, but it is accurate to the extent that we know the functional requirements for the system. The name for each of the use cases gives us some idea of what the goal of the use case is. Creating an actor list does not require a lot of effort, making it easier to change or drop proposed use cases. This list also helps us try to keep the *goal level* of each use case the same. It is easier to see at a glance if there are use cases that do not fit in with the others. In this example, *Open Passenger Profile* and *Close Passenger Profile* stand out because their goal level appears to be lower than the other candidate use cases. With little effort, these are quickly pruned out from the use case set or merged into other use cases.

Once the writers have finished the list, they may try to write simple, one-paragraph stories describing the main success scenario for the use case. These are often called *briefs* or *high-level use cases*. For example, see Use Cases 3.1 and 3.2.

Use Case 3.1   Brief for *Reserve Flight*

Reserve Flight

Actor: Agent

The agent specifies a client's desired travel itinerary. The system searches for a suit-able flight routing and presents it to the agent. The agent selects a routing that best matches the client's desires. The system verifies availability and then reserves the seats. The system calculates the fare price for the class of service requested by the agent.

Use Case 3.2   Brief for *Book Flight*

Book Flight

Actor: Agent

The agent retrieves a client's reservation and books the flight. The agent examines the aircraft seat map and selects the client's preferred seats in the aircraft. The agent enters the client's payment information, and the system books and assigns the seats. The system prints the tickets.

Briefs allow us to refine the actor list and incrementally increase the precision of our use cases. These briefs tell us which actions the use case author believes are essential for reserving and booking flights. From them, we can tell that reserving a flight does not include paying for the flight or even selecting a seat; that is part of *Book Flight*. Briefs do not specify detailed steps, alternatives, preconditions, or post-conditions. Rather, their intention is to quickly cover the broad scope of the system, that is, its breadth, before we dive into the depths of the details. Briefs are easy to write, available for early review, and easy to fix. They allow you to detect and correct problems quickly, before problems gain a foothold and become ingrained in the system.

Once we have defined a broad system view, then we can expand a subset of the briefs and begin to fill in their details. We include step-by-step descriptions of the main success scenario, alternative courses of actions, preconditions, and post-conditions. It is important to note that we define only a subset of the briefs. Perhaps each use case writer takes one brief and simply enumerates the alternatives. Then, with this addi-tional information added to the use case, the team may once again review the use case to determine what effect it may have on the other candidate use cases.

We call this technique *Surface and Dive,* where we take one or just a handful of use cases and dive down into the details once we have developed the broad scope of the system. Once at the bottom, we surface again to see what effect the detailed use cases have had on the rest of the use cases. We carefully adjust the model, select another subset of briefs, and dive down into the details of the use cases. Using this approach, even Sitra and Ralph may be able to come to a consensus.

A More Literary Example

Dictionaries and encyclopedias contain immense amounts of information, which their publishers are constantly revising. But the volumes are so large that the publishers don't want to start new editions from scratch and completely rewrite them every few years. Instead, they are written iteratively, reusing as much of the previous edition as possible, adding new words or articles as needed, and modifying or eliminating the obsolete entries. This method considerably simplifies the writing process, and greatly reduces the time to market. As an added bonus, the publisher can resell much of the same information every few years to the same customers.

◆ **SpiralDevelopment and UML Models, by Dan Rawsthorne**

It is especially important to realize that you do not need to develop your Use Case Models all at once. As you are iteratively improving your use case set, you should be iteratively improving your use case diagrams as well.

Also, there is no requirement that all your use cases belong on the same diagram. Your diagrams must be understandable. As you progressively increase the quality of your use case set, you may find the need for a number of different models that focus on different things, such as:

- Diagrams based on actors
- Diagrams based on similar functionality
- Diagrams based on abstraction level

Mrs. Ryan's dogs

3.3 MultipleForms

You are writing use cases with a **SharedClearVision** (p. 80).

> Different projects need different degrees of formality in their work, and various people have different preferences for the template. Requiring everyone to use the same use case template is counterproductive.

Taste in music is a highly personal thing. What is good for one person may not be acceptable for another. Some people like rock and roll, some like country, and never the twain shall meet. People will refuse to buy a particular album because they see it in the wrong section, or think it might be the wrong genre. When I was growing up, it was common for older people who would never buy a Beatles album ("It's not music") to snap up Perry Como's or The Boston Pops' renditions of Beatles songs without a second thought. Music companies take advantage of these differences. They don't snub any type of popular music, but instead package each album to maximize sales in its particular market segment.

People and projects are different. Everyone is unique, and each person has his or her own way of looking at the world. Our personalities, experiences, and training shape our individual natures, and as a result, each of us sees things differently from other people. Similarly, each development organization has its own people, history, and culture that differentiate it from any other group.

Different projects have different needs. Projects may be large or small, simple or complex, and represent either new functionality or a remake of an existing system. For these projects, use cases might describe a business process, focus discussion about a future software system, describe functional system requirements, or document a system's design. You could develop your project locally, or be distributing the work over several teams in several geographical areas. Each of these factors affects the amount of formality you need in your use cases, and choosing the most appropriate form for your use cases must be done on a project-by-project basis.

You want to avoid getting caught up in unnecessary precision and rigor, costing your project a lot in expended time and energy. This risk needs to be balanced against the potential damage of missing key requirements. A format that is too lax will cause you to omit important details, but a format that is too rigid can create a lot of busy-work that adds nothing to the qualities of the model.

Different teams want different amounts of formality. Different methods for documenting use cases exist to fulfill different needs. At one extreme, an organization may require very formal use cases that rigorously define all possible system behaviors, while at the other end of the spectrum, an organization may require very simple use cases. Any of these approaches can be correct, as long as they adequately describe what the developers and stakeholders need to know, with an appropriate level of detail.

Using a common form within an organization facilitates communication. A standard use case form or template makes it easier for people to know what information to put in their use cases as well as what information to expect from one. More important, because this form is usually well defined, it is easier to use and easier to understand the purpose of each of the use case's components.

Although templates are useful, some people have an insatiable urge to fill in all the boxes in one go. This depth-first approach can sap your energy and cause you to lose focus. Worse, it can waste a lot of time by forcing you to do unnecessary rework revising and refactoring your use cases as you learn more about the system. It is important to realize what needs to be completed at the desired level of precision.

Therefore:

> **Select the format based on the risks associated with the project and the preferences of the people involved.**

Be open-minded when choosing a format for your use cases, and don't fall into the rut that all use cases should look alike. Use cases are only a tool for describing a system's behavior to your stakeholders and developers, and therefore need to meet only their needs for precision and content. Any more information is unnecessary.

Base your template selection on the purpose and level of risk associated with each use case. For critical use cases, write more formalized use cases containing a generous amount of information, and pay close attention to **ExhaustiveAlternatives** (p. 129) and **PreciseAndReadable** (p. 138). For less critical or better understood ones, be less formal and use less detail.

While it can be tempting to use different templates on the same project, it is not a good idea; multiple templates are way too hard for a team to wade through. Choose a standard template for any one project, and stay with it. The template will help the team handle the **SpiralDevelopment** (p. 52) of the use case set. A team of advanced practitioners may find it appropriate to write with differing amounts of formality and rigor for different use cases in the same set, but they should still use the same template to avoid confusion.

Examples

Batch Job Distribution

Sometimes, the name is all you need. I helped my team write use cases for a system that would distribute large "batch" jobs across a set of workstations and personal computers. During the course of the project, we identified approximately seventy use cases covering a wide range of system behavior. Because we had a strong understanding of the system from working on its predecessor, we annotated only the ten or so use cases that described the various ways the users would use the system. We left the rest blank (Use Case 3.3) because they described familiar behavior (for example, job monitoring, logging on to and off of the system, and so on). These sixty "textless" use cases were very valuable to us, as we used them to define the system servers and the boundaries between them. We could have annotated them, but our team was very small, and this effort would not have helped our already tight schedule. However, the annotated job flow use cases were very useful, because they significantly described interesting behavior that we would have to understand when we built the system. We referred to these use cases often, both with customers and in design meetings. Accordingly, we were able to build a successful system with a small team in a short period of time.

Use Case 3.3   Use Cases for the Workstation Monitor Server

Actor	Description
Administrator	Person monitoring and controlling job control system

Use Case	Description
Login	Log Administrator onto server*
Logout	Log Administrator off of server*
Set Monitor Parameters	Allow Administrator to specify boundaries and precision of items being monitored
Select Monitor	Choose something to monitor (such as throughput, processes, or wait queue)

Monitor Workstation	Collect the performance statistics for the jobs using the workstation
Display Results	Display the performance results that the user selected according to the Administrator's specified preferences

* Some methodologists debate whether login and logout in general constitute valid use cases. We defined them in this case because we knew we would have to implement functionality for logging users on and off the server.

Purchasing for a Business

The key question is how much information does your audience need? Use cases 3.4 and 3.5, taken from *Writing Effective Use Cases* (Cockburn 2001), demonstrate different forms for the same use case. The first use case is appropriate when describing a high-level view of the process, or in those instances when the stakeholders already possess a good understanding of the feature.

Use Case 3.4 *Buy Something* (Casual Version)

Buy Something (Casual Version)

The Requestor initiates a request and sends it to the Approver. The Approver checks that there is money in the budget, checks the price of the goods, completes the request for submission, and sends the request to the Buyer. The Buyer checks the contents of storage and finds the best vendor for the goods. The Authorizer validates the Approver's signature. The Buyer then completes a request for ordering and initiates a PO with the Vendor. The Vendor delivers the goods to Receiving and gets a receipt for delivery (out of scope of system under design). The Receiver registers the delivery and sends the goods to the Requestor. The use case ends when the Requestor marks the request delivered.

At any time prior to receiving the goods, the Requestor can change or cancel the request. Cancelling it removes it from any active processing (delete from system?). Reducing the price doesn't affect the request's status, while raising the price sends it back to Approver.

Often your use cases require more detail or formality, as demonstrated by Use Case 3.5.

Use Case 3.5 *Buy Something* (Fully Dressed Version)

Buy Something (Fully Dressed Version)

Primary Actor: Requestor

Goal in Context: Requestor buys something through the system, gets it. Does not include paying for it.

Scope: Business—The overall purchasing mechanism, electronic and non-electronic, as seen by the people in the company.

Level: Summary

Stakeholders and Interests

  Requestor: Wants what he/she ordered and an easy way to do that.

  Company: Wants to control spending but allow needed purchases.

  Vendor: Wants to get paid for any goods delivered.

Precondition: None

Minimal Guarantees: Every order sent out has been approved by a valid Authorizer. Order was tracked so that company can be billed only for valid goods received.

Success Guarantees: Requestor has goods, correct budget ready to be debited.

Trigger: Requestor decides to buy something.

Main Success Scenario

1. **Requestor:** Initiate a request.
2. **Approver:** Check money in the budget, check price of goods, complete request for submission.
3. **Buyer:** Check contents of storage, find best vendor for goods.
4. **Authorizer:** Validate Approver's signature.
5. **Buyer:** Complete request for ordering, initiate PO with Vendor.
6. **Vendor:** Deliver goods to Receiving, get receipt for delivery (out of scope of system under design).
7. **Receiver:** Register delivery, send goods to Requestor.
8. **Requestor:** Mark request delivered.

Extensions

1a. Requestor does not know vendor or price: leave those parts blank and continue.

1b. At any time prior to receiving goods, Requestor can change or cancel the request.

  Canceling it removes it from any active processing. (Delete from system?)

  Reducing price leaves it intact in process.

  Raising price sends it back to Approver.

2a. Approver does not know vendor or price: Leave blank and let Buyer fill in or call back.

2b. Approver is not Requestor's manager: Still okay, as long as Approver signs.

2c. Approver declines: Send back to Requestor for change or deletion.

3a. Buyer finds goods in storage: Send those up, reduce request by that amount and carry on.

3b. Buyer fills in Vendor and price, which were missing: Request gets re-sent to Approver.

4a. Authorizer declines Approver: Send back to Requestor and remove from active processing. (What does this mean exactly?)

5a. Request involves multiple vendors: Buyer generates multiple POs.

5b. Buyer merges multiple requests: Same process, but mark PO with the requests being merged.

6a. Vendor does not deliver on time: System does alert of nondelivery.

7a. Partial delivery: Receiver marks partial delivery on PO and continues.

7b. Partial delivery of multiple-request PO: Receiver assigns quantities to requests and continues.

8a. Goods are incorrect or improper quality: Requestor refuses delivered goods. (What does this mean?)

8b. Requestor has quit the company: Buyer checks with Requestor's manager, either reassigns Requestor, or returns goods and cancels request.

Technology and Data Variations List: None

Priority: Various

Releases: Several

Response Time: Various

Frequency of Use: Three times a day

Channel to Primary Actor: Internet browser, mail system, or equivalent

Channels to Secondary Actors: Fax, phone, car

Open Issues:

When is a canceled request deleted from the system?

What authorization is needed to cancel a request?

Who can alter a request's contents?

Children playing on a jungle gym

3.4 TwoTierReview

You have been writing use cases in a series of **SpiralDevelopments** (p. 52).

> Many people may need to review the use cases. This is an expensive, time-consuming proposition.

Representative democracy is a system of government in which citizens elect people to represent them in a deliberative body. These representatives study the issues as they arise, and vote on them based on their understanding of the subject and their constituents' feelings. If a citizen has a concern about an issue, she can talk to her representative about it, potentially influencing the legislator's decision. The system isn't perfect, but it is certainly more efficient than having millions of people debating every issue or voting on each and every decision, big or small. While the representatives make the decisions, the voters have the final say. Voters can remove from office those representatives that they feel are ineffective or who have failed to represent them.

This system provides a good model for reviewing use cases, especially those intended for large, diverse groups of stakeholders. It allows every interested group to have its say as to the use case's contents, without overwhelming everyone, or requiring excessive time.

Reviews are necessary to verify and validate writing and content. Reviews are a good way to validate the correctness and completeness of a piece of work early in the development process. People tend to believe their work is better than it really is, often thinking that the quality of work is proportional to the effort spent on it. But inadequate, inaccurate work can distract the audience from a document's purpose; your stakeholders expect professionalism in business documents. It is harder for writers to catch their own mistakes because they are familiar with their work and tend to draw inferences from it that aren't necessarily there. People reading a document for the first time are more likely to notice errors because the errors distract them from understanding it.

The stakeholders have a vested interest in the use cases. Many different groups have a vested interest in a set of use cases and depend upon the use cases to help them do their work. It is in your best interest as a writer to consult with these groups early and often, to simplify your effort and minimize the amount of rework required to produce acceptable use cases that adequately address the stakeholders' issues.

It is expensive, tiring, and slow to involve everyone in the writing process. Teams with too many people tend to get in their own way, they are inefficient, and they require a lot of effort to coordinate. A **SmallWritingTeam** (p. 31) helps keep the process manageable and tends to cut down on feature creep.

If only a small writing team is doing the review, not all stakeholders' interests are incorporated. It is very difficult, if not impossible, for a small writing team of two or three people to represent the views of a large, diverse audience. A **SmallWriting-Team** without a **ParticipatingAudience** (p. 35) doesn't have the experience or the diverse knowledge base to understand or represent all of the stakeholders' views on a large project. It is likely that such teams will miss key parts of the system without this help.

Reviews can be expensive, tedious, and time-consuming. For a review to be effective, the participants need to invest a great deal of time and energy. The time spent on frequent or long reviews, with many people, quickly adds up to significant manpower. Therefore, we need to be judicious when conducting reviews, by scheduling them only when needed and requiring as few people as absolutely necessary. Also, while some people like reviewing development material, others despise it. You can allow all interested parties to attend, but keep the required attendance to a minimum.

Therefore:

> Hold two types of review: The first by a smaller, internal team, possibly repeated many times; the second by the complete group, perhaps just once.

First, review the use cases internally to verify their readability, implementability, precision, and accuracy. These "inner" reviews can be informal desk reviews, formal meetings, or a combination of both. Any kind of review is appropriate as long as it allows the reviewers to catch errors and verify that your use cases are sufficient as far as they are concerned. One of the purposes of these initial reviews is to eliminate the "noise" caused by spelling, grammatical, formatting, and technical errors, which when left uncorrected are distracting.

You may need to hold several of these inner reviews when the system is large or overly complex. Because people tend to lose interest in detailed discussions outside of their own area of interest, consider holding separate group reviews for different functional areas when formally reviewing use cases aimed at a large, disparate customer base. That way, each group of stakeholders can review the use cases in depth from their particular point of view without distraction.

At the end of these inner reviews, the teams are asserting that it is **QuittingTime** (p. 68), and that the use cases are complete, correct, and as implementable as they need to be at this point. The use cases are then ready for the bigger group to check.

Hold at least one meeting with the complete group once the use cases pass internal muster, to review the system as a unified whole. Trust the first tier of reviews to validate the internal workings of the system, so that the second tier can focus on how the pieces fit together.

The definition of "complete group" varies by project. It should be all the people who review the requirements before development gets too far underway. In some cases it is just the development team; sometimes developers plus an executive; sometimes it is the business analysts and the lead programmers; sometimes it is users, executives, and the entire programming team. The purpose of the "outer" reviews is to determine the following.

- Is this really the appropriate thing for the developers to spend time building? (business-value check)
- Is this correct as a specification? (Are the business rules correct, and does it leave open the proper allowed variations in implementation? Does it lock down the important decisions? Does it identify the appropriate set of open issues that can be handled later?)
- Can the developers really build it?

Examples

Wings Over the World (Continued)

Many of the stakeholders are grumbling about the frequent reviews, and some are even refusing to participate. Is it necessary that every review be an all-hands effort? Of course not! **SpiralDevelopment** (p. 52) requires regular reassessments of the use cases to verify (1) that the use cases are a fair representation of the functional requirements and (2) that structurally the use cases exhibit the signs of quality advocated by the patterns listed in this book. The majority of stakeholders are only interested in reviewing the use cases to verify that the use cases protect their interests. Although all the stakeholders or their representatives want to participate in the project, they certainly don't want to spend long hours in formal and tedious use case meetings each week to review minor changes.

TwoTierReviews allow the writers to preview the use cases first, removing obvious errors and much of the "noise" that can be distracting and time-consuming in formal reviews. More important, they provide a "safety-valve" for the review process, ensuring that most of the stakeholders only see the use cases when they are hopefully complete, somewhat polished, and actually ready for review.

The Programmer Who Cried Review

Once upon a time there was a programmer who was designing a new system for a large company. It was an important system that would alter the jobs of many people. The programmer wanted to make sure the interests of all the people affected by the system were protected, so soon after he finished a draft of the system vision, he cried out, "Review!" The moment he cried out, all the people came running to the conference room, because they knew that the last person to arrive would have to take minutes. For the next two hours, they reviewed the draft of the system, taking down action items. At the end of the meeting, all the people thanked the programmer for allowing them to verify that the vision addressed their interests.

The programmer incorporated all the action items into the second draft of the system vision and once again cried out, "Review!" Just as quickly as before, all the people came running into the conference room. For the next two hours, they all reviewed the updated draft. Some people grumbled this time that they had better things to do than sit in a review, but still most of the people thanked the programmer for allowing them to verify that the vision still addressed their interests.

The programmer incorporated all the action items from the second review into a third draft of the system vision and once again cried out, "Review!" As quickly as before, all the people came running into the conference room. For the next two hours, they all reviewed the updated draft. This time, most of the people grumbled that they had better things to do than sit in a review. They complained that they did not want to be called into another review unless there was something more than just document structure to look at.

The programmer incorporated all the action items from the third review into a fourth draft of the system vision and once again cried out, "Review!" But this time, no one came running to the conference room, not even the interns. "Review! Review!" cried the programmer. Still no one came. So the programmer decided to baseline the system vision anyway.

Unfortunately, this situation let an important feature fall through the cracks, and the company's CEO was embarrassed at a live demo when it was not there. The programmer ended up in the Call Center gulag because he had cried, "Review!" too often.

Day shift lining up before the time clocks to punch out. Bethlehem-Fairfield shipyards, Baltimore, Maryland

3.5 *QuittingTime*

You have written a set of use cases in a **BreadthBeforeDepth** (p. 48) manner.

> Developing a use case model beyond the needs of the stakeholders and developers wastes resources and delays the project.

Engineering history is full of stories of heavily overspecified and overdesigned systems. The military has often borne the brunt of these stories because they have a tendency to rigorously overspecify the requirements for any acquisition. We always hear about hammers and toilet seats procured by the military costing tens and sometimes even hundreds of times the price of their off-the-shelf cousins. While these incidents make entertaining news stories, they point to the real problem of overspecification.

We specify requirements to reduce the risk of creating the wrong system for the stakeholders, and many methodologies prescribe rigorous requirements specification procedures that must be closely followed. However, this rigorous approach to requirements specification does not take advantage of shared experience or common sense among the project participants. Consider buying a hammer: Most people simply walk into a hardware store and say, "I need a hammer," trusting that the salesperson knows what they mean. If they want to be really precise, they might say, "I need a claw hammer."

In contrast, military procedures may require the procurement officer to disregard common shared knowledge and say

> I need a MIND—Manual Impact Nail Device. The MIND shall have an impact face between 15 and 20 millimeters in diameter and must be made from dropforged tungsten steel. The MIND shall also have an integrated NRU—Nail Recovery Unit—consisting of twin 30-millimeter carbon steel prongs, set apart in a V formation with a maximum gap spacing of 5 millimeters. Lastly, the MIND shall have a human-machine interface of oak or equivalent hardwood. . . .

It is easy to see how this practice delays simple acquisitions and escalates costs.

Good use cases are balanced, describing essential system behavior while providing only the necessary details about the interactions between a system and its users. They are complete enough so that their readers can easily understand what the system does, but they are not formal tomes that describe the system to the *n*th degree. Knowing when to quit writing use cases can be difficult, because deciding when to stop involves balancing some complex forces.

A paralyzing fear of overlooking important requirements encourages builders and stakeholders to prolong the requirements-gathering activity. Because it is much easier to fix requirements than it is to fix code, many developers will drag their heels and put off designing a system until they are absolutely sure that their requirements are correct. Some developers believe that the later a requirement error is found in the project, the greater the cost associated with rectifying the problem. Others fear the potential embarrassment and loss of stakeholder confidence if they overlook an important requirement.

Many technical professionals place an unwarranted high priority on model formality. Technical professionals are trained and indoctrinated in problem-solving techniques that require formal, precise descriptions. Formality is important from their point of view because it provides a "liberating form" for guiding and channeling the thought process, and it also minimizes ambiguity and omissions.

Ambiguity can destroy a project. Common engineering school dogma in the 1970s held that a slight miscalculation of less than one-tenth of one percent would have caused the *Apollo* spacecraft to miss the Moon completely, and send the astronauts into eternal orbit. Small details matter, and leaving the interpretation of vague requirements to the implementers' imagination can lead to missing functionality as well as some highly innovative features that take the product into unforeseen and unwanted areas. When writing use cases, stopping too soon is an easy way to introduce all kinds of ambiguity into a system.

Most people can work with a fair level of ambiguity. Many organizations possess "core competencies." These attributes represent the shared knowledge and experience of the people within the organization that give the organization an advantage over its competitors. Core competencies help the organization reduce the risk associated with projects. For example, when a carpenter tells an apprentice to get a hammer and some nails, he probably does not have to explain the full details of what kind of hammer and what kind of nails to fetch. The context of the situation in which they are working and the shared background help the apprentice understand the specific needs of the situation.

Overspecification of requirements may convince stakeholders that the requirements are more accurate than they actually are. In high school science, many of us were taught the importance of experimental error. For example, we could not write in our laboratory notebooks that the mass of a specimen was 10.3482727 grams if our scale could only measure to a tenth of a gram of accuracy. We did not want to imply more precision in the result than we could actually measure. Stated another way, telling detailed lies does not make them any more accurate or truthful. Likewise, there is a tendency to assume that detailed requirements are more accurate (truthful) than less detailed requirements. Writing detailed requirements will hide the uncertainty associated with the requirements.

The cost of a mistake is quite small if it is caught early; often the cost of not moving ahead is exorbitant. Human beings make mistakes and have misunderstandings in the best of circumstances. The challenge is to discover quickly that a mistake has been made and exploit the knowledge gained from the mistake. Mistakes caught early in the project are less costly to fix. Delaying a project until all requirements are known can be dramatically more expensive.

Therefore:

> **Stop developing use cases once they are complete and satisfactorily meet audience needs.**

You need to know what your goals for writing use cases are before you can determine if your use cases are complete. It is important to communicate clearly to all involved why you want to write use cases in the first place, as well as what problems and risks you need them to resolve.

To determine if your use cases are complete, ask the following questions:

1. Have you identified and documented all actors and goals?
2. Has the customer, or someone representing the customer, acknowledged that the use case set is complete, and that each use case is readable and correct?
3. Can your designers implement these use cases?

If the answer to any of these questions is no, then chances are you need to do more. Take advantage of the core competencies of the organization and the shared knowledge of the stakeholders to flesh out your use cases. Always keep in sight what the stakeholders need to see in the model. Once the stakeholders agree that the use cases adequately reflect their vision of the system, you are close to being finished, but it is important to satisfy all three questions.

Don't fuss too much about quality, and avoid excessive attention to adornments. There comes a point beyond which further development of the use case model will not yield any more understanding about the system. At this point you should exercise your **WritersLicense** (p. 73), "put your pencil down," and move on.

You can always add more details later, as you learn more about the system. If moving on reveals ambiguities and uncertainties in the model, do not hesitate to pick up the pencil again and exploit the newfound knowledge. Be careful to consider the consequences to the entire system. Don't add the new details all at once to completion, but do it in an organized manner (that is, **BreadthBeforeDepth**), applying this information throughout the set of use cases where appropriate.

Examples

Wings Over the World (Continued)

Ahmed and Ralph are arguing over the completeness of the use cases the team has written. Ahmed states that the use cases cannot be complete until all details are filled in. Ralph says that it is a waste of time and that they should just get on with it. Who is right?

"How do you know when you're done?" is one of the toughest questions to answer on a project. Many wonderful textbooks offer absolute answers to this question, but unless you have the financial resources of a federal government, you usually must push something out the door long before the completion criteria recommended by the textbooks. Like any real company, our fictitious Wings Over the World operates in a very competitive world and needs to deploy systems quickly.

QuittingTime is about balancing the risk of delaying the project with the risk of incomplete requirements. Software engineering textbooks often place a very high risk premium on incomplete requirements because they assume the development organization has little or no expertise in their problem domain, nor is there some level of trust between project members. But all of these factors usually exist in a company. The term "core competency" was coined in the 1990s to describe the advantage that knowledge and trust give to a company. Fast-moving, agile development methodologies such as XP take this to the extreme, where they take advantage of corporate knowledge for a high level of development agility. For example, XP requires a customer representative to be part of the development team to quickly resolve requirement shortcomings.

What the Wings Over the World story never makes clear is what the purpose of the use cases actually is, and who is going to use them. For example, if the intention is to outsource the development of the system, then the use cases require a great deal more rigor and completeness. The slow pace of communications between a client and its vendor would increase the risk in any of the ambiguities in the requirements. On the other hand, if the system is being developed in-house, the developers will have easy access to users and domain experts. If the developers take advantage of that close relationship, then they can tolerate a great deal more ambiguity.

Wings Over the World has decided to outsource a portion of the development of their new system. This decision implies that we need more rigor because of the higher potential for misunderstandings and the slower rate at which discrepancies are found in this type of situation. It is likely that the outsource vendor will have a template it uses for writing use cases. That template will be one part of a methodology used by a consulting company. But team members should be cautious that they do not fall into the trap of filling in every detail in the template for the sake of doing so.

The **BreadthBeforeDepth** (p. 48) approach facilitates an early **QuittingTime**, because it does not demand that every use case be written to a predefined level of detail. In fact, it may in some cases be acceptable to leave some use cases as briefs, when adding more detail does not add any new knowledge—the problem and solution are well known in the organization. This is an approach that relies on trust.

Bust of Shakespeare

3.6 WritersLicense

You are conducting **TwoTierReviews** (p. 64) on your use cases, and are questioning whether it might be **QuittingTime** (p. 68).

> Excessive emphasis on style issues unnecessarily impedes the effort of writing use cases.

Each year, film and television companies produce movies and TV programs based on true stories. Most of these productions take a creative license with the story to make it more appealing to a wider audience. For example, the film *The Serpent and the Rainbow* (1988) was based on a book by Wade Davis about a medical researcher looking for a new anesthetic in Haiti. When asked about the liberties the movie had taken with his story, Davis simply replied, "It's not exactly the story I wrote, but then I doubt that my story would have opened on 1700 screens."

We should allow some freedom in our use case style to suit each unique system and audience.

We would like a consistent writing style, to simplify reading. A familiar style can be reassuring to readers when they are trying to understand something new. An inconsistent style, however, can confuse readers and make it difficult for them to find information; the mix of styles forces them to readjust to each use case. It can be especially frustrating to look for some information that appears in a different place in each use case.

It is costly and impractical to get everyone to write in exactly the same style. Writing is highly individualistic, and everyone has his or her own personal style. You could revise the use cases until they are similar, but this practice wastes time, energy, and money, and leads to sending the manuscript around and around and around. There comes a point when the law of diminishing returns takes effect, and the results aren't worth the effort. Style guides are useful, but they only solve part of the problem, because it is impossible for them to document every potential issue. A common style is "frosting on the cake," but not worth substantial extra effort.

There is value in getting the use cases into development sooner. The sooner the developers have the use cases, the sooner they can start developing the product, and the sooner they can finish it. Every delay in moving use cases into development can cause project slippage, which costs money. It doesn't matter if the use case's style contains some minor variances; the developers can still use them.

We still need to meet the basic completion criteria of a use case being readable, logically correct, and detailed enough for the developers. The purpose of use cases is to provide information that accurately describes a system in an easy-to-read format. Use cases should correctly document enough knowledge so that the people depending upon them can easily find enough information to help them do their jobs, whether they are working with the big picture or implementing the low-level parts of the system.

Therefore:

> Small differences in writing style are inevitable. Once a use case passes the tests for **QuittingTime**, the writer can claim "writer's license" on small stylistic differences.

Write each use case so that it passes the following tests.

- It follows the organization's writing template and basic style.
- It is logically correct.
- It is readable to the end evaluators.
- It is precise enough for the implementers to use.

Once the use cases meet these tests, allow each author to have final say on smaller stylistic matters. Small differences in writing style are up to each use case writer. Writers can claim "license" to make any changes they think appropriate and ignore other style changes they do not find worthwhile.

Style guides can be useful within a limited context, for a specific purpose, by describing a common "look and feel" for your use cases, and informing the writers about standard use case properties. Just be sure to treat such manuals as *guides,* not as a set of iron-clad rules. They should be flexible enough to promote individual creativity and not hinder the exchange of information.

Examples

Wings Over the World (Continued)

Chief Architect Ahmed is suggesting a rigid style manual that specifies the rules for writing use case descriptions. While his intentions are good, they defeat the utility of a use case. Use cases are meaningful to the project participants because they are semi-formal artifacts. They have enough structure so that the readers can ferret out the inconsistencies and gross ambiguities in the requirements, but not at the expense of making them unreadable to someone who is not expertly trained in the methodology.

All project participants have gone through a basic one-day use case course, so they do know what a use case is about. But can you imagine trying to get a travel agent or marketing manager to understand pseudocode? For requirements to be useful, they must be well understood by those who must review those requirements.

Use case writers frequently abuse templates. Templates represent a good checklist of items that may be included in the final use case, not a prescription for everything that must be in the use case. One of our personal peeves is with the preconditions section of a use case. Easily 90 percent of the use case preconditions that we have seen state something to the effect of "User is logged on." While this may be valid, does it really add value to the use case? Writers should determine what helps the audience understand the use case, and what words or phrases contribute nothing.

3.7 Trade-offs and Collaborations

Following the right development process is critical to writing quality use cases. This process doesn't have to be elegant or "high powered," but it does need to cover all the bases. For developing use cases, good process means balancing discovery versus writing and content versus need. Although it would be nice to have one, there is no one-size-fits-all process for creating quality use cases. Writing use cases is highly personalized; everyone has his or her own style, and every organization has its own way of doing things, based on its culture and business needs. Yet, while there are multiple ways of writing quality use cases, the better processes share several common elements. The process patterns presented in this chapter describe the characteristics of effective use case development, and are intended to help you create your own process.

These patterns are closely related to each other, each describing a different aspect of use case development. As a result, they tend to work together rather than conflict with each other, and we don't really see any trade-offs among them. **MultipleForms** (p. 58) recommends formatting use cases in a style that is appropriate to the project and the audience's need, instead of using a companywide standard form. Everyone writing use cases for a particular project should use the same template, but choosing which one should be the team's own decision. **BreadthBeforeDepth** (p. 48) and **SpiralDevelopments** (p. 52) are very tightly coupled, and form an efficient basis for developing use cases. Working across a set keeps the set balanced, and keeps you aware of the relationships among its various members. If you determine that two use cases really address the same issue, or that some are unnecessary, you can react sooner in the writing cycle, minimizing the amount of unnecessary work. But this method by itself can be overwhelming, unless you do it in reasonably sized chunks, developing the use cases incrementally in a series of cyclic expansions. Writing use cases is a discovery process in which you often learn things affecting several use cases while researching others. Breadth-first development is an efficient way to keep from getting ahead of yourself on any particular use case, and avoid revising it continually as you learn more about the system.

This iterative approach also allows an organization to determine when its use cases are "good enough" for its purposes, and stop writing them before reaching the point of diminishing returns. Yet, to stop with any degree of confidence, writers need to have some well-defined criteria. The pattern **QuittingTime** (p. 68) says you can quit writing use cases when (1) you believe that you have identified and documented all actors and goals, (2) the customer has approved the use cases, and (3) you believe that the developers can implement the system from these use cases. **TwoTierReview** (p. 64) prescribes an efficient review process that helps verify that the use case collection is correct and complete, and it facilitates **ParticipatingAudience** (p. 35). **Writers-License** (p. 73) states that small stylistic details are not that important, and that you can stop writing once you have addressed all of the system issues, even if some stylistic issues remain.

Process is only half the battle of writing high-quality use cases. Effective use cases are organized into a structure that clearly identifies certain key features of the system and allows readers of various backgrounds to use the various pieces easily. This structure is the subject of the next few chapters.

Chapter 4

The Use Case Set

◆ **Red-eye**

You seem to have a knack for doing it to yourself. No one asked you to hop the red-eye; no one told you to fly to the East Coast. You just blurted out to Wings Over the World's CIO, "Sure, I can be there tomorrow. I'll just see if I can book tonight's red-eye." It's now hour three of a five-hour flight east to Wings Over the World's corporate office. At nine in the morning, you're supposed to sit down with their requirements team and help them dig themselves out of the hole they've fallen into. Your mission is urgent because they are starting to develop a bad case of "silver-bullet syndrome"; believing that the use cases you hooked them on represent their ticket out of their requirements woes.

That's why you scrambled to get on the red-eye, to deal with the problems early, and reset their expectations before this case of silver-bullet syndrome becomes terminal to the project.

Like any project, this one is experiencing a lot of birthing pains. The first thing you noticed was that not everyone was clear on why Wings was taking on this multi-million-dollar project. During your last conference call with Ahmed, their chief architect, all he could gush about was how excited he was to be opening their system to the World Wide Web. "Everyone is looking forward to learning IBM's WebSphere, JSP, and EJB," he said.

You don't recall Wings Over the World's management caring one whit about the implementation technology. Rather, they were more interested in reducing ticketing costs and opening new revenue streams. Excitement about new technologies and methodologies is admirable—that has you excited about this project too—but there already seems to be a conflict between the tech team's vision and the rest of the management's vision.

The red flags really started popping up when you read the first use cases from Wings Over the World. The first major problem was that everyone seemed to have a different idea about what belongs in the system and, more important, what does not. Some of the programmers had already started writing use cases for managing customer complaints. You recall that only an interface to a CRM system was ever discussed; the CRM system itself was supposed to be out of scope. When you suggested that these features might be out of scope, you got the classic, "But we may need it in the future." At the other extreme, some of the programmers assumed that the scope of the system was just the Wings Over the World wholesale ticket operation, and that none of the flight-planning features were part of the system.

The spillover from a lack of a clear boundary is that there are actors all over the place. It looks like someone simply took all of the possible Wings Over the World's job descriptions and declared them to be actors. Most of the jobs have huge overlaps in responsibilities. You see use cases with names "Booker: Find Flight," "Agent: Find Flight," and "Consultant: Find Flight." The only difference you can see between these use cases is just who is trying to book the trip.

Worse, though the team doesn't know the scope of the system, it seems that they have simply assumed that everyone in the company will need to use the new system to do their job. That's probably the source of all those customer service use cases that you think belong outside of the system.

You get a little restless smile as you read other use cases. CRUD must be one of the most aptly defined acronyms ever, because it best describes so many of the use cases you have seen. Easily 70 percent of the use cases are of the form *"actor create data," "actor read data," "actor update data," "actor delete data."* None of these use cases tells you why the actor is performing that action or what he hopes to accomplish from it. How can the use cases ever help the company discover if the system is going to do anything meaningful or satisfy its stakeholders' expectations?

The use case set patterns are the signs of quality for a well-written set of use cases. These signs of quality are not directly attributable to a single use case; rather, they describe the emergent properties of all the use cases taken together. These patterns answer the question, "What are the signs of quality that are visible in a good set of use cases?"

First and foremost, the use case writers must have a **SharedClearVision** (p. 80) of the system's purpose and goals. Why are you building this system, and does everyone know and share the same vision? The need for a vision goes beyond use cases because if project participants are unclear about its purpose, they are likely to assume one, correctly or incorrectly. A clear, well-defined vision significantly simplifies development by enabling everyone working on the system to understand what they are trying to do, and why they are doing it. Everyone involved with the system must share the same vision to enable them to work in unison.

The vision must be bounded by a **VisibleBoundary** (p. 86) that limits the scope of the system. This boundary clearly delineates what belongs in the system and what does not. What are the responsibilities of the system? Which people and what other systems will interact with the system?

Together, a **SharedClearVision** and a **VisibleBoundary** should provide readers with a good grounding for understanding the project's vision and scope.

The **VisibleBoundary** helps us discover who or what can interact with the system, who on the outside requires services from the system, and who on the outside helps the system provide these services. We call these people or things *actors* in use case terminology, and we need to know who they are, what they want from the system, and what they offer to it. These actors are the **ClearCastOfCharacters** (p. 90). The cast includes people, organizations, and computer systems or hardware. This list provides a very concise and useful picture of the system, defining the initial negotiating point between the user representative, the financial sponsor, and the development group.

What are the services the system must offer the actors if the system is to realize the objectives and goals specified in the **SharedClearVision**? These services are the **UserValuedTransactions** (p. 95), the services that yield measurable value to the actors of the system.

We structure our use cases with higher level use cases referencing lower level use cases in an **EverUnfoldingStory** (p. 102). This organization allows readers to focus on the system at varying levels of detail, depending on their need.

Lower Manhattan seen from the S.S. Coamo

4.1 *SharedClearVision*

You have decided that writing a set of use cases will help you and your stakeholders understand a system's functional requirements.

> The lack of a clear vision about a system can lead to indecision and contrary opinions among the stakeholders and can quickly paralyze the project.

In a special session before the U.S. Congress, President John F. Kennedy made the challenge "that this nation should commit itself to achieving the goal, before this decade is out, of landing a man on the moon and returning him safely to earth." These words became a mantra to NASA and much of the nation. The scope of the project was enormous, and presented many technological, manufacturing, and management challenges. Inspired by President Kennedy's dream, the United States spent over 25 billion dollars (that's close to 100 billion by today's inflated standards) and used the services of several hundred thousand people for eight years. The well-focused vision was realized on July 20, 1969, as people all over the world watched Neil Armstrong step onto the moon and utter the famous words, "That's one small step for [a] man . . ."

Effective use case writers have a clear vision of the system's purpose and make sure that everyone involved shares that vision.

Time pressures can encourage people to start developing a system prematurely, basing their work on erroneous assumptions. Getting them back on track can be expensive. Often, builders simply enumerate the system's basic services, creating use cases without understanding their value to the actor requiring the service. This approach fails to reflect accurately the users' needs and can paradoxically result in features that are unnecessary or deficient. Many of the so-called CRUD (Create, Read, Update, and Delete) use cases originate from a lack of a clear vision.

Builders have a natural tendency to expand the scope of the system. Without some guiding principle that can be used as criteria for evaluating and scrubbing features, there is a danger that the development team will expand the scope of the system. The vision provides a mechanism for removing vague, ambiguous, or poorly defined requirements from the scope of the project. It is an objective filter for scrubbing requirements, and helps to define what is in or out of the system's scope.

Stakeholders have competing visions. There are usually competing visions of the actors' needs and responsibilities, and stakeholders often have very little knowledge to help select the most appropriate vision of the system. Most projects are under time pressure and cannot simply evaluate a countless number of alternatives. Team members must begin to limit the solution space quickly. If there is no clear vision, then project participants may substitute their own vision for the project, which may conflict with the corporate mission. For example, without a vision, the software developers may create their own vision for the product that emphasizes scalability and flexibility in the software architecture. Although these are highly desirable architectural characteristics, they may conflict with the corporate need to deploy a system quickly and cheaply.

People in the trenches don't know what the goal of the project is. An interesting experiment on larger projects is to go around and ask the participants why they think the project is important. If you're fortunate, most people will understand how their specific piece of the project contributes to the overall project. But does anyone understand what the goal of the project is beyond making money or reducing costs? What does the system allow its users to do that they couldn't do before? Why is this important? Simply, is it clear to all project participants why someone is willing to pay money for the system?

People don't communicate. Despite an organization's best efforts to encourage communication—by replacing private offices with cubicle hell, for example—there remain many barriers to informal communication in any organization. The larger the organization, the stronger these barriers are. When there are strong barriers to informal communication, then the formal communication channels must be strengthened.

Therefore:

> Prepare a statement of purpose for the system that clearly describes the objectives of the system and supports the mission of the organization. Freely distribute it to everyone involved with the project.

In the vision statement, include the following:

- The objectives of the system
- The problems that the system will solve

- The problems the system will not solve
- Who the stakeholders are
- How the system will benefit the stakeholders

Maintain consistency in the vision by making a small team of people responsible for creating the vision (**SmallWritingTeam** [p. 31]). A characteristic of many successful projects is the appointment of a single person who champions the vision of the system and is responsible for maintaining the consistency of that vision. This responsibility usually falls on someone in a marketing role, such as the product manager. This person must also actively communicate with all members of the development team, to ensure that they share the same interpretation of the vision.

Validate the vision and seek support for the vision by obtaining advice from those who will be affected by the system (**ParticipatingAudience** [p. 35]).

Strengthen and constrain the vision by clearly specifying what is outside of the system and what is part of the system (**VisibleBoundary** [p. 86] and **ClearCastof-Characters** [p. 90]).

Ensure that the vision is supportive of the stakeholders' mission and shows up in the **UserValuedTransactions** (p. 95). Even a truly excellent system vision will fail if it defines a purpose that works against the organization's mission.

Finally, when there are changes to the vision, make sure that all project participants learn about the changes immediately.

Examples

Wings Over the World

There are few things short of an extinction event—like a huge asteroid hitting the Earth—that can derail your project as quickly as the lack of a shared clear vision. Most modern methodologies emphasize the need for a vision statement or document. Unfortunately, when people produce a typical vision statement, they do so only to satisfy the requirements of the methodology or to fulfill a contractual obligation with the client. The vision is rarely shared or clear.

Consider what happens when our long-suffering consultant asks Ahmed, "Why are you building this system?" Ahmed answers by itemizing the technology that's being used to implement the new system. After further probing, Ahmed offers only, "Well, to allow people to book their travel on-line."

It is hard to believe that the company's directors would launch a project simply to "allow people to book travel reservations on-line." (Maybe this was acceptable during the dot-com bubble, but we certainly hope it is not the case anymore.) Why is this feature important to the mission of the company? Does the company see itself as a market leader, trying to increase market share by offering clients the option of booking on-line? Is it playing catch-up with its competitors to preserve market share? Or is it trying to reduce the cost of bookings in a highly competitive marketplace?

By failing to communicate the objectives for the system to all project participants, the directors are creating a void that others may fill with their own agendas. Technical teams are notorious for this.

Ahmed is envisioning a high-performance, scalable, Web-based system. There is nothing sinister in this practice, it's just human nature. Maybe Ahmed's vision happens to align with the corporate mission. But what if the company is playing catch-up and needs to deploy a system quickly and cheaply to stay abreast of its competition? Then Ahmed's vision may run counter to the corporate needs. Without a **SharedClearVision**, the development team will create one based on their core belief; reliability, scalability, and expandability are the important characteristics of a high-quality system. Without a clear vision for the system, developers will bias their design efforts toward these goals rather than those of the overall organization.

What is an appropriate vision statement for the Wings Over the World project? See Figure 4.1.

In Figure 4.1, we have something. We won't claim that it's perfect, but we do at least see the corporate vision for the system. This statement will help structure our thinking as we begin the process of discovering the use cases.

Fortunately for Ahmed, this corporate vision seems to support his technology vision.

Wings Over the World endeavors to maintain its reputation for innovation by increasing access to our travel services and by offering new and innovative services that are unmatched by our competitors. Specifically:

- Increase brand awareness of Wings Over the World with the creation of a public Web site.
- Increase market share by 15 percent and lower the cost of booking tickets by letting 30 percent of our clients book on-line.
- Open the Wings Over the World travel system to independent travel agents by offering premium booking services and therefore create a new revenue stream.
:
:

Figure 4.1 *The Wings Over the World vision statement*

Automated Railway Signaling

The Vehicle Control Center (VCC) guides automated trains for city mass transit systems in Canada. The original software for this system was nearly twenty-five years old, and it was becoming difficult to find replacement parts for its aging sixteen-bit mini-computers. Finding programmers who could, or even wanted to, program them was also difficult. Furthermore, the capacity of the system was fast approaching its design limits. With rapid growth in the mass transit marketplace, it was time to consider replacing this tried-and-true legacy system.

Replacing such legacy systems is fraught with risks. According to Frederick Brooks (1995), the second system is the most dangerous system a person can ever build, because it provides an opportunity to release all the pent-up desires to fix the perceived shortcomings in the first system. Naturally, this desire translates into "gold plating," adding features of little value that make the product look better. However, the VCC replacement project organizers controlled this desire with a well-defined project vision statement (see Figure 4.2).

This vision statement clearly states what the project's participants could and could not do, effectively preventing gold plating. Possibly the most important statement in this vision is the last statement. Rigorous enforcement of that final sentence led to the success of the project (Adolph 1996).

The purpose of the project is to lower costs associated with the maintenance and modification of the Vehicle Control Center by:

- Porting the system from aging sixteen-bit minicomputers to modern thirty-two-bit machines
- Recoding the original assembly code in a high-level language to make it easier to recruit developers
- Adopting a development methodology that complies with railway industry requirements
- Quadrupling the capacity of the system
- Incorporating new features identified in reference document DOC-XXXX

No changes shall be made to the system's fundamental architecture or algorithms.

Figure 4.2 *The vision statement for the Automated Railway Signaling System*

Mobile Dispatching

Contrast the Vehicle Control Center legacy replacement project with another one whose aim was to replace a mobile dispatch system. The circumstances surrounding the decision to replace this legacy system were similar to those for the Vehicle Control Center; however, the results were different. A year after the project's inception, it was cancelled without delivering anything of worth (Adolph 2000).

The project began with a well-defined vision statement, shown in Figure 4.3.

Replace the existing mobile dispatch system with one that:
- Lowers software maintenance costs
- Supports a relational database
- Supports new client features as specified in document DOC-XXXX

Figure 4.3 *The vision statement for the Mobile Dispatching System*

The "Lowers software maintenance costs" clause was probably the spark that contributed to the project's explosive downfall, because management and development understood it differently. Management believed that the clause meant reducing the time it took to perform standard system customizations for a client. The developers, however, felt that it meant completely rewriting the dispatch system using leading-edge technology. Both sides had a clear vision, but it wasn't a shared one—not even close.

Checkpoint Charlie, Berlin

4.2 VisibleBoundary

You have a **SharedClearVision** (p. 80) for a system.

> The scope of a system will grow in an uncontrollable manner if you do not know its boundaries.

The late 1950s was probably the golden era of the so-called B-films. One of the films that all connoisseurs love is the 1958 science fiction film *The Blob*. In this movie that launched Steve McQueen's career, a group of teenagers discovers an alien creature from outer space that has no form or shape. The creature grows rapidly as it absorbs everything and everyone around it. As expected in a film of this genre, the teenagers attempt to warn a doomed town of the danger it faces, but no one believes a bunch of kids until it's too late.

Few other films have been used as extensively as a metaphor for the dangers of uncontrolled or unmanaged growth. *The Blob* has symbolized everything from urban sprawl to poor software architecture (Brown et al. 1998).

Different people have different points of view regarding where a system's boundary is. Some stakeholders such as business owners are often more interested in how the business runs than in how the software works. Developers often care more about the software than the business. For the stakeholders the system is the business and the environment is the world in which the business operates, with customers, suppliers, and competitors on the outside of the system. Resources such as the sales staff and customer service clerks are inside or part of the business. On the other hand, the developers may regard the sales staff and customer clerks as users, and therefore outside of the system.

Poorly defined boundaries lead to scope creep. Many stakeholders have "pet" problems they want a new system to resolve. Sales and marketing staff often load features onto a system in the hopes of capturing customer interest. Developers love to enhance or add features to even well-defined systems. Poorly defined or undefined boundaries exacerbate these problems. Without a clear definition of the system boundary, everyone tries to add features they deem even slightly necessary. But these extra features often don't add any value to the system. If anything, they make the system more complicated and less useful.

Imprecise and conflicting objectives early in the project often make it difficult to determine the boundary of a system. When a project is beginning, there may be insufficient information to identify what belongs to the system and what is part of its environment. The system may be large, or its purpose may not be clearly defined.

People believe that defining a boundary is unnecessary. Programmers often feel that analysis activities only get in the way of the real work (coding) and don't offer them any real value. This perception is especially true in the start-up world, where companies operate on a shoestring budget and their very livelihood depends heavily on the time it takes them to get their product to market. But this approach can quickly result in unnecessary and missing features, inadequate products, and excessive costs.

Therefore:

> Establish a visible boundary between the system and its environment by enumerating both the people and equipment that interact with the system.

The **VisibleBoundary** limits and supports the **SharedClearVision** by:

- Specifying what external systems and personnel the system must collaborate with, establishing a **ClearCastofCharacters** (p. 90)
- Specifying what resources the system has available to accomplish its purpose

In the early stages of development, the visible boundary may be fuzzy because the vision for the system may not be clear. Start by putting a stake in the ground and documenting the system boundary based on the information you have available to you. As you develop your use cases and learn more about the system, you can refine and sharpen the system boundary, that is, perform **SpiralDevelopment** (p. 52).

Examples

Wings Over the World: Context Diagrams

A context diagram is a useful tool for documenting the visible boundary between a system and its environment. It is a simple but information-rich diagram consisting of a circle and boxes connected by lines and arrows. The circle represents the system, and the boxes—called terminators—represent anything that is outside of the system. The lines running between the circle and the boxes represent the flow of data between the system and its terminators. In short, a context diagram shows what the system interacts with in its environment.

The context diagram, which can be drawn in UML as a deployment diagram, is a simple, effective tool for identifying potential actors and use cases, because it helps us focus on the things that interact with a system while ignoring the services that those things require.

In addition to simplicity, the benefit of using this kind of diagram is that it is based on information that is readily available early in the development cycle. With use cases, you must find actors and the services they need. On the other hand, with context diagrams, you need to find only the physical things that the system will talk to. You do not need to know what services it will require or deliver to the system.

The context diagram provides an excellent starting point for building the use case set. To find actors, we ask questions such as, "What are the different roles played by terminators such as customer, bank, and ticket wholesaler with respect to the system?" The diagram also identifies invalid actors. For example, Figure 4.4 shows that the system is the company. Since travel agents are part of the company, they are also

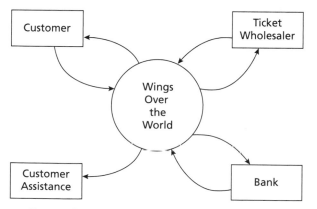

Figure 4.4 Context diagram for Wings Over the World

part of the system. For this specific example, travel agents cannot be actors: any use case that portrays travel agents as actors will be inappropriate.

Just as important, context diagrams show what does not interact with the system. For example, the Wings Over the World system does not interact with independent hotels or car rental agencies. According to this diagram, actors and use cases for independent car rentals and hotels are outside of the system's scope.

The types of interactions that are outside of the system's scope can also be documented. For example, while this system does interact with customers and with the customer assistance system, it has no business getting involved in any direct interactions between the customer and customer assistance. A use case describing a scenario in which the customer phones customer assistance to complain about an airline or some other service is outside of the system's scope.

◆ **VisibleBoundary and UML Models, by Dan Rawsthorne**

The context diagram is a lovely thing, and it can be drawn with standard UML. A good context diagram goes a long way to help "scoping" discussions, as well as provide the vocabulary necessary to develop a use case set.

I love drawing context diagrams and putting them up on the wall. Being constantly reminded of the environment the system lives in, the developers can stay focused on what's important, and realize what isn't. The context diagram is a natural counterpoint to the use case diagrams you have drawn for **SpiralDevelopment** (p. 52) and **BreadthBeforeDepth** (p. 48).

These diagrams make obvious the scope of the system's functionality from the inside and the outside. The context diagram shows the scope from the outside—what the boundaries of the scope are, while the use case diagrams show the functional scope from the inside—what functionality you consider important and will implement.

Group of Shakespearean players on stage

4.3 ClearCastOfCharacters

You have a **SharedClearVision** (p. 80) of the system's purpose and are establishing a **VisibleBoundary** (p. 86) that specifies who and what is outside of the system.

> If we analyze only the users of the system, and ignore the roles they play with respect to the system, then we can miss important system behavior or introduce redundant behavior.

An actor is a person who plays a role, whether on stage, on TV or radio, or in movies. Some actors are so good that they make it hard to believe that they are not the role they are playing. Actors frequently get typecast into a role they play particularly well. For many people, it is difficult to distinguish Clint Eastwood from "Dirty Harry" or Sean Connery from "James Bond." When actors play unexpected roles, such as when Clint Eastwood portrayed a caring, sensitive man in *The Bridges of Madison County,* viewers can come near to experiencing culture shock.

The craft of acting becomes stunningly clear when one actor plays several radically different roles in the same play or movie. In Stanley Kubrick's classic Cold War movie *Dr. Strangelove* (1964), Peter Sellers plays three distinct roles: the calm, rational Group Captain Mandrake, who is trying to prevent a nuclear holocaust; the ineffective, milquetoast President of the United States, Merkin Muffley; and the very mad scientist Dr. Strangelove. In acting, it's the role that we are interested in, not the person doing the acting. We don't follow Peter Sellers in *Dr. Strangelove,* we follow Mandrake, the President, or Strangelove. Each of these characters has his own traits and develops in different ways throughout the movie, and each role contributes to the development of the movie's plot.

Just like actors in a movie or on the stage, users may play many roles with respect to a system. If we do not understand all the roles a user plays, then we cannot understand the system.

To be useful, a system must satisfy its users' needs and protect the interests of its stakeholders. If the system is not to be deficient in its requirements, then we must find all the services its users need. A development organization can suffer a damaging loss of goodwill when it fails to provide the services that the users actually need instead of what they think they want.

Tying services to users may make the system so rigid that services cannot be reused. Different users may have overlapping sets of responsibilities. A single user can play many different roles with respect to the system. Many different users may actually share a single role with respect to the system. If we consider only the different users, then we may create a system with different interfaces for similar operations. Failure to discover overlapping responsibilities and separate them from the users will lead to bloated, rigid systems.

The narrow focus of subject matter experts can obscure all the services a user requires. Subject matter experts are quite vocal on the topics they care about, but they often have little interest in areas outside of their specific expertise. Unless we have a mechanism to probe and elicit from the subject matter experts all the services required by the user, the system will be deficient. (See the example "Centre A," on p. 92.)

Focusing on users may bog us down with implementation details, rather than provide understanding of the services the user needs. Engineers love to solve challenging, detailed problems; that's why they became engineers in the first place. Focusing on users rather than the roles they play in the system runs the risk of prematurely introducing implementation details into our analysis (the "how" rather than the "what"). It is tempting to do so, because users are real. Engineers can grab on to them immediately and attack a big problem: How should the system communicate with the user? How should we lay out the user interface? What happens when the user asks for a nonexistent part number? It is not so easy to pull from thin air the services the system must offer the user.

Many people find it easier to comprehend concrete concepts rather than abstract ones. We hear this comment frequently: "If I can't point to it, then I don't want to know about it." A person, machine, or even another piece of software is easy to point to and identify. The roles played by that same person, machine, or software are much more abstract and therefore more difficult for people to visualize. Furthermore, abstract concepts may sometimes mask fuzzy or imprecise thinking.

Time pressure and expediency encourage us to analyze only the users. Once the boundaries of the system have been identified, the users are relatively easy to find. After all, it is easy to identify users by name and job description. It is relatively simple to point to a box at the end of a cable that must communicate with your system. It takes more time and effort to find out that that box and that person play the same roles.

Therefore:

> Identify the actors the system must interact with and the role each plays with respect to the system. Clearly describe each.

Analyze the system by focusing on the **UserValuedTransactions** (p. 95), or the set of services the system must offer the users. You should know at least who the users are because the **SharedClearVision** gives you a statement of the system's purpose and the **VisibleBoundary** gives you a glimpse of the scope of the system.

For each user, identify and list the services that the user requires from the system. Try to organize the services into cohesive sets, and then name those sets. Look carefully for users that have overlapping sets of services, and then collect those services into sets. Examine the sets of collected services to see if they are complete. Are any services missing? Once complete, these sets are the actors of the system and represent the roles that entities play with respect to the system.

Give each actor a clear, crisp noun or noun phrase name. If you cannot provide a good name for the actor, then the odds are that you have not identified an actor. Write a description for the actor specifying the services it requires from or offers to the system.

In the early development phases, it can be difficult to find the roles of the actors. Finding the roles of the users is often an emergent characteristic of creating the use cases. So don't get bogged down if you cannot find all of the roles right away, because they should naturally emerge as part of the **SpiralDevelopment** (p. 52) cycle.

Examples

Centre A: The Museum for Contemporary Asian Art

Centre A *(www.centreA.org)* is the Museum for Contemporary Asian Art in Vancouver, British Columbia, Canada. Its directors hope to create a museum that is more open and responsive to the needs of the community. One of the authors helped them write use cases to model the museum's mission and operation.

During the design of the Centre A use case set, our subject matter experts focused on the activities of the museum curator, specifically the curator's scholarly activities, such as the search for and acquisition of art for the museum. These experts were either artists or curators themselves. What we missed and had to recover from was that the curator also has the tedious, day-to-day job of simply running the museum. This role consists of the very mundane tasks of fighting the board of directors for funding, soliciting bids from contractors, authorizing purchase orders, and hiring and firing employees. In larger museums, some curators have only a scholarly role, while others have only a managerial role. Had we completely missed this management role, our system would have been grossly deficient. Yet this role of the curator as manager was largely hidden because it did not interest the subject matter experts (see **BalancedTeam** [p. 39]).

The Pharmacy Receptionist

In a pharmacy, there are three main actors: the Receptionist, the Pharmacy Technician, and the Pharmacist. Any one of these three actors may greet a Customer and take a prescription order. Either the Pharmacy Technician or the Pharmacist may fill the prescription, but only the Pharmacist can check and authorize the prescription. If we analyze only the users of the pharmacy system, then we risk overlooking the overlaps in responsibility between the Receptionist, Pharmacy Technician, and Pharmacist, and end up creating the model shown in Figures 4.5 and 4.6.

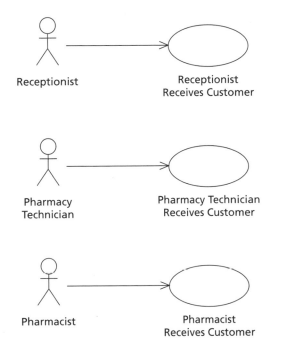

Receptionist   Receptionist Receives Customer

Pharmacy Technician   Pharmacy Technician Receives Customer

Pharmacist   Pharmacist Receives Customer

Figure 4.5 *The* Receive Customer *use case when all users are treated as different actors*

Receptionist	The Receptionist welcomes Customers to the pharmacy. He or she takes the Customer's prescription.
Pharmacy Technician	The Pharmacy Technician assists the Pharmacist by filling prescriptions but is not authorized to dispense the prescription. The Pharmacy Technician may also welcome the Customer to the pharmacy and take the customer's prescription.
Pharmacist	The Pharmacist fills and dispenses prescriptions for customers. Only the Pharmacist can check and authorize the prescription. The Pharmacist may also welcome the Customer to the pharmacy and take the prescription.

Figure 4.6 *The actor list for the pharmacy system*

By overlooking these shared job roles, we can lose the opportunity to simplify the system by capturing a common role. We need to understand and model the roles played by the system's users rather than model the users. In the worst case, we would design separate reception interfaces for the Receptionist, the Pharmacy Technician, and the Pharmacist without realizing that these three users play a common role and could share the same interface. We would be much better off by realizing this commonality, as shown by the model in Figures 4.7 and 4.8.

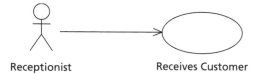

Receptionist   Receives Customer

Figure 4.7 *The* Receive Customer *use case, with the actor's role defined as Receptionist*

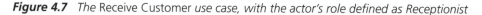

Receptionist The Receptionist welcomes Customers to the pharmacy. He or she takes the Customer's prescription. Anyone on the pharmacy staff can play the role of receptionist.

Figure 4.8 *Revised pharmacy system actor list*

Bookies taking bets at the horse races. Warrenton, Virginia.

4.4 UserValuedTransactions

You have established a **SharedClearVision** (p. 80) of the project and have defined a **ClearCastOfCharacters** (p. 90) who need services from the system.

> A system is deficient if it cannot deliver services that are valuable to its users and it does not support the goals and objectives specified by the system vision.

A few years ago one of the authors bumped into a colleague who was working for a start-up firm that was building a radio advertising distribution network. The idea was simple: Advertisers were using couriers to distribute tapes of their ads to radio stations, but even with overnight delivery, it could be two to three days before a new ad was actually playing over the radio. The colleague's company had built a continent-wide private network to distribute advertising spots to radio stations nearly instantaneously. Furthermore, with the company's proprietary protocols and compression hardware, they could guarantee quality of service to their clients.

It seemed like a license to print money. Offer a service that is cheaper, faster, and more reliable than what is currently available and the world will beat a path to your door. This was a case right out of Marketing 101. But the market never developed, eventually the company succumbed to the inevitable, and it was taken over.

A while later this story was mentioned to a radio DJ at a local station. "Doesn't surprise me that they failed," he said. "Radio is a local media. Almost no one does national campaigns."

A well-written set of use cases clearly and accurately describes the essential actions that a system provides. This information allows customers to preview a system before it is built and determine whether it offers the kind of services that they find valuable.

A set of use cases should capture the fundamental value-added services that users and stakeholders need from the system. An organization commissions the development of a system because that system will return some benefit. Use cases allow the organization's project team to inspect a system before it is built, so that they can verify that it is what they want, request changes, or decide that it doesn't meet their needs. Use cases should describe the kinds of things that users find valuable, so they can present the system in its best light. A system that does not deliver needed valuable services to its actors is deficient, can lose money, and will sully the reputation of the development organization.

It is relatively easy to identify low-level transactions, but it can be difficult to identify useful services. It is usually easier to describe the individual routine transactions that a system may provide than it is to discover what the user really wants to do with the system. Doing it the easy way often leads to "CRUD" (Create, Read, Update, and Delete) style use cases. It is not unusual to see use cases with names like *Create Employee Record, Read Employee Record,* or *Delete Employee Record.* While such use cases may be technically correct, they do not capture what is valuable to the user. Is creating an employee record important, or does the user really want to *Hire Employee*?

Use cases need to be relatively stable because they form "anchor points" for the rest of the product development process. Constant changes to use cases can ripple through the rest of the development process, creating havoc for the developers and significantly increasing the cost. To keep this cost low, we want to write each case at a level high enough to insulate it from inconsequential changes. Otherwise, the writers will constantly be updating their use cases every time someone changes some trivial detail. Worse, the readers will have trouble understanding the use cases, because their meaning will be constantly changing.

Readers want to see easily how the system will meet its goals. (See **Shared-ClearVision**.) Just as a picture is worth a thousand words, a use case is worth a thousand pages of system specifications. But even pictures can be hard to understand when they are too complex or abstract. Concise use cases that stick to the point are easier to read than long, flowery ones.

People tend to work at a level that is either too high or too low. People tend to use excessive detail when describing things they understand or find interesting. Conversely, they tend to gloss over details they don't understand or find boring. Use cases should be somewhere in the middle, containing enough information to describe system behavior adequately, without describing it in great detail ("what" versus "how"). If we write them at too high a level, then they are not useful to the system developers, because they do not describe the system in enough detail. However, if use cases contain too much detail, then it is difficult for non-programmers to understand the system from the 50,000-foot level. In the words of Ian Graham (1997), use cases should contain only necessary but essential information.

Therefore:

> **Identify the valuable services that the system delivers to the actors to satisfy their business purposes.**

Ideally, a set of use cases should contain all of the information necessary to depict a system but no more. Each use case should describe some unique, essential service that is valuable to at least one user or stakeholder.

Use the **ClearCastOfCharacters** and **SharedClearVision** to identify those services that the system should provide. Define as many valuable services as you can for each actor in your cast of characters. Each service must help at least one actor reach a goal. Being unable to identify any service for an actor may indicate that the actor might not represent a valid system user; you may need to remove that actor from the cast. Conversely, if you identify a service that doesn't map to an actor in your cast, it may indicate that you have not identified all of the actors.

For each service that you identify, ask "What value does this service provide to the users or stakeholders?" Get rid of those services that fail to add value to the system. You don't want to waste valuable time writing use cases or implementing code for a feature that no one will use or cares about.

Users and stakeholders prefer to see the bottom line rather than an itemized list of CRUD-style services, so examine each service and determine whether each one stands by itself or is part of a larger, more valuable service. Fold those services that cannot stand by themselves into more comprehensive ones that address one key objective, and then eliminate duplicates. A client booking an airline reservation is interested in getting a good flight at a good price. The client doesn't care how many times the system updates its databases or files as the travel agent books a seat.

Write use cases around these goals. While you want to minimize the number of use cases in your collection, each use case should be a cohesive unit that describes one and only one key concept between an actor and the system, a **CompleteSingle-Goal** (p. 118). Describe this collection in sufficient detail to adequately convey its purpose, yet at a high enough level so as to be insulated from simple changes.

This singleness of purpose does not prevent a use case from addressing more than one goal, as long as the use case is cohesive and achieves a unified purpose. For example, a high-level use case can reference several subordinate use cases in an **Ever-UnfoldingStory** (p. 102), but these use cases must work together to accomplish a common purpose.

Note: In **BreadthBeforeDepth** (p. 48), the actor names and the names of the user-valued transactions make up the original depth to which use cases should be taken before **SpiralDevelopment** (p. 52) is applied.

Examples

Wings Over the World and UserValuedTransactions

What are **UserValuedTransactions** for Wings Over the World? Where would our analyst look to find them? The vision statement is a great place to start, because it is supposed to state the objectives for the system. If the system is going to be successful, then its use cases need to support those objectives. The vision statement for Wings Over the World is repeated here as Figure 4.9.

> Wings Over the World endeavors to maintain its reputation for innovation by increasing access to our travel services and by offering new and innovative services that are unmatched by our competitors. Specifically:
> - Increase brand awareness of Wings Over the World with the creation of a public Web site.
> - Increase market share by 15 percent and lower the cost of booking tickets by letting 30 percent of our clients book on-line.
> - Open the Wings Over the World travel system to independent travel agents by offering premium booking services and therefore create a new revenue stream.

Figure 4.9 *The Wings Over the World vision statement*

What are some of the valuable services the system may offer to support this vision? Some examples are:

- *Book Trip*
- *Search for Flights*
- *Promote Vacations*
- *Create Trip Itinerary*
- *Update Trip Itinerary*
- *Delete Trip Itinerary*

But are all of these services valuable? *Book Trip, Search for Flights,* and *Promote Vacations* are the kinds of things that successful travel agencies do to stay in business. But *Create Trip Itinerary, Update Trip Itinerary,* and *Delete Trip Itinerary* probably do not represent those goals a user would consider valuable. Each is a part of a larger service. *Book Trip* involves *Create Trip Itinerary, Change Booking* includes *Update Trip Itinerary,* and *Cancel Booking* involves *Delete Trip Itinerary.* These changes reduce the list to the following services.

- *Book Trip*
- *Change Booking*
- *Cancel Booking*
- *Search for Flights*
- *Promote Vacations*

Does this small list imply that a complex on-line travel Web site may have only ten or fifteen use cases? At the 50,000-foot level, the answer is yes: There will be only a few summary use cases. We can then unfold these use cases into their sea level use cases later. But what is most important is that we know the important and **User-ValuedTransactions**.

Wings Over the World and Avoiding Form-Focus

Many use case writers make the mistake of creating a use case for each user interface form or external protocol message (Lilly 1999). The result is a set of many small use cases that add minuscule value to the primary actor. Following such a strategy could result in the set of use cases for booking an airline ticket shown in Figure 4.10.

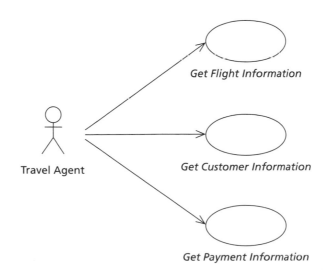

Figure 4.10 *A forms-based use case set*

Each of these use cases describes the steps required to obtain a piece of information from some form and process it. Each use case may have a well-defined goal, but the goal is only a small step in booking an airline ticket for a customer. If we tried this approach for a larger system with many forms, we would end up with hundreds of small use cases, and we would lose the story context that is so valuable to our understanding the system.

It is easy to lose the context when writing these kinds of use cases, even in this small example. Are these three use cases all that is done to book a ticket? How do you know these are related to booking a ticket?

Furthermore, these use cases do not have goals that reflect the actor's point of view. This style of goal encourages writing use cases from the system's perspective rather than the actor's perspective. Note how each use case is named *Get XXX,* and would most likely describe how the system acquired information from the actor, rather than how the actor used the system to perform a useful task.

To the travel agent, the valuable transaction is not *Get Payment Information,* but *Book Ticket. Get Customer Information, Get Flight Information,* and *Get Payment Information* are really steps in the *Book Airline Ticket* use case. The goal of the travel agent is booking a ticket and making a sale, not gathering payment information, as Figure 4.11 shows.

If the steps *Get Customer Information, Get Payment Information,* and so on represent important and complex behavior, you can write them as lower level use cases (**EverUnfoldingStory** [p. 102]). *Book Airline Ticket* now gives a context into which these use cases fit, and makes it easier to comprehend the use case set.

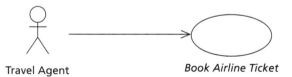

Travel Agent   *Book Airline Ticket*

Figure 4.11 *Booking an airline ticket as a valuable transaction*

The Cruddy Mortgage Origination System

A banking client was developing its next-generation mortgage origination system. This was the first project their team was tackling with use cases, and after their first cut they had come up with use cases such as these:

- *Create Customer*
- *Update Customer*
- *Delete Customer*

The *Create Customer* use case described the steps a loan officer took to add a customer to the customer database. The *Update Customer* use case described the steps to update customer information, and *Delete Customer* described the necessary steps to—well, you get the general idea. In short, the team was well on its way to building a CRUD-dy use case set: it would accurately describe behavior, but it would not be useful. For example, how is creating a customer a goal of measurable value to the loan officer? Or updating a customer? Or deleting a customer? The question here is "Why?" Why are you creating a customer? Why are you updating a customer? Why are you deleting a customer?

When asked about creating a customer, the loan officer replied, "Well, that's part of what I need to do when I open a new customer account. I have to create a customer." *Poof,* the light bulb goes on in everyone's head: Creating a customer is part of a very valuable transaction called *Open Customer Account.* Now that's a goal that has measurable value to the loan officer.

Now what about that *Update Customer* use case? Still talking to the loan officer, we find out that updates are done in two situations: (1) making simple changes to the customer account such as changing an address or correcting misspellings; (2) adding documents that support the customer's request for a loan. So the two valuable transactions that result are *Correct Customer Information* and *Acquire Supporting Documents.*

Finally, why is a customer deleted from the database? "Well," says the loan officer, "they're never quite really deleted. After we've approved or declined the loan, we archive the customer account." So out of this comes *Archive Customer Application.*

Our three CRUD-dy use cases now become the much more valuable four:

- *Open Customer Account*
- *Acquire Supporting Documents*
- *Correct Customer Account*
- *Archive Customer Account*

Reduction gears, Pratt and Whitney Aircraft Corporation, East Hartford, Connecticut

4.5 EverUnfoldingStory

You are organizing the **UserValuedTransactions** (p. 95) so that the context in which they sit, and their structure, are clear.

> **The number of steps needed to describe the behavior of the system exceeds both the memory and the interest of the various types of readers.**

Imagine for a moment if all maps could be drawn at only one scale. If the uniform map scale was very fine, say, 1 centimeter equals 1 kilometer, then we could probably create a usable city street map. But then maps of the world would be totally unusable: a globe built to this scale would be some 40,000 centimeters in diameter! (That's about a quarter of a mile in diameter, for the metrically challenged.) If we changed from a fine scale to a very coarse scale, say, 1 centimeter equals 100 kilometers, then we could build a very serviceable globe, but we could never build a usable street map. This is why maps are drawn to a variety of different scales, such that the users of the map can easily use the map for the information they require: fine-scale street maps for finding an address in a city, and coarse-scale world maps for finding a city on the planet.

Different stakeholders view a system differently. If we limit our use cases to a particular viewpoint, we risk leaving much of our audience behind.

Each use case can have many readers and many uses, all requiring different levels of detail. Some use case readers are interested in system architectural issues and need a set of use cases to help them understand the big picture. Other readers care about business issues and need a set of use cases to help them understand the business layer, including details about system installation and testing. Still other readers will be involved in implementing the system and need the use cases to help them understand the complex interactions the system will allow. Each of these readers needs to see a different level of detail in one set of use cases. Accordingly, the use cases must contain enough information to satisfy all of them. If, for example, the use cases contain only high-level system descriptions, then the subject matter experts will not have the information that they need.

Use cases need to show how every function contributes value to the business. Every part of a system needs to directly add value to the business or support a process that does. Unnecessary functionality is expensive, adds extra cost to the system, and hinders performance. Accordingly, each use case needs to demonstrate this value to the readers, so that they can determine easily whether the functionality is required or not. It is much cheaper to eliminate unnecessary functionality early in the product development cycle, preferably in the requirements phase, because this pruning prevents the unnecessary allocation of precious resources during subsequent cycles.

It is, however, confusing to write at multiple levels. Writing at different levels requires an understanding of these levels. Not only must the writers know how the system should operate at different levels, but they must also comprehend the appropriate domain requirements and what the readers need to be effective at each level.

Writers need a principle to follow for organizing the requirements. Readers need an easy way to navigate through the use case set. Simply presenting the use cases en masse can overwhelm readers as they attempt to make sense out of the model. Good organization simplifies this task for the reader by allowing him or her to easily locate needed information. But good organization doesn't happen in a vacuum; it requires the writers to define comprehensive principles so that the readers can understand what they are trying to accomplish.

Therefore:

> **Organize the use case set as a hierarchical story that can be either unfolded to get more detail or folded up to hide detail and show more context.**

Just as maps are drawn at different scales to reveal or hide details, use cases can be written at different levels of abstraction. A good set of use cases contains several cohesive levels of related use cases that completely describe the system in different levels of abstraction, where each subordinate level closely resembles the level above it, albeit with greater detail.

Each individual use case captures a **CompleteSingleGoal** (p. 118) at whichever level it is placed. That goal may be found as a single step, the **ActorIntentAccomplished** (p. 156), in a higher level use case. The lower level use case shows the unfolding of that accomplishment.

A good way to describe unfolding use cases is to include several levels of use cases in your collection, where each level describes the system at a different level of detail.

In his book *Writing Effective Use Cases,* Alistair Cockburn (2001) suggests three levels of use cases.

- **Summary Level** takes multiple user-goal sessions to complete—possibly weeks, months, or years.

- **User Goal Level** satisfies a particular and immediate goal of value to the primary actor. It is typically performed by one primary actor in one sitting.

- **Subfunction Level** satisfies a partial goal of a user-goal use case or of another subfunction. Its steps are lower level subfunctions.

Figure 4.12, adapted from Alistair Cockburn's book, illustrates the relationships among these levels. The higher level use cases provide the context for the lower level use cases. Or more simply, higher level use cases answer the question "Why is the actor doing this?" for lower level use cases. The lower level use cases answer the question "How is this going to happen?" for the higher level use cases.

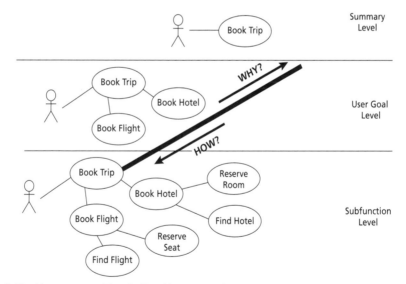

Figure 4.12   *Use case goal levels (Cockburn 2001)*

Examples

Wings Over the World and Use Case Levels

The system developer's desire to have detailed specifications is a force driving us toward detailed use cases. But detailed specifications are long-winded and confusing to most people outside of the development community. If the use cases describe the system from only the programmers' level, they won't meet the needs of the stakehold-ers who also need them to understand the system.

This was one of the problems our consultant for Wings Over the World ran into. In our story, the analyst was told that the Wings Over the World development teams were "just tearing into the use cases, and had already written a thirty-page use case for booking a flight." We don't know how you like to spend your time, but reading a thirty-page use case is not our idea of fun. Consider the use case fragment in Use Case 4.1 and Figure 4.13.

Use Case 4.1   Use Case Horror: The Thirty-page *Book Flight* Use Case

---

Book Flight

Level: User Goal

Main Success Scenario

1. This use case begins when a customer contacts the travel agency and requests a flight.
2. The customer proxy captures the customer's trip origin and destination.
3. The customer proxy looks up the airport codes for the origin and destination.
4. The customer proxy captures the preferred departure times for the customer.
5. The customer proxy captures the customer's preferred class of service.
6. The system requests from the airline proxy a list of the flights available that match the customer's preferences.
7. The system retrieves the customer's profile to get her preferred airline and fre-quent flyer number.
8. The system sorts the list of available flights first by the customer's airline prefer-ence and those that are closest to the customer's preferred departure times.
9. Etc., etc., for the next twenty-nine pages.

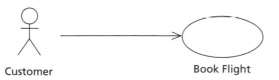

Customer   Book Flight

Figure 4.13 Book Flight

Would you want to read these steps for thirty pages? One solution to this problem is to maintain two parallel sets of use cases: one set written at the very detailed level required by the programmers, and a second set written at a much higher level of abstraction, much like a corporate report and its executive summary. Unfortunately, this approach has several problems. First, the use case set would remain relatively flat and without any context explaining why a given use case adds value to the business. Second, the scope of these use cases is often ambiguous, whether they are modeling the business or a supporting system. In our example, we have both business-level functions and system-level functions in one use case. To get around the problem of scope, many use case writers add a pseudo-actor they call *the proxy*. Finally, it is highly unlikely that the parallel use cases will remain parallel for very long.

A better approach (shown in Use Case 4.2) is to create a hierarchy of related use cases, organizing them as stories within stories that unfold as you need to discover more detail.

Use Case 4.2 Shortening *Book Flight* with EverUnfoldingStory

Book Flight

Level: User Goal

Main Success Scenario

1. This use case begins when a customer calls and requests a flight.
2. The customer describes her flight needs by specifying her origination, destination, travel dates, and preferred departure times.
3. The system looks up all flights that match the customer's travel preferences and presents the travel options to the customer.
4. The customer selects a flight.
5. The system builds a flight itinerary for the customer.
6. The system reserves the flight for the customer.
7. The customer provides a credit card number and charges the price of the flight against it.
8. The system issues the ticket to the customer.

When we need more details, we unfold the story and follow a more elaborate version of the use case set, as shown in Use Case 4.3 and Figure 4.14.

Use Case 4.3 A Lower Level Use Case for *Find Flight*

Find Flight

Level: Subfunction

1. This use case begins when a customer contacts the travel agency and requests a flight.
2. The travel agent captures the customer's trip origin and destination.
3. The travel agent looks up the airport codes for the origin and destination.

4. The travel agent captures the preferred departure times for the customer.
5. The travel agent captures the customer's preferred class of service.
6. The travel agent confirms that the customer's preferences are correct.
7. The system requests from the airline reservation system a list of the flights available that match the customer's preferences, which is presented to the travel agent.

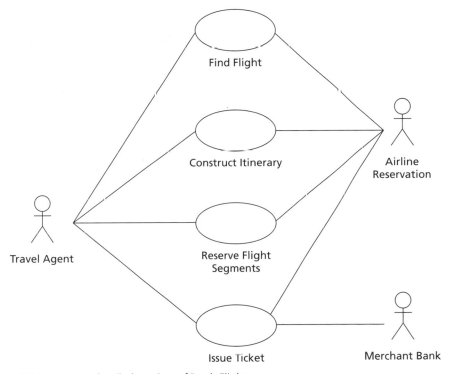

Figure 4.14 *A more detailed version of* Book Flight

Someone who is interested only in understanding the steps involved in booking a flight and the possible alternatives (for example, flights unavailable, bad credit, restricted fares, and so on) can read the *Find Flight* use case and see if the right process is captured. They can unfold *Find Flight* and look at the lower level use cases if they wish to know the details of how we find a flight or build an itinerary.

The benefit of this approach is that it maintains the thread of the use case goals from the system vision to the lowest level use case. It helps us answer the question "Why is this use case here?" For example, why is there a *Construct Itinerary* use case?

Because it is an essential step for the *Book Flight* use case, which is a **UserValued-Transaction** (p. 95).

Many use case writers implement this solution by using the *includes* and *extends* relationships. In UML terms, when you reference a lower level use case from a higher level use case, the higher level use case includes the lower level one. That is, the steps from the lower level one could, in principle, be placed directly into the higher level one. Figure 4.15 shows how to structure a use case set with *includes* to show how lower level use cases are related to a higher level use case.

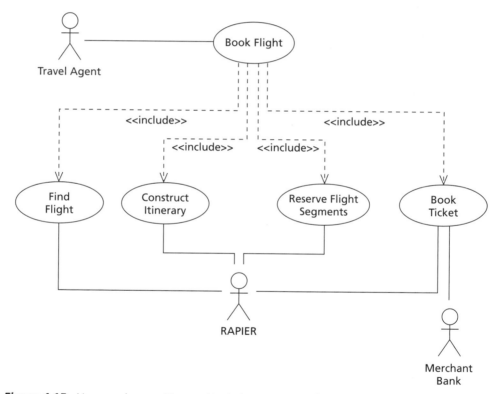

Figure 4.15 *Use case horror: Distorted* include *association for* EverUnfoldingStory

A lot of people like this approach because it provides a very satisfying drawing that clearly reveals a relationship between *Book Flight* and the other use cases. However, use case sets constructed in this manner can be confusing because of the myriad interpretations people have for *includes* and *extends*. We believe the application of *includes* and especially *extends* should be limited (see **InterruptsAsExtensions** [p. 182], **CommonSubBehavior** [p. 176], and **PromotedAlternative** [p. 190]).

Centre A: The Museum for Contemporary Asian Art

Centre A is an example of a use case set with the **EverUnfoldingStory** pattern. At the highest level is the use case *Engage Art,* shown in Figure 4.16.

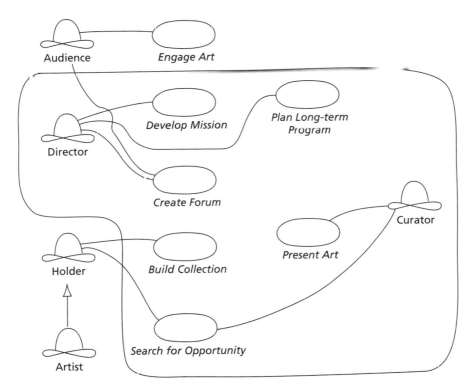

Figure 4.16 *An artistic rendering of* Engage Art

For those of you who are mystified by an artist's hand-drawn use case, we present a more traditional UML diagram in Figure 4.17.

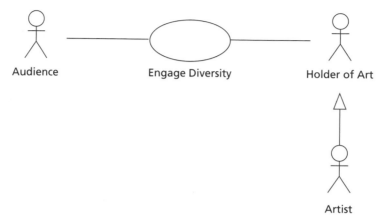

Figure 4.17   Engage Art

Use Case 4.4   *Engage Diversity*

Engage Diversity

The museum creates a forum in which the interests and cultures of everyone on the planet may be discussed.

Level: Summary

1. Audience bemoans the lack of diversity in society.
2. Curator develops a mission.
3. Curator conducts research for an event by creating forums to seek the input of the audience.
4. Curator produces event.
5. Curator hosts event.
6. Audience participates in the event.

The *Engage Diversity* use case (Use Case 4.4) provided the context for *why* a museum of art exists in our society. From this we could create a set of lower level use cases that described *how* the museum would accomplish this.

You will note in Figure 4.18 that Centre A took some liberties with the UML notation for use cases. Being artists, they were not too impressed with Ivar Jacobson's stick figures for actors. They were far more comfortable with the idea of a hat representing a role that someone plays. What is truly exciting about the Centre A model is that it has withstood nearly two years of debate and argument. The stakeholders have found it to be an excellent description of how a museum of art operates.

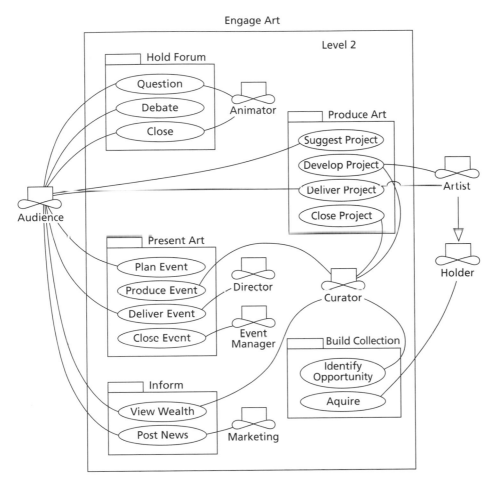

Figure 4.18 *Centre A use case model*

◆ **EverUnfoldingStory and UML Models, by Dan Rawsthorne**

One way to deal with multiple levels is to have only one level of abstraction on each use case diagram. If you insist on drawing something like the diagram shown in Figure 4.15, then do the relations between abstraction levels with a *trace* relationship. The *trace* relationship is a predefined UML stereotype of a dependency (dashed arrow) that is used specifically to trace between different abstraction layers in a model. Figure 4.19 shows how Figure 4.15 can be revised to reduce the confusion caused by an *includes* relationship.

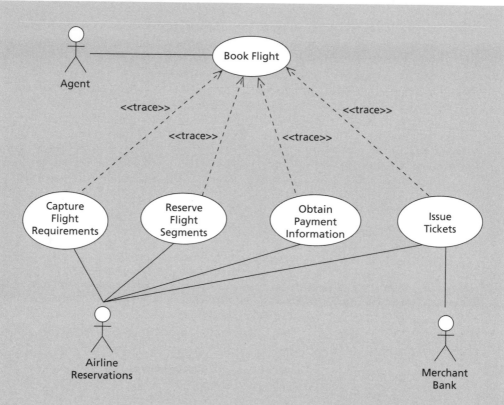

Figure 4.19   Book Flight

Of course, if your drawing tool will not allow you to use the *trace* relationship as shown, then you must do what you can. Just keep in mind that using an *includes* relationship may cause confusion—and at least you know what it should look like.

In the textual representation of the lower level use cases, you may want to show the traceability if the route through the **EverUnfoldingStory** is not enough. For example, the use case *Reserve Flight Segments* may look like Figure 4.20.

Reserve Flight Segments
Traces to: *Book Flight*

1. The Agent validates that the Flight Segments are available for the Customer's preferred class of service; the reservation system returns all applicable restrictions.

2. The Agent validates with the Customer that the restrictions are acceptable.

3. The Agent reserves the segments with the Customer's name and payment information.
4. ...

Figure 4.20 *The Traceability of* Reserve Flight Segments

This representation indicates that the *Book Flight* use case is being expanded, and that *Reserve Flight Segments* is part of the expansion. The *Book Flight* use case will simply have the reference to *Reserve Flight Segments* that one would expect by constructing the **EverUnfoldingStory**.

4.6 Trade-offs and Collaborations

Properly organizing your use cases can return a lot of bang for your buck. An efficient, well-thought-out structure makes it much easier for everyone, readers and writers alike, to follow your use case. Organization requires effort, and everyone writing use cases needs to fully understand the system's purpose—what it does and does not do, who will use it, and what its boundaries are—so that they can accurately describe these facts to their audience. Furthermore, they should organize their use cases so that their audience can easily follow them and understand their value. While it requires some effort to write this way, structuring use cases is fairly straightforward and quickly pays for itself.

The first level of organization is as a set or collection. We want to organize its contents in a friendly, easy-to-use manner that allows the user to first see the system as a whole, then shift his or her focus to its individual pieces. A good way to do this is to describe the system as an **EverUnfoldingStory** (p. 102), which consists of several complete levels of use cases that present the system in increasing levels of detail. Each of these levels can stand alone and allow the reader to examine the system from a particular level of precision. Yet each subset expands into the next level of detail, allowing readers to "zoom in" on the parts they find interesting. This style allows some readers to examine the system from the 50,000-foot level and then focus on some of the low-level details of the system.

Creating an **EverUnfoldingStory** requires the writers to have a **SharedClearVision** (p. 80) of the system, so that they can clearly describe its purpose and tell their audience what the system will and will not accomplish. To successfully craft this story, the writers need to answer three questions clearly. We have identified three patterns to help them do this. First, we need to know *who* will use the system. We need a **ClearCastOfCharacters** (p. 90), describing everyone's role in the system. Second, we need to know *what* actions the users expect the system to do, actions that are **UserValued-Transactions** (p. 95). Last, we want to know *where* these actions are meaningful to the user; we want to know the system's **VisibleBoundary** (p. 86).

These latter three patterns are tightly coupled. If the system's boundary changes, then its cast of characters will grow or shrink as more actors move inside or outside of the boundary. The converse also holds: adding or removing actors from the cast will expand or decrease the system's scope and shift its boundary accordingly. Changing the cast of characters also affects the need for services. New actors require new services; removing actors usually reduces the number of services required.

The next chapter describes the characteristics of good use cases within the context of a set as the **EverUnfoldingStory**.

Chapter 5

The Use Case

♦ **Precise but Unreadable**

After flying through the night, you've finally arrived at Wings Over the World's corporate headquarters in New York. You're not feeling too bad considering your lack of sleep, and you take it as a good omen that you were actually able to hail a cab during a rainstorm.

After the initial meeting with the chief information officer, you decide to sit down with their chief architect, Ahmed, and step through his thirty-page use case, which you spent most of the night reviewing. He's been with Wings for three years and graduated from Cornell about four years ago. You remember meeting him during your sales presentation weeks ago; he's got a keen mind and a wonderful supply of terrible jokes. In a way you feel guilty tearing his masterwork apart, knowing that he must have spent two weeks writing it. But Ahmed is the type who likes to learn. He's a little hurt that he's wasted so much effort, but you see the excitement growing in his eyes as he learns.

You: OK. If there was just one problem that I could single out, it would be the inclusion of the business rules into the *Change Seat* use case. Easily seventy percent of the steps here relate to the rules for seat assignment and upgrades. Just taking those steps out shrinks the use case down to ten pages.

Ahmed: But in the travel industry, the rules are everything. That is what our reviewers will be looking for. I have to capture that information, and the use case is perfect for that because it shows the circumstances for when the rule is applied, and I can write alternatives that describe what happens when the rule is not complied with.

You: That's true, but the use case should anchor this information rather than incorporate it. We can adorn the use case with business rules, constraints, and everything else. The information is still there, it's just that it won't hide the essence of the use case.

Ahmed: OK, I like that. That's great. What else?

You: The other thing that we have to look into is the goal of this use case, because it seems that it really addresses two separate goals.

Ahmed: What do you mean?

You: The use case begins when the traveler wants to either change his assigned seat or upgrade to the next level of service. That seems like two distinct goals to me.

Ahmed: On the surface it may, but when we constructed an object-oriented-analysis model of the seat change, we discovered that an upgrade is just a seat change—to a nicer one, mind you—but still just a seat change. So we thought if we used the *Change Seat* use case to do the upgrade, then we could reuse the *Change Seat* components when we build the system.

You: That's not what we're trying to do here. We just want to describe the black box behavior of the system. How that system implements the behavior will come out in analysis later. Our concern right now is just trying to capture user needs and stakeholder interests—you know, that stuff I told you about the **UserValued-Transactions** (p. 95). Trying to combine the two goals into one use case really bloats it up and makes it much more complicated and difficult to comprehend. Right now, half your alternatives are based on whether the seat change is for an upgrade request. The upgrade seat should in my opinion be a separate use case.

Ahmed: Even so, there would be a lot of steps in common between *Change Seat* and *Request Upgrade*.

You: Well, if that really is the case, then we can factor out the common courses of action into a use case that is included by both. We have a principle for doing that, which we can discuss later. One last thing. Why are you using Object Constraint Language [OCL] in your descriptions? Is there anyone here besides you who can read this?

Ahmed: Well, Ralph and I are having a bit of a disagreement. He really likes use cases, but thinks that writing all the details is just busywork. The use cases he's written are pretty ambiguous. He's assuming that the only people who'll read his use cases are billing experts. I'm trying to explain to him that precision is important because we're outsourcing a large part of the project to you guys, and the more precise I can be, the easier it's going to be for you, and the less chance there'll be any miscommunication. So I thought I would use OCL in my use cases as an example that Ralph and the others can follow.

You: I'm probably the only one in my group who can read OCL, and your travel agents certainly won't be able to. How are you going to get them to review these use cases?

Ahmed: Well, I thought we could have a few seminars and teach them OCL.

You: You're already having a hard time getting the agents on board for this project. Do you think making them learn OCL is going to help you?

A use case is a story that describes how an actor uses the system to obtain a specific measurable benefit. Like all stories, a use case can be a good story that clearly expresses the author's vision and is well received by the audience. Or it can be confusing, obscure the author's vision, and be rejected by its audience.

What are the properties that make a use case easy to read and comprehend? Like a good story, a use case should not have multiple plots or plot fragments. Rather, it should address a single and complete goal that supports the system vision, which we call a **CompleteSingleGoal** (p. 118). The actor will either succeed in reaching this goal or fail to completely reach it.

One difference between a use case and a story is that a use case has more than a single story line. There may be numerous alternative ways the actor can reach, or fail to reach, the goal. The use case must describe all the different courses of action possible as **ExhaustiveAlternatives** (p. 129).

How should we present all these different story lines in a use case? Should we exhaustively write every possible alternative as its own story? Or should we try to write the use case story like a computer program with nested ifs, loops, and other complex logic? Neither approach is satisfactory because people find the exhaustive scenarios redundant, and most readers prefer not reading anything that looks like program logic. The favored approach is to structure all the different alternatives as **ScenarioPlusFragments** (p. 125), where we write the expected path for achieving the **CompleteSingleGoal** as a simple single story line called the scenario, and then write each alternative as an incremental addition to that story, the so-called fragments.

All good stories should have a catchy title, and a use case is no different. The title should be a **VerbPhraseName** (p. 122), that reminds the readers of the use case's goal.

Good stories do not distract their readers with background information or references. Rather, they include these details as supplements, such as the list of references or an appendix. The same is true of use cases: we should not distract the reader with technological details, business rules, and constraints. Rather, we can use supplemental specifications, **Adornments** (p. 133), to adorn the use case.

Finally, all good stories must be readable. A use case is supposed to be a work of nonfiction and serves as the basis for comprehending a system. Therefore, it is important that it be **PreciseAndReadable** (p. 138).

Solitary country road

5.1 CompleteSingleGoal

You are working on the **EverUnfoldingStory** (p. 102), focusing on a **ClearCastOf-Characters** (p. 90).

Improper goals will leave the writers uncertain about where one use case ends and another begins.

One of the most painful events in American history was the Vietnam War, in which tens of thousands of young lives were lost, and many more tens of thousands of lives ruined. The Vietnam War made a powerful and proud nation look inward and doubt itself. Many armchair generals theorize about why the United States failed to succeed in Vietnam, but a consensus always seems to form around a lack of a clear moral purpose.

The United States had never declared war on Vietnam; its involvement started with sending advisors to assist the South Vietnamese. Slowly the United States was drawn into the quagmire that had previously swallowed France. Battles were fought; some were won, and others were lost. But it always seemed that the effort was fragmentary, with no goal.

Use cases that fail to address any goals are tangential and don't add value to the system. Those that fail to completely address one goal are insufficient, and leave the developers no choice but to look for other use cases, or guess at some parts of the system. Those that address too many goals tend to be too complex.

To build the correct system, we need to understand how an actor achieves some accomplishment of value. A story is organized into chapters. In each chapter, we want to show the hero or heroine overcoming some obstacles and achieving some particular accomplishment related to the overall story. In the same way, each use case should describe one significant accomplishment of interest to the primary actor.

We want to control complexity by partitioning our use cases into pieces that make sense to the stakeholders. A use case should describe a manageable unit of work. It should be a self-contained, logically cohesive unit that describes or references all relevant facets of a particular behavior. At the same time, it should be small enough so the reader can grasp its meaning, and not be overwhelmed by size or detail. We must consider several factors for controlling the complexity of our use cases, dealing with time and size.

- *The duration of the actor goals may vary.* An actor can have some goals on the minute-by-minute level, some on the one-sitting level, and some that take multiple days to accomplish. Use case developers often miss this observation. Many people tend to focus on goals that an actor can complete rather quickly in a short session; such an approach can result in small, fragmented use cases. Worse, they can completely overlook services that are important to the actor.

- *Excessively large use cases can bury the stakeholder in an avalanche of details and obscure the purpose of the use case.* The longer a use case, the longer it takes to write, and the harder it is for the reader to keep all the details straight. Use cases resembling Russian novels are bad because they are too complex, contain too much information, and provide too many alternatives. The readers and even the writers can lose sight of the use case goal, implement the wrong service, and emphasize the wrong characteristics of the system, resulting in additional features of no value to anyone. Once again, the purpose of the use case set is to convey how the system brings value, rather than exhaustively describing everything.

- *Large use cases can inhibit reuse.* Both size and detail make it hard to reuse basic features. Larger use cases can hide important system properties, making it hard to identify reusable services. Larger use cases tend to contain implementation details because writers have a tendency to substitute details for completeness. Such an approach is likely to offer solutions rather than address stakeholder needs. The result is rigid, narrowly defined transactions that are too precise to reuse in other contexts. It is simply easier to reuse smaller pieces than larger ones.

- *Excessively small use cases will describe only a fragment of some accomplishment of value.* If writing use cases like Russian romantic novels is not appropriate, then what about writing them as partial stories? Unfortunately, this type of use case will cover only a portion of the overall behavior of the system, so the reader will not see its overall purpose. This style of writing results in cliffhanger endings, which are wrong because each use case needs to represent a "complete usage of value" to the actor.

◆ *The narrow knowledge of subject matter experts may push us toward small use cases.* Experts often have a narrow focus, so they tend to propose those use case transactions with which they are familiar. Many experts favor smaller transactions because they are well versed in some particular process, but don't necessarily understand the purpose or goal behind that process. Yet these transactions only partially satisfy the actor's need, and often require one or more additional transactions to satisfy the goal of the actor.

Therefore:

> Write each use case to address one complete and well-defined goal. That goal may be at any level in the **EverUnfoldingStory** (p. 102).

Select and name the primary actor goal with a **VerbPhraseName** (p. 122) that you wish to highlight. This goal may require a few seconds, days, weeks, or months to accomplish, and can be at any level. If you cannot come up with a good **VerbPhraseName**, then you may not have a goal after all. Good characteristics of a goal are:

◆ It is associated with a well-defined actor.

◆ It is valuable to the actor or the stakeholder on whose behalf the actor is working.

◆ It is consistent with other goals that you have identified for the system at this level. If the goal is not appropriate for the level of abstraction that you are working at, consider reorganizing the use case model as an **EverUnfoldingStory**.

Be **PreciseAndReadable** (p. 138). Describe the different ways the primary actor can either reach or fail to reach this goal. To accomplish this, structure the use case as a **ScenarioPlusFragments** (p. 125), with a main success scenario describing the nominal case. This is followed by a set of fragments describing all reasonable alternatives that can affect the actor as he or she attempts to achieve the goal.

A use case should leave the system in a well-known state when it ends: either the primary actor fully obtains the goal, or the system state is the same as if the use case never happened. Use cases should not contain cliffhanger endings. The initiating and terminating events should be clear and unambiguous to the actors.

Occasionally, your use case may need to address more than one goal. This can be done without violating the spirit of **CompleteSingleGoal**, as long as the use case is cohesive and achieves a unified purpose. It is much better, however, to write the use case to address a higher level goal that encompasses subgoals, as well as any other issue associated with the higher level goal.

Examples

Wings Over the World

Our consultant has reviewed the *Change Seat* use case that Ahmed had written. Its goal was to change a traveler's seat, either as a normal exchange or an upgrade.

We can immediately see that this use case really addresses two goals: obtain a different seat or upgrade a seat. Ahmed may have correctly argued that a seat upgrade is just the same as a seat change from a system point of view, but we want to write use cases from the actor's perspective. For most air travelers, an upgrade is a very different goal from a seat change.

Combining these two goals will likely lead to long, complex alternatives that can obscure the differences between them. You can capture any steps that are truly common to both in lower-level *included* use cases to avoid redundancy (see **CommonSub-Behavior** [p. 176]).

Select Exit Row Seat is another example of a poor use case goal. It says:

Select a seat in a designated exit row for the traveler.

The qualification in this example should make us question whether this statement represents a complete goal or just a fragment of another. Most airlines will not assign a seat in a designated exit row until the passenger checks in and airline staff can confirm that the passenger is physically capable of opening the exit door in an emergency. Most likely, this use case should be an alternative to *Change Seat*.

A frequent cause for writing fragmented use cases is that many writers tie each of their system-level use cases to specific interface details, with one use case per user-interface form. This practice frequently results in numerous system-focused use cases, such as *Capture Traveler's Desired Itinerary, Present Itinerary to Traveler, Capture Traveler's Preference, Capture Traveler's Personal Information,* and *Capture Traveler's Payment Option.* Do these examples truly reflect a useful goal for a traveler, or are they all just fragments of the goal *Book Flight*? The use case is inappropriate for capturing user-interface details. Such information should supplement a use case as an **Adornment** (p. 133).

Writing use cases around goal fragments leads to the creation of numerous closely related use cases without any structure tying them together. In this example, if you were reviewing twenty or more use cases, would it be obvious to you that *Change Seat* and *Select Exit Row Seat* are closely related? Probably not. You would lose an opportunity to simplify the system and make it more comprehensible by consolidating closely related behavior.

Sign for frog company, Rayne, Louisiana

5.2 VerbPhraseName

You have identified a use case associated with a **CompleteSingleGoal** (p. 118).

> Meaningless, generic names will not set reader expectations or provide a convenient reference point.

Names convey meaning. A picture may be worth a thousand words, but descriptive names can say much, much more. Just the name "The Grand Canyon" instantly evokes vivid images of colors, plateaus, rock formations, mules, and snow-covered vistas accompanied by the gentle strains of the "Grand Canyon Suite."

Businesses recognize the value of a good name, and they will spend millions of dollars researching good ones. They want something "snazzy" that instantly catches people's attention and draws customers to their product. They also want to avoid names with negative connotations that hurt their product's image. A popular business school example of a bad product name was General Motors' attempt to introduce the Chevrolet Nova into Spanish-speaking countries. Unfortunately, Nova sounds like the Spanish for "no-go."

Using descriptive verb phrase names for your use cases is a good practice, because they accurately reveal the intention of each use case.

The name sets the tone and association for the audience and can provide a focal point for the writer. A name should reveal the use case's intention and reflect the **CompleteSingleGoal** that the actor is trying to achieve. A meaningful name that adequately describes a use case's purpose can give the reader more insight into a use case than several paragraphs of text. The name should offer a preview of things to come, and be descriptive enough to stand by itself, allowing the reader to work at the use case set level without having to delve into the contents of the use cases composing the set.

A descriptive, goal-based name can also help the writers understand the essence of the use cases that they are writing, and it can constantly remind them of the goals that they are trying to accomplish.

An appropriate name provides a handle for the use case. One of the benefits of software patterns is that the names of the various patterns convey sufficient meaning to become part of the development nomenclature. For example, developers can use the terms "Visitor," "Bridge," or "State" to describe fairly complex components to their audience with very few words. In the same way, a meaningful name can adequately describe a use case so that the audience doesn't need to read the full use case to use it.

Appropriate use case names allow you to see the big picture and work on the whole set. People working with a system at the 50,000-foot level don't care about the low-level details of the individual use cases. In fact, such details would hinder their efforts because they would quickly obscure the abstract concepts they are trying to understand or explain. Meaningful use case names assist those working at a high level by revealing the intent of the various use cases to the audience. People don't have to stop and read each one; they can instead focus on the system as a whole, without distraction.

Therefore:

> Name the use case with an active verb phrase that represents the goal of the primary actor.

Begin each name with an active verb that describes the use case's goal, and follow this verb with a phrase describing its object. Be terse, yet descriptive enough to capture the use case's essence. For example, a good name for a use case describing paying an accident claim is *Pay Claimant.*

Choosing a good name for a use case is important, because it conveys the use case's purpose to the audience. Descriptive names are easy to work with and can significantly improve the cohesiveness of your use cases. If you have trouble coming up with a name, then you should reconsider your use case.

Examples

Insurance Claims

Use Case Naming Horrors
Consider the following names for some insurance use cases:

- *Main Use Case*
- *Claim Process*

- *Use Case 2*
- *Process Stuff*

It's nice to know that *Main Use Case* is apparently the important one, but what does it do? This kind of name is okay for those who already know what the system does, but it doesn't help anyone who is unfamiliar with the system. Names like this are not evocative of the use case goal; they force the audience to read most of the use cases to determine which ones interest them.

Claim Process appears to be a better name, but what does it imply? This use case name doesn't define how the system handles all claims or how users enter claims, nor does it tell what kind of claim the use case defines. It forces the reader not only to read the use case to determine its purpose, but also to look through the whole set to find the ones about the claims in which they are interested.

Use Case 2. Believe it or not, some of us have seen use cases named *Use Case 1, Use Case 2,* and so on before. Of course, no one had any idea what they covered, but at least we knew that there were at least two of them.

Process Stuff. Someone actually used this one too. This could be about anything, but at least it can be used in almost any context.

Good Use Case Names

- *File Accident Claim*
- *Approve Property Damage Claim*
- *Report Fraudulent Claim to Police*

Each of these names is descriptive and conveys some meaning to the audience, so that they don't have to read every use case in the collection to understand each one. The names also serve as a convenient reference, so that the readers can easily locate only the ones in which they are interested.

You can number use cases for organizational purposes. For example:

Use Case 42: Approve Property Damage Claim

allows us to use descriptive names and organize our use cases numerically. Very short comments are also acceptable. If the use case you are describing drives the rest, then you could describe it as:

Use Case 1: Book Airline Reservation (Main)

We still refer to it as *Book Airline Reservation,* but we also know that it is the first use case in our collection, and it is the main one as well.

Newspaper clippings from the Electric Institute of Washington

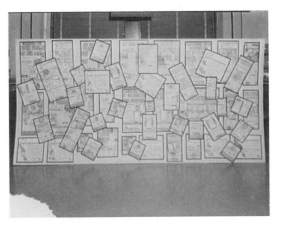

5.3 ScenarioPlusFragments

You are writing a use case description for the primary actor's **CompleteSingleGoal** (p. 118).

> **Readers must be able to follow the path easily through the specific scenario or story that they are interested in; otherwise, they are likely to become frustrated or miss important information.**

A delightful style of children's book is the "choose your own adventure" story. These books draw the reader into the story by asking him or her to choose the hero's course of action. Do you heed the warning of the old gypsy and avoid the dark path into the forest, or do you venture into the forest to seek the legendary magic amulet? The reader must choose one alternative. If you heed the gypsy warning, then the reader turns to page 59 to continue the thread of the story. If you choose to venture boldly into the forest, then the reader turns to page 112. One choice advances the hero closer to his goal, while the other may lead to failure and death.

A "choose your own adventure" story is a good style for writing use cases, because it makes it easy for the readers to follow the various paths in a use case.

An interesting use case needs to capture alternatives to the main success scenario. Many different things can happen as an actor attempts to attain a goal. Things don't always go right. Sometimes, if the system is prepared, it can detect the problem and take the steps necessary to rectify it. Other times, however, things can be screwed up too much to continue, and the best course of action is to stop. The system should be able to handle these situations gracefully. To do so, the developers need to know all the things that they can reasonably expect to go wrong before they build the system.

The difference between a use case and a "choose your own adventure" story is that the adventure story has no "main" success story line, so the reader must make the choices at various moments while reading the book. Unlike the story, a use case is a description that should reveal the crisscrossing structure, not hide it. There are several ways we can show this structure:

- *Writing every alternative as a complete story will obscure the differences between story variations.* We could write every possible variant of the plot as an entire story. This has the advantage that the reader can simply read any complete variation of the story from top to bottom. However, there will be a great many of these to read, and at some point the reader will have trouble telling the difference between, say, plot variant 17 and plot variant 18. The two variants might be almost entirely similar, perhaps differing in only two sentences. At that moment, the structure becomes a drawback, since the reader will get more, not less, confused over time.

- *Separating out every variant also makes the writer's life difficult.* Any change in the story line usually affects a number of the variants, and the writer must find and change every variant, trying to be consistent and accurate in the change. This is both tiring and error-prone, so we want to keep the number of variants to a minimum.

- *A large number of* if *statements will clutter the story.* A second alternative is to put *if* statements into the story, which shortens the writing. Programming languages are constructed this way, and many people have been trained to write in the form, "If such and such is the case, then so and so happens."

  If our story had only one of these *if*s, then this would indeed be a practical way to proceed. However, most of the stories that get written into use cases have a large number of variations, from a half dozen up to several dozen, sometimes with *if* inside *if*s. This structure quickly gets out of hand, and the reader is soon unable to follow the story lines. It is important that every reader, from end user to executive to programmer, be able to understand the crisscrossing story, and so the "if . . . then. . . , but if . . . then . . ." story line structure is no longer recommended.

- *People cope well with incremental complexity.* There is a surprising third alternative that has shown itself to be effective. People seem to be quite adept at modifying and adding complexity to a base concept a little at a time. We often see people describing a simple concept, and then saying, "Well, actually, it isn't that simple. This can also happen. . . ," adding a twist to the story. The listeners to these explanations are able to build up a complex understanding, a small piece at a time. We can use this idea to convey the intertwining story line (Cockburn 2001, p. 87).

The main success scenario needs to be clearly identified. If all threads are written as scenarios, then which scenario is the most important one? The readers and the builders need to know which scenario is the main success scenario that you expect the primary actor typically to seek.

Therefore:

> Write the success story line as a simple scenario without any consideration for possible failures. Below it, place story fragments that show what alternatives may occur.

The main success scenario describes how the primary actor accomplishes the goal in a straightforward manner. It doesn't have to be the shortest possible path or the only possible successful path, but it should be the normal desired path for reaching the goal, that is, the one the users are most likely to follow.

For each of the **Exhaustive Alternatives** (p. 129) that has to be considered, create a header after the main success scenario. First, describe the **DetectableCondition** (p. 148) that cause the actor to take the branch. Then describe what happens in this branch, and how it ends: either rejoining the main story or ending in failure.

Each scenario in a use case should have a clear purpose. Write each scenario in the use case as a set of **LeveledSteps** (p. 153), each showing the **ActorIntentAccomplished** (p. 158), making **ForwardProgress** (p. 162) toward the use case's **CompleteSingleGoal**.

Usually, the fragment ends in a fairly obvious way, by retrying the step that preceded the branch, fixing up the step so that it can rejoin the next step in the main success scenario, or simply failing altogether. On occasion, it is necessary to name explicitly where the story picks up again.

Occasionally, some of the fragments become long and complex enough to obscure the rest of the use case. To make the use case **PreciseAndReadable** (p. 138), at this point it would be useful to create a **PromotedAlternative** (p. 190). Extract the alternative and put it into a separate use case.

You will occasionally want to associate other information with the use case: performance information, business rules, or possible screen designs. Create places for such information as **Adornments** (p. 133) to the use case in the template.

Note: In terms of **BreadthBeforeDepth** (p. 48), this pattern identifies these stopping points:

- Main success scenario
- Naming the conditions
- Finishing some of the fragments

Examples

Auto Insurance Claim Handling

Use Case 5.1 illustrates a main scenario with several alternative fragments overriding some of its steps. While this example is fairly straightforward, we can often identify many viable alternatives for a scenario.

Use Case 5.1   *Get Paid for Car Accident* (from Cockburn 2001)

Get Paid for Car Accident

Primary Actors: Claimant   Accident victim making claim

                Insurance Company   Company insuring Claimant

                Agent   Insurance Company representative processing claim

Level: Summary

Main Success Scenario

1. Claimant submits claim with substantiating data.
2. Insurance Company verifies that Claimant owns a valid policy.
3. Insurance Company assigns Agent to examine case.
4. Agent verifies that all details are within policy guidelines.
5. Insurance Company pays Claimant.

Extensions

1a. Submitted data is incomplete:

     1a1. Insurance Company requests missing information.

     1a2. Claimant supplies missing information.

2a. Claimant does not own a valid policy:

     2a1. Insurance Company declines claim, notifies Claimant, records all this, and terminates proceedings.

3a. No Agents are available at this time:

     3a1. (What does the Insurance Company do here?)

4a. Accident violates basic policy guidelines:

     4a1. Insurance Company declines claim, notifies Claimant, records all this, and terminates proceedings.

4b. Accident violates some minor policy guidelines:

     4b1. Insurance Company begins negotiation with Claimant as to degree of payment to be made.

Railroad roundhouse turntable

5.4 ExhaustiveAlternatives

You are writing a use case as a **ScenarioPlusFragments** (p. 125).

> A use case may have many alternatives. Missing some alternatives means the developers will misunderstand the system's behavior, and the system will be deficient.

We had just moved, and this was our first winter in our new home. For two days it snowed, dumping nearly three feet of heavy, wet snow. Even with chains, there was no way my car would get out of the driveway, and I was forced to begin shoveling. After an hour I had managed to clear my driveway, feeling quite satisfied with my accomplishment. That is, until I saw the municipal snowplow barreling down the street, pushing a wall of snow in front of it, directly into my freshly shoveled driveway. Swearing mightily, I cleared the snow away, and then I noticed the wall of snow that the plow had pushed into my neighbor's driveway. He was an older gentleman, and I thought it would be neighborly to clear the snow out of his driveway.

Halfway through clearing his driveway, I heard the rumble of machinery down the block. I thought, "Oh no, not again. The plow's coming back to finish me off." Then I saw that the city was using a small front-end loader to clear away the snow that the plow had pushed into people's driveways! I didn't know whether to laugh or cry, because I could have just waited, warm and cozy, in my house for this plow to come by.

Later, when I told my neighbor, he laughed and apologized profusely. "I'm sorry. I forgot to tell you that the city clears the driveways after the plow comes through." I had gone out and gotten cold and soaking wet because I did not know that the alternative of just sitting and waiting was available to me.

A good use case describes all important alternatives, so that the developers can properly address potential problems, protecting the users from unpleasant surprises.

Developers need to know how to handle errors. Error handling and exception processing constitute the bulk of most software-based systems. Certain classes of errors are well known and easy to handle, but a significant number of errors are hard to predict and difficult to detect. For example, it is easy to detect missing data, but not so easy to find problems with boundary conditions or subtle interactions between seemingly unconnected fields. It is difficult for a system's developers to identify potential errors because they are working under time constraints, and good error finding requires "out-of-the-box" thinking. Developers focus on using the system correctly, and they often fail to consider cases of incorrect system use because these actions break the rules. But users do not share this constraint and often, through unfamiliarity, necessity, or experimentation, attempt to use the system in ways the developers never considered. A robust system must be able to handle these types of situations without failing. But the only way to handle these errors is to identify them before building the system, so that the system knows how to recognize and handle them. One of the most important facets of the analysis process is identifying potential error situations that the system is likely to encounter, and then developing uniform policies for handling them.

Schedule pressure limits the time developers can spend identifying variations. Identifying variations requires time, creativity, and out-of-the-box thinking. It can be mentally tiring to think about many of them and keep them straight. Developers often fail to see the value in this exercise, especially when many of the differences are so minuscule that they appear to be meaningless, and when there is intense schedule pressure. But this kind of thinking is backwards, because this information is absolutely essential for estimating the scope of a project. Variations represent a significant, and possibly a majority, portion of the effort involved. Acknowledging them helps to determine an accurate schedule for the project.

Some of the variation-handling policies need significant investigation. Identifying errors is often the easy part. Handling these errors can be much more difficult and often requires significant time and effort. It is easy to decide that certain input fields should allow only integers, but it requires a coordinated policy and potentially complex components to implement this feature efficiently for tens or hundreds of similar fields. Moreover, other input fields may have somewhat similar constraints, and it is highly desirable to use the same mechanism to handle these fields as well. But designing this kind of feature requires real work.

Having information about the variations helps developers build a robust design. The better the developers understand a system, the easier it is for them to design and build it. Even when using iterative development processes, it is often much cheaper and simpler to build a system when its developers are aware of error conditions at the beginning of the development process. Having this knowledge allows them seamlessly to incorporate exception handling into their system architecture and handle these conditions in an effective manner, providing a much more robust and user-friendly system. They can still add functionality later on, but it is hard to incorporate these add-ons seamlessly into the system's architecture. As a result, the add-ons are often not as well structured as they would have been if they were part of the original system.

Therefore:

> Capture all alternatives and failures that must be handled in the use case.

Once you have identified all of your use cases and their main courses, identify as many variations from the main course as you can. Capture all of the variations that you want the system to handle, yet be selective. These variations should be **DetectableConditions** (p. 148) that result either from the user using the system differently or from error conditions. Eliminate all the variations that begin with conditions that the system cannot or does not have to detect, and then merge all the variations that produce the same resulting behavior.

Document the remaining variations in the use case using the **ScenarioPlusFragments** (p. 125) format, listing the appropriate **DetectableConditions** as the first step of each scenario or fragment.

Note: This is a good time, when doing **BreadthBeforeDepth** (p. 48), to find all the alternative conditions that will force different paths, before spending much time on the extension handling. The list of conditions will act as a table of contents of issues that need to be researched over the following days.

Working **BreadthBeforeDepth** is the third place at which to pause and examine your work. (The first is after you have named the actors and **UserValuedTransactions** (p. 95). The second is after writing the main success scenario.)

Examples

E-mail Access

Use Case 5.2 demonstrates how to itemize a use case's alternate courses. Instead of defining a separate use case for each of the alternate and error courses, we itemized each as a deviance from the original. This format nicely encompasses those situations in which the user performs several separate actions, such as saving some e-mail, forwarding some e-mail, and replying to still other e-mail.

Use Case 5.2 *Access E-mail*

Access E-mail

Primary Actor: Reader   Person reading e-mail

Level: User Goal

Main Success Scenario

1. Reader initiates use case by logging on to the system and requesting e-mail.
2. Server displays Reader's e-mail screen.
3. Reader and server repeat the following sequence indefinitely.
4. Reader selects e-mail.
5. Server displays e-mail and marks it read.
6. Reader selects "Quit" option.
7. Server updates Reader's e-mail account information and logs off the Reader.

Alternate Courses

Reader Saves E-mail

4. Reader selects "Save E-mail" option.
5. Server marks e-mail as unread.

Reader Replies to E-mail

4. Reader selects "Reply" option.

5a. Server prompts Reader for a reply.

5b. Reader enters reply and instructs server to send e-mail.

5c. Server sends e-mail to address of message's originator.

Reader Forwards E-mail to Another Reader

4. Reader selects "Forward E-mail" option.

5a. Server requests address.

5b. Reader supplies information and instructs server to send e-mail.

5c. Server forwards e-mail to specified address.

Error Courses

Invalid Login

1. Reader supplies incorrect login id or password.
2. Server displays error message and initiates a new login sequence.

Cadet dressing for Sunday dinner, Selma, Alabama

5.5 Adornments

You are writing the use case description as a **ScenarioPlusFragments** (p. 125), keeping the steps **TechnologyNeutral** (p. 167).

> **The inclusion of nonfunctional requirements in a use case can quickly clutter and obscure the use case.**

Okay, I admit that I am an opera fan. (Can you guess which one of us?) I enjoy listening to people shout at each other in a foreign language while wearing strange costumes. Most people say they don't understand opera. But the stories behind the operas are often fairly simple, usually something about young romantic love thwarted by meddling parents or the patriarchy. An adequate synopsis of an opera can usually fit on two pages of a program.

Of course, there is a great deal more information available about an opera that can help you understand it. For example, what are some of the critical interpretations of the opera? Or, what were the historical influences on the composer that led to the creation of the opera? The answers to these questions are never included in the synopsis because they would clutter and obscure the synopsis. Rather, separate articles in the program answer these questions.

A use case is similar to a program synopsis because it offers an understandable explanation of a complicated production. You should be able to read a use case and understand how a system delivers value to its actor without worrying about user-interface details, data storage details, or other nonfunctional requirements.

The purpose of a use case is to express clearly the functional requirements of a system. A use case should show what a system does, not how it does it. It should provide a clear, concise description of the services that a system provides its users in plain, everyday language (Jacobson et al. 1992). A reasonably intelligent person, regardless of his or her technical background, should be able to pick up a use case and quickly understand the functionality that it describes.

We often discover nonbehavioral information while researching functional requirements. It is very common to collect all kinds of valuable information when gathering system requirements. Some portions of this collected data, such as the types of actions to perform or the number of users to support, form a basis for the resulting requirements. Other portions, including such items as sample reports, example GUIs, or generated data files, don't directly map into the requirements, but instead serve to illustrate and clarify them.

Inclusion of nonfunctional requirements in the use case is distracting. Excessive detail makes use cases harder to comprehend and forces readers to wade through more material and grapple with issues that they don't need to understand. Therefore, we don't want to include this extra information in the use case proper. The most common type of unnecessary information is user-interface details, which can quickly bloat an otherwise simple use case into an incomprehensible monster. Likewise, a detailed description of how the system captures and validates customer shipping information usually does not help your understanding of a use case describing how a customer makes a purchase.

But we do not want to lose information that aids in understanding the use case or is valuable to the developers. Just because some data describe specific details or are highly technical doesn't mean that the information isn't valuable. Many of these nonfunctional requirements offer insight into the use case and could well be information that the developers need to implement the system. Because much of this information is either specific or relevant to a use case, we need to keep it close to the use case so that the readers are aware of its existence. The information could be captured in separate documents, but then we would lose a lot of the context that comes from the close association of the nonfunctional requirements with the use case.

Therefore:

> Create additional fields in the use case template that are outside the scenario text to hold the supplementary information that is useful to associate with the use case.

Nonfunctional details such as business rules, a user-interface sketch, external interface protocols, data validation rules, and even outstanding issues (so-called TBDs—To Be Determineds) can be added to the use case in a supplementary section. This helps keep the use case **PreciseAndReadable** (p. 138) and the steps **Technology-**

Neutral. Nonfunctional information does not clutter up the basic use case, but it is still associated with the relevant use case.

Examples

Wings Over the World with Adornments

Our consultant is explaining to Ahmed, the chief architect, the consequences of including the business rules in the use case. A fragment from Ahmed's *Change Seat* use case appears in Use Case 5.3.

Use Case 5.3   Use Case Horror: *Book Flight* with Business Rules

Book Flight
1. Traveler selects preferred seat.
2. The system verifies a seat has been assigned to the traveler.
3. The system verifies the seat is not in a designated exit row.
4. The system verifies the ticket is a full-price economy ticket, class Y, or is a business-class ticket, class J. If not, the system verifies the ticket is either class L, M, or N, and the traveler is a platinum member of the frequent flier program. The system verifies the seat assignment was not issued as part of a companion ticket. If not, the system verifies . . .
5. The system . . . yada yada yada . . . and the use case terminates.

Use Case 5.3 is a simplified fragment, and we should remember that airlines tend to have Byzantine rules regarding changes to tickets. We have seen simple use cases bloated by business rule descriptions into thirty-page monstrosities. Yet, the actual *Change Seat* use case may be as simple as the one shown in Use Case 5.4.

Use Case 5.4   *Change Seat* Adorned with Business Rules

Change Seat
Level: User Goal
Main Success Scenario
1. This use case begins when the traveler specifies that she wishes to change her seat assignment.
2. The system verifies that the traveler is eligible for a seat change.
3. The traveler specifies her flight number and day of departure.
4. The system displays the current seat map for the aircraft.
5. The traveler selects her preferred seat.
6. The system verifies that the seat is still available.

7. The system releases the traveler's existing seat and assigns her chosen seat.
8. The system confirms to the traveler her new seat assignment.

Alternatives

2a: Traveler is not eligible for seat change

    2a1. The system . . .

Business Rules:

Seat Reassignment Eligibility

1. Unconditional seat reassignment is allowed for full-fare economy, and business class tickets, ticket classes J and Y.
2. Unconditional seat reassignment is allowed for discount fare codes L, M, and N if passenger is a platinum-tier frequent flier.
3. Ticket classes L, M, N may request seat reassignment 72 hours prior to departure time to Premium Economy seats.
4. Ticket class K may request seat reassignment 24 hours prior to departure time to Premium Economy seats.
5. Award tickets, class C, may not request reassignment.

    .
    .
    .

In this revised version of the *Change Seat* use case, we test to see only if the traveler is eligible for a seat change. In a separate section of the use case—or even in a separate document—we capture the eligibility rules for seat changes. There are several advantages to this approach:

1. The reader can clearly see the flow of events because the use case description is not cluttered with the business rules.
2. There are fewer alternatives in the use case. There may be dozens of rules regarding whether a traveler is eligible for a seat change. If we try to capture all of these rules as part of the use case, we risk specifying an entry in the alternatives section for each situation where we can fail the rule. But in this example, the net result of failing any of the rules is the same: the seat is not reassigned. So we have only one alternative, **DetectableConditions** (p. 148).
3. Whenever the business rules change, we do not have to update the use case scenario.

One of the most frequent mistakes use case writers make is that they believe the use case replaces all other tools for system specification. Business rules, data formats, and user-interface navigation have no place in the use case description. But these items are important and valuable pieces of information that we want to associate with the use case. While this information should not be part of the use case description, it can be written up in supplementary documents that are anchored by the use case. Figure 5.1 conceptually shows how nonfunctional requirements revolve around the relevant use case.

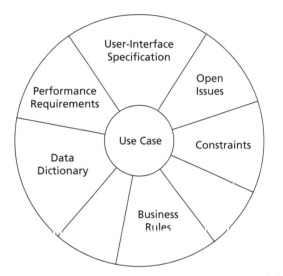

Figure 5.1 *The use case anchors other supplementary requirements (adapted from Cockburn 2001).*

Engineers discussing blueprints. Wilson Dam, Alabama, Tennessee Valley Authority (TVA).

5.6 *PreciseAndReadable*

You are writing the text for a use case as a **CompleteSingleGoal** (p. 118).

> Use cases that are too complicated for nontechnical readers, or too imprecise for developers, are deficient and likely to result in poorly built, inadequate systems.

Beginning guitarists quickly learn that it is difficult to determine how to play a song correctly from traditional sheet music, as it is possible to play any given note or chord at a number of different locations on a guitar. Traditional musical notation shows what notes to play, but it can't always show where or how to play them. For this reason, many guitarists prefer a specialized notation called tablature, which is very precise and easy to learn, demonstrating where and how to play a lick or riff in such a manner that a novice can try it. The lick may be very complex, and require much practice, but any player can at least see how it is done.

In a similar way, a use case should be written with an easy-to-understand precision that meets the knowledge level of most members of the use case audience.

A use case should be readable by both the stakeholders and the developers. Any use case can have several different audiences with varying needs and technical abilities. Higher level audiences, such as customers, can get turned off if the use cases are too difficult to read or too technical to follow easily. Likewise, lower level audiences such as developers will not use use cases if they contain too much "fluff" or fail to describe the system adequately. Well-written use cases address the needs of several different audiences without unduly favoring any.

Developers tend to add detail and solutions. This tendency is natural, and hard to control, as people believe extra details add clarity. Unfortunately, these details are often unnecessary, adding little value to a use case. Worse, they can complicate it, making it more difficult for the reader to understand. Problem solutions are especially unnecessary in use cases, because the people writing use cases are still trying to understand and describe system behavior. They are hardly in a position to propose meaningful designs, because they haven't fully determined the problems associated with this behavior. Well-written use cases describe the essential characteristics of a system's behavior without specifying technical details or favoring a specific implementation.

Nontechnical stakeholders are likely to miss necessary considerations. Nontechnical people have difficulty understanding highly technical documentation. Those without an understanding of the problem domain are unlikely to make the proper inferences from it, because they are unaware of all of the nuances of the problem domain. Well-written use cases specify the issues involved with a system's behavior and spell out the consequences of its various actions.

We want to encourage a dialogue between the stakeholders and the developers to ensure the accuracy of the requirements. One of the greatest benefits of use cases is that they make it easy for stakeholders, many of whom are nontechnical, to understand a system's behavior and determine if it is what they really want. If not, they can work with the system's developers to describe the system better so that it meets their needs. Unfortunately, developers often ignore this benefit because they are in a hurry to build the system. But use cases are meaningless to the system developers until they correctly describe a system that the users really want. Well-written use cases contain a consensus of people having different system views (**ParticipatingAudience** [p. 35]).

Dual models are unacceptable because they can become disjointed and are difficult to maintain. Having different sets of requirements documents for the customer and the developers is a project nightmare. Project teams are under too much pressure; the documents will soon become disjointed and difficult to maintain. Updating multiple copies of a document is not only unnecessary, tedious, and time-consuming, but it also becomes unworkable on most projects. Even worse, multiple versions of design documents unnecessarily introduce ambiguity. When someone refers to a use case, how do you know which one she is referring to? Are your tests based on what the developers did, or what the customers want?

Therefore:

> Write the use case to be readable enough so that the stakeholders bother to read and evaluate it, and precise enough so that the developers understand what they are building.

Every use case you write should accurately and fully describe a **CompleteSingleGoal**, without being so verbose that the audience cannot read it or so high level that it fails to communicate enough information.

The cardinal rule for writing is "know your audience." Determine who needs these use cases, and write each one using your audience's terminology, in a style that they can easily understand. The correct level of precision and readability presents a moving target, so it is important that you understand your audience's needs and abilities when writing each use case.

Do not substitute detail and verboseness for precision. A good general rule to use is "Never expect your audience to fill in the gaps." Use plain language to describe essential system behavior, keeping the steps **TechnologyNeutral** (p. 167). Include only that information necessary to describe the system's behavior. Describe the behavior clearly and precisely enough so that an uninformed reader can fully understand its consequences, without missing important events. This precision benefits not only the customers, but also the developers, who should not have to make guesses when building the system.

Examples

Wings Over the World: Readable but Imprecise

Ralph is the Wings billing expert, and he believes that formality in writing use cases is just busywork that delays getting down to the real work of building the system. Frustrated with the formality advocated by Ahmed, he wrote his own version of the *Change Seat* use case, shown in Use Case 5.5.

Use Case 5.5   Informal Version of *Change Seat*

> *Change Seat*
> **Primary Actor:**   Traveler—Person flying on airplane
> **Level: User Goal**
> *Change Seat*
> Actor: Traveler
>
> *Main Course*
> Traveler specifies her seat preference and the system reassigns her to the new seat.
>
> *Alternatives*
> Traveler is not eligible for a seat change.
> Traveler is informed that a seat change is not available.

This use case is written as a brief or high-level use case. It uses free-flowing prose to describe the exchange between the traveler and the system. In a tight-knit workgroup, this level of precision may be suitable. After all, you do not want to waste a lot of energy writing detailed specifications if you do not have to (**BreadthBeforeDepth** [p. 48]), **QuittingTime** [p. 68]). On the other hand, the Wings project is being outsourced, and this brief does not provide enough precision for a distant team to implement this feature correctly.

Wings Over the World: Precise but Unreadable

While imprecision results in ambiguity, excessive precision results in unusable use cases. Ahmed had used UML Object Constraint Language (OCL) in his use case description. OCL is a formal language for specifying object constraints and is intended for situations in which natural languages are too imprecise. He has used OCL to describe the following rules for seat change eligibility:

> *t : Traveler*
>
> *f: Flight*
>
> t.seatAssignment->notEmpty **and**
>
> t.ticketClass = #J **or** t.ticketClass = #Y
>
> t.ticketClass is In set and f.departureTime < 24 hour

Ahmed suggests that using OCL will reduce ambiguity in the use cases. There is justification for this point of view, because Wings Over the World is outsourcing the project, and the more precise the specifications are, the less opportunity there is for misunderstanding on the part of the developers. Some software developers believe that using formal languages in specifications can greatly reduce the potential for ambiguity.

But this level of precision is too complex for most readers to follow. On the topic of formal specifications, a noted software methodologist is reported to have said, "I like writing these, but I really hate to read them!" Even though stakeholders and designers may have different interpretations of the requirements using natural language, the real problem may be that the stakeholders do not fully comprehend the formal language or, worse, are intimidated by it. Therefore, we may not know if we have the correct specification in the first place. We may in fact precisely capture the wrong specifications because no one can clearly understand the language—but few people are willing to admit they cannot understand a spec.

A good specification is one that the stakeholders can read and then clearly tell you, "No, this is completely wrong. You do not understand my operation. Let me tell you how things really work here . . ." Although your description was incorrect, it was clear enough for the stakeholder to comprehend and tell you that it was wrong. On the other hand, if the stakeholder reads the spec and then tells you hesitantly, "Well, OK. I guess so. You're the expert in this stuff after all," then you are heading for trouble. The stakeholder might not understand the specification and may be withdrawing, leaving you holding the bag.

Higher levels of formality in specifications can often give the developers a false sense of security that there is less opportunity for problems resulting from ambiguity. Nothing can replace a good ongoing dialogue with the stakeholders.

5.7 Trade-offs and Collaborations

As its name would suggest, the use case is the key component of use case modeling. Its purpose is to illustrate how a system enables an actor to meet a particular goal by showing all of the appropriate paths that the actor might take, as well as those situations that could cause the actor to fail. The use case is primarily organizational in nature, providing order and structure so that the reader can easily identify and follow the different paths, or scenarios, as the actor progresses toward his goal.

UserValuedTransactions (p. 95) tells us to capture the smallest set of goals that delivers all necessary services to the actors. A well-written use case presents a story describing how the system helps the primary actor completely reach a particular goal, a **CompleteSingleGoal** (p. 118). The most important factor to consider in this regard is granularity. A use case that addresses multiple goals becomes awkward, confusing to read, and hard to develop from. A use case that addresses a partial goal will likely force readers to wade through multiple use cases to follow a single thread of thought, making it easier for them to miss important actions.

There are several factors to consider when writing **CompleteSingleGoal**, and we have identified several patterns to help. A well-written use case contains a main success scenario and an orderly, well-structured collection of fragments. We call this style **ScenarioPlusFragments** (p. 125). The scenario describes a singular and complete sequence of events that the actor follows while attempting to achieve some goal; it results in either success or failure. The fragments are a list of **Exhaustive-Alternatives** (p. 129) that describe any and all plausible alternative situations that the system can reasonably expect to encounter when attempting to meet this goal. This list is important because it enumerates the situations that the developers need to handle, and helps them to quantify the effort that will be involved.

Aim to keep these various pieces simple and free of clutter. If you have some information that doesn't really belong in the use case but you feel is still valuable, then you append it to the use case as an **Adornment** (p. 133).

A meaningful use case name is also important. Every use case should have a **Verb-PhraseName** (p. 122) that gives the reader a hint of the use case's contents and provides a word association, similar to a pattern name, that the audience can use to describe the use case's purpose in the course of subsequent conversations. The name is tightly coupled to the **CompleteSingleGoal**. If the goal changes, you should consider changing the name as well, or if you want to keep the name, you need to verify that the goal is correct. If you have trouble coming up with a name, then you should question whether your use case really represents a **CompleteSingleGoal**.

Finally, a use case should be **PreciseAndReadable** (p. 138), written so that it is tailored to its audience. Every use case should accurately and completely describe some behavior, but at the same time it should not contain so much detail, nor be so verbose, that the audience cannot read it. The correct level of precision and readability presents a moving target, so it is important that you know your audience when writing each use case.

These guidelines are important because they describe a structure for organizing the details associated with multiple complex scenarios. Use cases without this structure can be very cumbersome, forcing readers to jump between seemingly unrelated sections of text or to read volumes of tediously repetitive sections that seem to differ little from each other. **CompleteSingleGoal** and **ScenarioPlusFragments** are important factors in writing quality use cases. The organization of the individual scenarios is just as important, and is the topic of the next chapter.

Chapter 6

Scenarios and Steps

◆ **Telling a Good Story**

There are few cities in the world where you can still get a terrific corned beef sandwich the way you can in New York. Despite the great outdoors lifestyle the West Coast offers, it still has not learned the fine art of the deli lunch. It almost makes what you have had to endure for the last twenty-four hours worthwhile. A red-eye flight from the coast, spending the morning tearing poor Ahmed's use cases apart, and now you are about to do the same to poor Sitra, Wings Over the World's resident expert on the RAPIER reservation system. Sitra is much like Ahmed, probably less than three years out of school, very smart, very eager to try out new technology. It also appears that Ahmed has warned her about "the consultant."

Sitra: Ahmed said that you shredded his use case.

You: Shredding wasn't my intention. We shortened it and made it more useful.

Sitra: That's what Ahmed said also, so I shouldn't be afraid of this. He was really happy with the results, and he says that you can really help us.

You: Good. I think I can help you, too. I was looking at your *Reserve Flight Segment* use case and it has a lot of the same issues that I discussed with Ahmed, such as the inclusion of business rules and excessive precision. I see Ahmed talked you into using OCL as well. The intention to make the use cases more precise is good, but it is inappropriate. There are also a few other things—for the most part this use case is quite low level—most of this is a description of the physical protocol between you and RAPIER.

Sitra: That's true, and most of my other use cases are like this one. They describe a transaction with RAPIER. But that's important because just about everything we do must go through RAPIER, and my subsystem provides a wrapper around it.

You: Fair enough, but consider this: *Reserve Flight Segment* is really a single step in the *Book Flight* use case.

Sitra: Yes, but it's a lot more complicated than that. The request can be rejected for a number of reasons, or even fail, and I thought the use cases were such a nice mechanism for capturing that.

You: I agree, but a big problem with this use case is that the steps are all at varying levels of abstraction. Some are at a business level: for example, you have one step here, Traveler selects flight. And then other steps are down to almost the program level: System formats RAPIER request header with request type set to booking. Really, what we would like is all the steps in a use case to be at the same level, what I call **LeveledSteps** (p. 153). That way, you do not have to do mental calisthenics jumping back and forth between the different levels of abstraction. The essence of *Reserve Flight Segment* is to send a message to RAPIER to make a reservation on a single flight. RAPIER is either able to make the reservation or unable to do so. The essence of this use case is about three or four steps.

Sitra: Yes, that may be true, but it is a lot more complicated than that. You have to first set up a transaction with RAPIER, then format a request, send the request, decode the response. There are literally dozens of return codes. . . .

You: OK, but that is not necessarily what we want to capture in a use case. What you have here is twenty pages of prose that as a use case I can distill down into about three or four steps, plus a couple of alternatives. That is the essence of the *Reserve Flight Segment* use case.

Sitra: But what about everything else? That's the meat of the problem. I can't design a RAPIER interface subsystem from four sentences of prose.

You: Of course not, but the same thing I told Ahmed applies here: We can use the use case as an anchor for all the details, business rules, protocol specifications, and technical constraints that are supplements to the use case. I like to call these **Adornments** (p. 133). Ninety percent of this use case is a protocol description. Maybe you want to draw a state transition diagram that would more succinctly describe the protocol. Also, what you have done is tied this use case to the RAPIER implementation. Really, the use case should be **TechnologyNeutral** (p. 167). After all, we're trying to capture the system's essence, not its implementation. I would publish the RAPIER interface as a separate external interface document and then reference it from the use case.

Sitra: So that way if we want to work with another airline reservation system, our model is not tied to one specific implementation?

You: That's right, the essence is still there, but if you have to change protocols, then only that portion of the model is affected. Also, this approach will reduce the number of alternatives your use case has. Right now you have some twenty alternatives, most of them based on the return code that you receive from RAPIER. But from what I can see, there are really only three outcomes. Either, one, you were able to reserve the segment, two, you could not book the segment because space is unavailable, or, three, you could not book the segment because of a system failure.

*That's it. But you have twenty alternatives. Ahmed had the same problem because he had incorporated the business rules into his use case, and had an alternative for each of the different failures. We have a principle called **DetectableConditions** (p. 148), which states that if the action you take as a result of a set of different conditions is the same, then they are the same condition. This really helps reduce the complexity of the use case by eliminating redundant alternatives.*

The scenario and step patterns capture the signs of quality for writing good stories about systems. A sign of a quality story is that it stays focused, steadily advances toward its climax, and does not distract the reader with arbitrary or optional plot twists. It does not bore its readers with long, descriptive narratives that don't add any value to the plot.

Like any good story, it must always be clear in each use case step who is speaking and acting. **ActorIntentAccomplished** (p. 158) recommends that each step clearly describe what is accomplished and who is responsible for accomplishing it. Furthermore, it's not enough just to know who is speaking or acting, but each step in a use case scenario must make **ForwardProgress** (p. 162) toward the primary actor's goal. Steps that don't advance toward the goal are meaningless, and don't belong in the use case; they can only distract the readers.

Wishes, fantasy, and magic are all part of good fiction, but they are certainly not part of good use cases. A system must operate in the real world. **DetectableConditions** (p. 148) recommends that each scenario be something that can actually happen or be detected by your system, as opposed to listing all conceivable alternatives.

While technology is part of the real world, technology or implementation dependencies are not part of a good use case. Each step and scenario should be **Technology-Neutral** (p. 167). Issues such as technology constraints or recommendations, user-interface requirements, and business rules are supplemental as **Adornments** (p. 133) and not part of the use case proper.

Finally, we should never ask a reader to cope with a mixture of complex and trivial steps written at different levels of abstraction. Good use case descriptions consist of scenarios with **LeveledSteps** (p. 153), where each step is similar in scope.

The U.S. Weather Bureau station at the National Airport, Washington, D.C.

6.1 DetectableConditions

You are structuring the **Exhaustive-Alternatives** (p. 129) for a use case that can happen under differing conditions.

Writers always wrestle with how many and which conditions to include.

Playing the stock market became very popular during the dot-com bubble of the late 1990s. Every investor had the same dream: timing it so that they bought stock at its absolute lowest price, and selling it at its peak, becoming enormously wealthy in the process. Many investors developed complicated methods for determining just where the market was in its cycle, but all of these techniques shared a flaw: It is absolutely impossible to detect if the market has either peaked or bottomed out until well after the fact, when it is too late to act.

A system cannot handle events that it cannot detect. If the system cannot detect an event, then it cannot take the appropriate steps to deal with it. Any code that is written to handle an undetectable event is wasted, because the system will never know to run it. It is possible that this condition may be a form of another detectable condition, but treating it separately can lead to repetition. For example, if you are writing a use case for a computer to operate a car, losing a key, having a bad starter, or finding no gas in the tank all lead to the same condition: the car will not start. Although the resolution of each situation is different, the onboard computer doesn't care, it just knows that the car won't start.

The developers need to know what conditions to detect. Effective use cases provide the stakeholders and developers with a complete picture of a system's behavior, enumerating all of the conditions that they can reasonably expect the system to encounter, and a brief description of their resolution. Otherwise, the readers may not realize that a particular event can happen, or if they do, they are left to guess at its resolution or to track it down themselves. We want to capture every reasonable possibility, so that the system developers know what business rules they need to incorporate.

Fear of overlooking an important alternative encourages developers to specify irrelevant conditions that cannot be detected by the system. If the people writing the use cases miss a condition, either the developers or the end users of the system will likely bump into those conditions later. Researching detailed business rules late in development is expensive. Discovering a forgotten condition after the system has been put into service is even more expensive. This reality, plus a natural tendency to feel that a thicker requirements document is better, tends to lead beginning use case writers to enumerate every circumstance imaginable as alternatives that the system should handle.

Many apparently different conditions can lead to writing unnecessary alternatives. Writing, reading, and reviewing a use case document is an expensive and tiring business. You don't want to write more than you have to, and it makes no sense to write scenarios that cannot happen. Also, if you write the same condition in several ways, the developers may implement what should be one handling procedure several different ways. Both situations can lead to code bloat.

Therefore:

> **Include only detectable conditions. Merge conditions that have the same net effect on the system.**

Each scenario in a use case must begin with an action that the system is able to detect. Otherwise, the system will never be able to execute the scenario, and you are only wasting valuable time writing it, and you risk introducing features that unnecessarily complicate the system. Being unable to come up with a detectable condition to initiate a scenario may indicate that the scenario doesn't belong in the use case.

If you find a scenario that begins with a nondetectable condition, ask, "What general condition is this scenario trying to handle?" If you can identify the condition, then use it to initiate the scenario; otherwise, eliminate the scenario, because it can't happen. Be careful, however, because a nondetectable condition quite often is a special case of a more general detectable condition, and several apparently different conditions may mask the same basic set of actions. While a use case should capture all of the conditions that the system must be able to handle while resolving a specific goal (**ExhaustiveAlternatives**), it should capture only those, without duplication.

Examples

The ATM JAD Session

Many things can go wrong when a customer accesses an automated banking machine. Let's eavesdrop on a group of ATM developers brainstorming alternatives in a Joint Application Development (JAD) session:

> "What are the situations that can get in your way while getting money from an ATM?"

> "Once, when I bent down to tie my shoelaces, before I straightened up again, the machine had both pushed out the money and sucked it back in again!"

> "I was picking up my crying baby, and the same thing happened!"

> "It ran out of ink on me, and I couldn't read the receipt!"

> "I accidentally put in my library card!"

> "There was some gum stuck in the card reader!"

> "I got all the way there and forgot my card!"

> "I got there and the power was out!"

> "I was in the middle of using it and the power went out!"

The note taker at the board says, "Right. So I'll set up different scenarios in this use case: One for bending down and tying shoelaces, and one for attending to babies."

At that, someone quickly pipes up, "Wait a minute. The machine can't tell why they didn't take the money. All it can tell is that that they did not take the money within a certain time period."

This speaker is right. It makes no sense to write down a condition that the system can't detect. In such cases, all the system can detect is that time went by and the money did not get taken.

> "What's the difference between sliding a card in upside-down and sliding one in that is badly scratched?"

> "None. Put them together: Card unreadable."

While you are at it, remove any conditions that the system does not actually have to handle. Each unnecessary condition that gets written into the requirements document increases the cost of the final system. Those that really must be detected must be written down, of course. But sometimes people get so creative and detailed that they include things that really don't need to be included.

"Hey! What about when the ink runs out?"

"It's expensive to build a low-ink detector. How about we just have someone check the machine once a day to see that the receipt is still printing well enough to be read, and otherwise wait for someone to complain?"

"Hey, what about when the printer accidentally pushes the receipt crooked and it bends back up into the machine and the person can't get it?"

"They don't need it."

Finishing off this ATM example, suppose that the main success scenario is written as shown in Use Case 6.1.

Use Case 6.1 *Withdraw Cash* **(Fast-Path Option) Use Case with DetectableConditions**

Withdraw Cash (Fast-Path Option)

Level: User Goal

Main Success Scenario

1. Customer inserts card.
2. ATM verifies card as readable and legitimate.
3. Customer enters PIN and selects "Fast Cash."
4. ATM sends account number, PIN, and cash withdrawal request to the main banking computer system (BCS), which returns an okay for the withdrawal.
5. ATM issues $40 in two $20 bills, returns the customer's card and a receipt, logs those actions, and sends to the BCS confirmation that the cash was given.
6. Customer takes the cash, card, and receipt.
7. ATM resets for the next customer.

Extensions [*Only the conditions are presented here.*]

a. Sudden power failure detected during operation.

1a. Card jams in reader.

2a. Unreadable card.

3a. Time exceeded on PIN entry or function selection.

4a. BCS is unreachable (off-line or line broken).

4b. BCS refuses transaction.

4c. Insufficient cash in cash dispenser.
5a. ATM detects misfeed of number of bills (too few or too many).
5b. Cash jams in dispenser.
5c. Customer does not remove cash within time limit.
5d. Customer does not remove card within time limit.

Notice how each alternative describes a distinct action that the ATM can reasonably be expected to detect. Because each step distinctly addresses a real condition, none are duplicates.

Wings Over the World

In Chapter 5, we considered the problems caused when Ahmed placed the business rules in the use case. His *Change Seat* use case was apparently thirty pages long because he had incorporated the business rules for checking for eligibility. He had then written alternatives for the failure of each business rule. But from the point of view of the traveler, she was either able or unable to change her seat. She doesn't care why.

Now Sitra has run into the same problem. She has incorporated technology details into her *Reserve Flight Segment* use case. For each of the different RAPIER failure codes, she thought she would have to create an alternative in the use case. This approach would lead to the creation of a large number of alternatives. However, it turns out that there are really only three outcomes: either (1) RAPIER was able to reserve a seat, (2) it failed because there were no seats available, or (3) it failed because there was a system failure.

Poe Lock, Sault Ste. Marie, Michigan

6.2 *LeveledSteps*

You are writing the steps of a use case as a **ScenarioPlusFragments** (p. 125).

> Excessively large or excessively small use case steps obscure the goal and make the use case difficult to read and comprehend.

Anything can be described in smaller and smaller steps, until it loses its sense. Consider the following alternative descriptions of something as simple as stepping up to the sidewalk:

- ◆ She steps to the sidewalk.
- ◆ She lifts her foot from the street to the curb.
- ◆ She lifts her foot, arcs it through the air, and lowers it to the pavement.
  1. She rocks her foot.
  2. Disengages her weight and frees the foot to be lifted.
  3. Lifts it in a curve higher than need be.
  4. Shifts her weight slightly forward.
  5. Brings the foot heel first down onto the curb.
  6. Adjusts to support her weight as it moves above.
  7. Then stands on it.

Excessively small steps make a use case long and hard to read, and they obscure the "why." The "stepping onto the sidewalk" example demonstrates how excessively small steps make the reading long and tedious. Worse, it hides the intent in the details.

Excessively large steps may bury important behavior. The opposite occasionally happens; the writer operates at a very high level of abstraction and makes large leaps in the narrative, omitting key actions the developers must know about.

Mixing levels of detail in a scenario is distracting. Occasionally, one must write adjacent steps at different levels of abstraction. Too much of this distracts the reader from what is supposed to be happening and makes correct interpretation of the instructions difficult.

Therefore:

> Keep scenarios to three to nine steps. Ideally, the steps are all at similar levels, and at a level of abstraction just below the use case goal.

> Write each step to show **ActorIntentAccomplished** (p. 158) with the actor making distinct **ForwardProgress** (p. 162) toward the goal. Keep each step **Technology-Neutral** (p. 167). Make the goal of the step at a level of abstraction lower than the **CompleteSingleGoal** (p. 118). The steps themselves are generally kept at similar levels. If you need to explain how a step is performed, then create a smaller use case that explains the details underlying the step using the **EverUnfoldingStory** (p. 102) to expand from a short description to a fuller description. The step's goal becomes the **CompleteSingleGoal** for a lower level use case.

Examples

A Long and Tedious Use Case for an On-line Store

All of the steps in Use Case 6.2 are legitimate, but the levels are too low. The result will be a very long and tedious document.

Use Case 6.2   Use Case Horror: A *Purchase Goods* Use Case with Unleveled Steps

Purchase Goods

Primary Actor: *User* Customer wanting to make a purchase
Level: User Goal
Main Success Scenario
1. System asks User for first name.
2. User enters first name.
3. System asks for middle initial.
4. User enters middle initial.
5. System asks for last name.
6. User enters last name.
7. System asks for first line of street address.

    .
    .
    .

[And so on—we'll spare you the details.]

The usual motivation on the part of the use case writer for creating long and tedious scenarios like this example is to specify all the fields of personal information the system should collect from the user: surname, first name, middle initial, and so on. Use cases are not interface specifications nor are they data dictionaries, although many use case writers unfortunately tend to write them that way. Such information should be expressed as **Adornments** (p. 133) to the use case. We can level this long and tedious scenario by simply consolidating the data capture steps, as in Use Case 6.3.

Use Case 6.3   Revised *Purchase Goods* Use Case with LeveledSteps

Purchase Goods
Primary Actor: *User*   Customer wanting to make a purchase
Level: User Goal
Main Success Scenario
1. User specifies his personal information.
2. [Some really interesting or useful step rather than an enumeration of every piece of personal information the user is supposed to enter.]

If the reader wants to know what data the system collects as personal information, then she can look up the definition for personal information in the data dictionary.

In general, we find that good writers keep a single scenario to less than ten steps. It seems that this is the number that readers can follow and understand easily.

A Use Case with Excessively Large Steps for an On-line Store

What if the steps are excessively large? Consider Use Case 6.4.

Use Case 6.4   Use Case Horror: A *Purchase Goods* Use Case with Excessively Large Steps

Purchase Goods
Primary Actor: *Visitor*   Customer wanting to make a purchase
Level: User Goal
Main Success Scenario
1. Visitor enters all the personal, product, and purchase information.
2. System presents visitor with final sums, charges credit card, and delivers packing list to the shipping department.

This example meets our less-than-ten-steps rule, but it really doesn't tell us any more about the system than we could deduce from the name.

We can expand these excessively large, or "overloaded," steps by asking, "How is that accomplished?" Breaking the two steps into smaller steps, we now notice that the system was supposed to perform some intermediate actions, as shown in Use Case 6.5.

Use Case 6.5   Revised *Purchase Goods* Use Case

Purchase Goods

Primary Actor: *Visitor*   Customer wanting to make a purchase
Level: User Goal
Main Success Scenario

1. Visitor enters customer information (name, address, etc.).
2. System retrieves customer's profile information, and presents product search and selection mechanisms.
3. Visitor selects products until satisfied. After each selection, system adds the selected product to the customer's shopping cart and presents the ongoing running total of products selected.
4. Visitor selects to purchase the selected items.
5. System presents contents of shopping cart and requests customer's payment information.
6. Customer enters manner of payment and other payment details.
7. System presents visitor with final sums, charges credit card, and delivers packing list to the shipping department.

A Use Case That Mixes Large and Small Steps for an On-line Store

What if we mix large and small steps? Consider Use Case 6.6.

Use Case 6.6   Use Case Horror: Mixing Large and Small Steps in a Use Case

---

Purchase Goods

Primary Actor: *User*   Customer
Level: User Goal
Main Success Scenario

1. The system displays the login screen.
2. User enters a username and password.
3. The system verifies the information.
4. The system sets access permissions.
5. The system displays the main screen.
6. User does one or more of the following: *Place Order, Return Product, Cancel Order, Send Catalog, Register Complaint.*
7. The system terminates the session and resets the screen.

While this scenario has less than ten steps, there is a vast gulf between the levels of the first steps and the sixth step. It would be better if the first five steps were merged into two or three.

We'll merge the first four or five steps by asking "Why were the user and system doing those things? What were they trying to accomplish?" The answer is that the user wanted to log in. So we can revise the steps as shown in Use Case 6.7.

Use Case 6.7   Revised Use Case for *Purchase Goods*

Purchase Goods

Primary Actor: *User*   Customer

Level: User Goal

Main Success Scenario

1   The User *Logs In* to the system.
2. The system presents the available functions to the User.
3. The User does one or more of the following: *Place Order, Return Product, Cancel Order, Send Catalog, Register Complaint.*
4. The system terminates the session and resets the screen.

Company dance given in Moose Hall, Lancaster, Pennsylvania

6.3 *ActorIntentAccomplished*

You are writing the steps of a scenario as **LeveledSteps** (p. 153).

> Both readers and developers get confused about a system's behavior if it is not clear which actor has responsibility for performing a step, and what the actor is trying to accomplish in that step.

Some time ago I was visiting friends who have young children. Their seven-year-old son was trying to tell me about a movie that he had just seen.

> It was so cool. These guys search for this monster that is sinking ships, and, well, they find it, only it's a submarine. They get captured and travel underwater in the submarine. There is this guy and he's really fascinated by the submarine and the submarine captain is this ex-prisoner guy and he's got an attitude and he's always mixing it up with this other guy. And then there is this giant squid that nearly eats him, but the other guy harpoons the squid and saves him.

If I had never seen Disney's version of Jules Verne's *20,000 Leagues under the Sea,* I would have had a lot of trouble following this synopsis. I would have been confused as to which "guy" was fascinated by the submarine, who had the attitude, and who saved whom when the *Nautilus* was attacked by the giant squid.

Writing quality use cases is hard work. It takes a lot of mental energy to create good prose. Often, people have trouble writing **PreciseAndReadable** (p. 138) use cases. Nonprogrammers tend to write ambiguous steps and miss the meaningful details the developers need to know. Programmers, on the other hand, tend to generously incorporate both design and technology details in their use cases, making them too hard for the nonprogrammers to understand. Often, programmers are told to write the use cases that they themselves will implement, leading them to write entirely from the system's perspective, leaving out what the other actors will do.

The developers need to know clearly what they are to implement, at what moments the system should wait for input, and when the system should take the initiative. Otherwise, they are left to make their own assumptions about these issues, or spend time tracking down details they should already have. The cost of miscommunication is high, so we aim to write use cases that are general enough for all of the stakeholders to follow, yet precise enough for the developers to use when building the system (**PreciseAndReadable**).

Therefore:

> Write each step to show clearly which actor is performing the action, and what the actor gets accomplished.

Minimize your writing effort by using a simple format for each step. We recommend a clear sentence with straightforward grammar: actor, verb, direct object, and prepositional phrase. "User enters name and address" or "System notifies user of results." When the actor is visible in each step, then it is clear to both the reviewers and the developers which actor must perform the step. This reduces ambiguity and helps protect the project from the problems that arise from miscommunication.

Use active verbs in the present tense to describe each actor making **ForwardProgress** (p. 162) toward the goal. Each step, except those at the lowest level, should address a lower level **CompleteSingleGoal** (p. 118), so that if necessary, you can create an **EverUnfoldingStory** (p. 102) by converting the step's verb phrase into a lower level use case.

Examples

The Actor-less ATM

Having programmers write their own use cases often results in system-oriented scenarios such as the one shown in Use Case 6.8.

Use Case 6.8 Use Case Horror: *Withdraw Cash* Description without ActorIntentAccomplished

Withdraw Cash
Primary Actor: *User* Account holder
Level: User Goal

Main Success Scenario
1. Read the ATM card.
2. Validate the card information.
3. Collect the transaction information.
4. Validate the transaction details.
5. Issue the cash and update the account.
6. Reset the system.

Although this scenario is clear to the writer, it leaves questions about what the customer's part is in the transaction. Use Case 6.9 is a better version of this use case because it clearly shows what the actor accomplishes.

Use Case 6.9   Improving *Withdraw Cash* Description with ActorIntentAccomplished

Withdraw Cash

Primary Actor: *User*   Account holder

Level: User Goal

Main Success Scenario
1. User inserts his ATM card [versus Read the ATM card].
2. System reads and validates the card information [versus Validate the card information].
3. User selects transaction and enters transaction details [versus collect the transaction information].
4. System validates transaction details [versus Validate the transaction details].
5. User collects cash and withdraws card. [After all, what happened to the User?]
6. System updates the account and resets the system [versus Issue the cash, and update the account, and reset the system].

This style clearly shows who is responsible for what action.

In a related style, some people like to write in the passive voice, again leaving out which actor is taking the initiative, such as in Use Case 6.10.

Use Case 6.10   Use Case Horror: *Withdraw Cash* Description Written in Passive Voice

Withdraw Cash

Primary Actor: *User*   Account holder

Level: User Goal

Main Success Scenario
1. The card gets inserted.
2. The card information gets validated.
3. The transaction information gets collected and validated.
4. The cash is issued, card returned, cash removed, account debited, screen reset.

Unfortunately, different actors initiate the actions. Though the steps in Use Case 6.10 are leveled and show **ForwardProgress** (p. 162), it is not clear to anyone other than the writer who is responsible for doing what. Readers can only guess.

A final mistaken style of writing is to name many, even technology-specific, movements the user of the system will take. See Use Case 6.11.

Use Case 6.11   Use Case Horror: *Access ATM* Description with Technology-Specific Steps

Access ATM
Primary Actor: *User*   Bank customer
Level: User Goal
Main Success Scenario
1. System asks for name.
2. User enters name.
3. System prompts for address.
4. User enters address.
5. User clicks "OK."
6. System presents User's profile.

Here we can improve the writing by combining the steps, making the use case **TechnologyNeutral** (p. 167), and capturing the intent of the actor instead of the technology-specific movements. The result is Use Case 6.12.

Use Case 6.12   Improved TechnologyNeutral *Access ATM* Use Case

Access ATM
Primary Actor: *User*   Account holder
Level: User Goal
Main Success Scenario
1. User enters name and address.
2. System presents User's profile.

Civilian defense workers marching in full regalia in the Labor Day parade, Detroit, Michigan

6.4 *ForwardProgress*

You are writing the steps of a scenario as **LeveledSteps** (p. 153).

> Writers have to decide how much behavior to put into any one step. They can easily write too much detail, making the use case long and tiring to read.

Creating a diversion is a simple plot technique to add conflict to what would otherwise be a very simple and straightforward story. Two or more rivals are pursuing a common goal and one of them attempts to slow or stop the other by creating a distraction. The "Star Trek" television series frequently used this technique. "Star Trek" would have been very uninteresting if all that happened when the *Enterprise* raced to answer a distress call from a damaged ship was that Captain Kirk and his crew rescued the troubled sailors and then headed off to the next starbase. To heat things up, chief engineer Scotty would shout his famous "She cannae take much mor o' this," or the Romulans would send a fake distress call that would force the *Enterprise* to break off and race to the rescue. Suddenly the story would focus on the efforts of the *Enterprise* crew to overcome the diversion. The original goal of the rescue mission became almost an afterthought.

While diversions help create good stories, a good use case should tell a story in a straightforward and simple manner.

Clear, succinct steps lower the mental cost of understanding and evaluating a use case. Each step in a scenario needs to be germane, succinct, and clear, to make it as easy as possible for the reader to follow. If you put too much information into a single step, you increase the chance that the reader will lose track of what is happening inside that step, perhaps missing a key business or implementation issue. If you put too little information within a step, you will need more steps to tell the story, making the use case longer and more tedious to read.

A desire for completeness and detail may lead to the inclusion of steps that are tangential to the goal of the use case. People like to add details to use cases because they feel that extra information improves our understanding of unfamiliar issues. However, tangential steps are more likely to cause the reader to lose focus. A good use case is much like a good movie: well paced and tightly plotted. Extraneous scenes and tangential steps only serve to clutter the description. Worse, someone may try to implement the tangents, wasting time and benefiting no one. Even when the step adds value to the scenario, unnecessary or overly complex details can distract the reader from the main path.

Therefore:

> Eliminate or merge steps that do not advance the actor. Simplify passages that distract the reader from this progress.

Writing long, complex, or tangential steps unnecessarily diverts the reader, who should instead see a clear progression within a scenario. Provide enough detail in each step to enlighten the reader of its purpose, but not so much that you describe the step in excruciating detail. Ensure that the steps stay relevant to the reader and that each step is a **LeveledStep**, contains a "bite-sized" amount of information, and shows the **ActorIntentAccomplished** (p. 158).

Many people have trouble reading technical documents because they are complex and contain a lot of unrelated details. Anything you can do to simplify your use cases (short of removing necessary information) will make them easier to use. If there are tangential steps that represent important alternatives, then incorporate them as alternatives to the scenario—**ScenarioPlusFragments** (p. 125). If there are details you believe are important to understanding the story, or are simply too important to lose, then attach them to the use case as **Adornments** (p. 133).

Examples

Wings Over the World: A Diversionary Scenario

The snippet of the *Request Upgrade* use case shown in Use Case 6.13 shows two blatant diversions in the main success scenario.

Use Case 6.13   Use Case Horror: *Request Upgrade* with Steps Diverting ForwardProgress

Request Upgrade

Primary Actor: *Traveler*   Ticketed passenger

Level: User Goal

Main Success Scenario

1. Traveler enters her account code for flight and requests a seat upgrade.
2. If the Traveler is a frequent flier, then the system displays her current mileage and recent flight activity.
3. The system verifies there are seats available for upgrading.
4. The system upgrades the Traveler's seat assignment, and the appropriate upgrade certificates are removed from the customer account.
5. The Traveler may also buy more upgrade certificates while requesting an upgrade. The system issues upgrade receipt to the Customer.

In this example, steps 2 and 5 are alternatives that divert attention away from the real story of how a traveler requests a seat upgrade. Step 2 is really an alternative to step 1, handling those instances where the customer is a frequent flier. Step 5 is an alternative available to step 4 when the traveler does not have enough upgrade certificates.

You can still show these diversions, but as alternatives. A better way to write this scenario appears in Use Case 6.14.

Use Case 6.14   *Request Upgrade* Makes ForwardProgress

Request Upgrade

Primary Actor: *Traveler*   Ticketed passenger

Level: User Goal

Main Success Scenario

1. Traveler enters her account code for the flight and requests a seat upgrade.
2. The system verifies there are seats available for upgrading.
3. The system upgrades the Traveler seat assignment, and the appropriate upgrade certificates are removed from the Traveler's account. The system issues an upgrade receipt to the Traveler.

Alternatives

1a: *Traveler is a frequent flier*

   1a.1 The system displays her current mileage and recent flight activity.

3a: *Traveler does not have enough upgrade certificates*

   3a.1 Traveler purchases additional upgrade certificates.

Insurance Claim: Not Enough Forward Progress

Use Case 6.15 shows a different example, in which the diversion is not as blatant as in the previous example but is still equally distracting. Its steps are not "leveled." There is no explicit diversion but there is not *enough* forward progress either.

Use Case 6.15   Use Case Horror: *Claim Insurance* Not Making Sufficient ForwardProgress

---

Claim Insurance

Primary Actor: Claimant—policyholder reporting accident claim

Level: Summary

Main Success Scenario

 1 Claimant obtains claim form.
 2. Claimant enters name and address on claim form.
 3. Claimant enters policy information on claim form.
 4. Claimant enters accident information on claim form.
 5. Claimant photocopies ticket and attaches it to claim form.
 6. Claimant photocopies claim form and puts it in file cabinet.
 7. Insurance company checks whether claimant owns a valid policy.
 8. Insurance company determines that claimant does own a valid policy.
 9. Insurance company assigns agent to examine case.
10. Agent verifies that all details are within policy guidelines.
11. Insurance company pays claimant.

The tip-off here is that several steps in a row refer to the same actor performing one action after another. When you see this, consider whether there is enough forward progress being made in each step. Ask, as in getting **LeveledSteps** (p. 153), "What is the actor trying to accomplish?" and "Can I find a way to express all this information in a single step?"

In Use Case 6.15, steps 1 through 5 are a necessary part of the process, but they waste a lot of the reader's energy by making very little overall progress. It would be more succinct, easier to read, and just as informative to write:

1. Claimant submits form with substantiating data.

Step 6 does not bring any forward progress to the use case; indeed, it is superfluous. Claimants may want to save copies of their claim forms (that is their prerogative). They may also want to post their insurance agent's picture on the wall for dart practice, or use one to line a birdcage. Again, that is their prerogative. These actions have nothing to do with the use cases; the insurance company will process their claim regardless. This step can be deleted.

Step 7 says, "checks whether." This commonly used phrase shows only half of the needed action. The check will either succeed or fail. Saying "checks whether" implies that the writer must write another sentence saying what the outcome will be. However, a use case step shows *accomplishment*—in other words, that the check succeeds. A failure on the verification will show up in an extension condition. Therefore, steps 7 and 8 should be merged, becoming the shorter, clearer:

2. Insurance company verifies that claimant owns a valid policy.

At this point, we can revise the preceding eleven-step scenario into a five-step scenario, in which each step carries its own weight, making distinct **ForwardProgress** toward a specific goal. The result is Use Case 6.16.

Use Case 6.16 *Claim Insurance* Revised to Make ForwardProgress

Claim Insurance
Primary Actor: Claimant—policyholder reporting accident claim
Level: Summary
Main Success Scenario
1. Claimant submits claim with substantiating data.
2. Insurance company verifies that claimant owns a valid policy.
3. Insurance company assigns agent to examine case.
4. Agent verifies that all details are within policy guidelines.
5. Insurance company pays claimant.

Testing the plumb of a bulkhead.
Bethlehem-Fairfield shipyards,
Baltimore, Maryland

6.5 *TechnologyNeutral* *

You are writing the steps of a scenario as **LeveledSteps** (p. 153), working to keep the use case **PreciseAndReadable** (p. 138).

> Including technology constraints and implementation details in a use case description increases the complexity and obscures the goal of the use case.

One of the less popular tasks that software developers do is called "porting" a system, which involves taking a software system that exists on one hardware platform and changing it so that it can run on another. This task is often tedious because it involves redoing the same system several times. One reason that the Java programming language is so popular is that it provides a "compile-once, run-anywhere" feature that allows programmers to write a program once, then run it on any computer that supports Java. (Or "compile once, debug everywhere," as some Java detractors say.) It accomplishes this feat by providing a standardized interface that hides the machine-dependent code from the programmers, so that programmers can call the interface without concerning themselves with platform-specific issues.

Good use cases should likewise insulate readers from system-specific details, leaving them free to focus on the system's essential behavior.

Many people like to think in concrete terms. While abstraction is key to good design, such thinking is difficult and requires a thorough understanding of the problem. People cannot abstract things they don't understand; instead, they seek concrete details to improve their knowledge. Only when they feel comfortable with a topic will they begin to think abstractly about it. It is not surprising that writers like to add low-level details to use cases, because they are often learning about the system as they

---

* This pattern was influenced by Rick Ratliff's **Sans GUI** pattern from the OOPSLA 98 Use Case Patterns workshop.

write, and these details make them feel comfortable by giving them a better understanding of what they are doing.

Technology is volatile; including details about specific technologies will cause rework. Technology is constantly changing. Vendors are constantly releasing new versions of their products, as those of us who have bought a top-of-the-line computer that became obsolete within a matter of weeks will attest. In theory, these changes should not present a problem, because they are hidden within a product. Unfortunately, many of them subtly and visibly do affect the product's behavior. Consequently, use cases describing these kinds of details become obsolete whenever the product changes, forcing an organization to either perpetually update its use cases or use obsolete ones.

Technological details impose improper constraints on future activities. Implementation details can bias the readers to a particular design by masquerading as requirements. Worse, they assume an undue aura of importance because they often require explanatory text. For example, mentioning a file in a use case might force the writers to include extra error and alternative courses for handling the file, turning the focus of the use case toward file handling, rather than providing a **UserValued-Transaction** (p. 95).

Adding technological details increases the cost of both reading and writing use cases. Use cases should capture essential system behavior without delving into its low-level structure. When they leave out technical details, use cases speak to a wide range of audiences, technical and nontechnical alike. If the readers can easily grasp the system's purpose, then they are free to use their own imagination to flesh out those details, often coming up with a better, more creative solution than the use case implies.

Sometimes technology is a requirement. Product development doesn't occur in a vacuum. Often, a new system must be able to interact with existing systems using specific protocols or access common data using a specific database engine. The product may also have to meet industry or government standards. Somehow, you need to include this information.

Therefore:

Write each use case in a technology-neutral manner.

Focus on essential system behavior such as what actions the system performs, or why someone might want to do them. Describe specific actions in neutral ways, avoiding details that might guide the readers toward specific implementations. Be especially cautious about specific terminology, because common words such as *database, file,* or *GUI* can subtly guide developers toward specific design decisions. Use phrases such as "The user requests information from the system" instead of "The user selects the Open button from the File pull-down menu." The former allows the developers the latitude to decide how best to store this information, while the latter leads them toward using files and a specific GUI. The developers may decide that a file is best after all, but that decision must come at a more appropriate time, when they have a better understanding of the system.

If there are implementation details and technology constraints that are relevant to the use case or help increase comprehension, then include these as **Adornments** (p. 133).

Examples

File Accident Claim: **Tied to Technology**

Developers constantly violate this guideline by tying their use cases to a particular graphical user interface (GUI). Yet this practice constrains the developers, and leads to a situation where the GUI drives use case development. But GUIs describe only a system's look and feel, not its behavior. Tying GUIs to use cases is putting the cart before the horse, because GUI developers should be using the use cases to help design the system interface, not the other way around.

Consider Use Case 6.17 for submitting a claim to an insurance office.

Use Case 6.17   Use Case Horror: The Technology-dependent *File Accident Claim* Use Case

File Accident Claim

Primary Actor: Claimant—policyholder reporting accident claim

Level: User Goal

Main Success Scenario

1. Claimant accesses Accident Reporting System.
2. Claimant enters name (first, last, middle initial) on form.
3. Claimant enters address (street, city, state, postal code) on form.
4. Claimant enters policy number on form.
5. System verifies that claimant owns a valid policy by checking policy database.
6. Claimant submits claim with substantiating data, including names of both parties, investigating officer, and citation number, if applicable.
7. System logs claim file and policy database, and sends e-mail acknowledgment to the claimant.

This example contains several flaws.

1. It presupposes that the system will store policy information in a database.
2. It presupposes that the system will store claim information in a data file.
3. It presupposes that the system will send e-mail to acknowledge a claim.
4. It presupposes that the system will use a specific form.

In short, this scenario makes some design assumptions. While these may or may not be requirements, they don't belong here. If they are not requirements, then they may prevent the developers from examining and implementing other, more efficient mechanisms for processing the claim.

For that reason, it is better to write the scenario as shown in Use Case 6.18.

Use Case 6.18   A Technology-neutral *File Accident Claim* Use Case

File Accident Claim

Primary Actor: Claimant—policyholder reporting accident claim
Level: User Goal
Main Success Scenario
1. Claimant accesses Accident Reporting System.
2. Claimant identifies self to system using name and policy number.
3. System verifies that claimant owns a valid policy.
4. Claimant submits claim with substantiating data, including names of both parties, investigating officer, and citation number, if applicable.
5. System logs claim and acknowledges its receipt to the Claimant.
6. Requestor: Mark request delivered.

This scenario describes the system's behavior without supplying any design information. It lists necessary information such as policy number and name, but it does not specify its format. It also informs readers that much of this data is persistent, but it doesn't tell them how it is stored. This format allows the developers to make these decisions in a manner that is best for the system.

It is incredibly easy to introduce implementation details into a scenario, and we often do so without realizing it. Just adding two seemingly innocent words to the end of Step 1—"via Internet"—completely changes the nature of this scenario.

1. Claimant accesses Accident Reporting System via Internet.

While the phrase "via Internet" seems innocuous enough, it subtly focuses the reader's attention on a Web-based solution. But who said that the Internet is the best solution for this system? What about customers without Internet access, either because they don't have access to a computer or because they've suffered an accident that requires lengthy hospitalization? It is quite possible that such clients might not be able to report the accident until they return home. This case is of particular interest to insurance companies, however, because most of them wish to know immediately when their clients are hospitalized in order to control costs. These two simple words could lead the developers to devise a solution that is in conflict with their client's most important goal of reducing costs.

6.6 Trade-offs and Collaborations

Like the old proverb, "A chain is only as strong as its weakest link," a use case is only as clear as its most ambiguous step. Organizing steps in scenarios and using a simple standard form for each step reduces the effort required in both reading and writing the individual step and the overall use case. The patterns in this chapter form the baseline for a simple standard form.

The two scenario patterns help us write **ScenarioPlusFragments** (p. 125). **DetectableConditions** (p. 148) tells us that we should describe only those kinds of situations that can really occur as the actors interact with the system. Otherwise, we waste our time writing scenarios that no one needs or that are redundant. Worse, someone may even try to implement the unnecessary scenarios, wasting valuable development time. **LeveledSteps** (p. 153) shows us how to balance our use cases so that no one scenario, especially an alternative one, can dominate. It recommends writing them in parallel styles so that the reader can easily follow them, without attaching undue importance to an overly complex one.

But leveling steps involves more than just writing steps with the same level of detail, and we have several patterns to guide us. Each step in a scenario must meet three conditions: First, it must add value by clearly making some **ForwardProgress** (p. 162) toward fulfilling the scenario's ultimate goal. Second, it must demonstrate purpose by showing the **ActorIntentAccomplished** (p. 158), showing who is trying to accomplish the action, and what it is that the actor is trying to accomplish. Last, it must be **TechnologyNeutral** (p. 167), neither bombarding the user with excessive details, nor implying a design. Steps that fail to meet all three of these conditions serve only to confuse the reader and add ambiguity to the scenario; they should be rewritten or removed from the scenario.

LeveledSteps is similar to **EverUnfoldingStory** (p. 102), bringing unity and parallelism to scenarios, just as **EverUnfoldingStory** does for a set of use cases. However, they are two different patterns, having different contexts and purposes. **EverUnfoldingStory** balances goal levels for sets of use cases, while **LeveledSteps**

balances the content of individual scenarios. In fact, using **LeveledSteps** makes it easier to write an **EverUnfoldingStory**, because it is a fairly simple matter to expand a series of leveled steps into a set of lower level use cases.

These three chapters—"The Use Case Set," "The Use Case," and "Scenarios and Steps"—have described the structure of well-written use cases. Sometimes, however, our well-written use cases can violate these guidelines for reasons beyond our control. System boundaries can change and goals can shift, causing some use cases to become redundant or obsolete, or to address the wrong scope. The following chapters describe what you can do to restore order to your use cases when these situations occur.

Chapter 7

Use Case Relationships

◆ **But I Thought You Said These Were Just Stories**

Yitka Dvorak is Wings Over the World's director of marketing and has just dumped a set of use cases on the table in front of you. "I thought you said these things were just simple stories. How am I supposed to figure them out if I have to keep jumping from one story to another?"

You glance at the diagram representing the use cases and immediately see the source of the confusion. It resembles the plans for an oil refinery's plumbing more than functional requirements. The use cases are loaded with *includes* and *extends* relationships, and even a couple of generalizations. Some of them contain a dozen *includes* relationships, and *includes* on *includes*. No wonder Yitka is so upset. You notice the author is Ahmed, and you assure her that you'll take of this.

You go over to Ahmed's cubicle and show him the use cases. "But that's how they show it in the book," he says, pointing to a textbook on his desk. "And besides, these are all standard UML relationships." You explain how many authors tend to over-emphasize *includes* and *extends.* You talk about the principle of one-stop shopping, which aims to minimize the need for your readers to jump all over the place to read one use case.

"The most important characteristic of a good use case," you explain to Ahmed, "is that the stakeholders understand it. Remember my success criteria for a good use case is that the stakeholder should be able to come up to us and say, 'No, this is not how it works. You guys are completely wrong.' When they can do that, it means they read the use case and understood it. If they come up to us and say, 'Yeah, I guess so. You guys are the experts,' or they refuse to read the use cases because they're hard to follow, then we're dead." *Includes* and *extends* should be used only when they simplify things, not to make things more complicated and confusing.

It's easy to start a riot at a use case conference. Simply walk up to an open microphone and ask, "What is the difference between *includes* and *extends*?" and then run for cover! How to apply the *includes* and *extends* relationships effectively in use cases is a question that has perplexed both beginning and experienced use case writers.

Includes and *extends* were originally intended to simplify the use case model by collecting and organizing common threads in the model. Unfortunately, these simplifying relationships seem to have the opposite effect, making the model more complex and difficult to understand. Many factors contribute to this problem. First, the definitions of *includes* and *extends* are ambiguous, leading to a wide variety of interpretations as to what they really mean. Second, software professionals tend to favor formality in the use case model over usability, creating models that follow all the rules but are hard to read. Finally, instructors tend to overemphasize these techniques when teaching people to write use cases.

The UML revision task force exacerbated this ambiguity in 1998 when they attempted to bring peace to the warring factions by introducing a new definition of the use case structuring relationships. They replaced the original *uses* relationship with the new *include* relationship, made *extend* a UML dependency relationship, and introduced the generalization relationship. While these changes helped to remove ambiguity in the formal grammar that supports the definition of use cases in UML, this revision has led to confusion and ambiguity in the practical applications of the use case structuring relationships.

◆ *Includes* **Versus** *Extends*

People waste too much time and energy debating when to use *includes* or *extends*. This is a debate that confounds both novices and experts. While we spent many evenings debating this over a bottle of wine, this is really not the topic you should spend a lot of energy worrying about. Rather, you should be focusing on whether it's appropriate to apply a relationship pattern. "Is the alternative sufficiently complex and distracting that I should create a **PromotedAlternative** (p. 190)?" Or, "Do these use cases have a common set of steps that I can break out as a **CommonSubBehavior** (p. 176)?" Debating these questions will make a difference to your project. Debating whether you should use *includes* or *extends* to draw these patterns will not. In situations where you can use either *extends* or *includes*, set a standard and stick with it. Save the *includes* versus *extends* argument for those nights when you and your colleagues gather over a bottle of wine to debate such things.

Consider this: While a programmer may understand the concepts behind these relationships, try getting the product manager, the lawyer, or the accountant who is a stakeholder in the system to understand them. These are intelligent, capable people, who have very little time to learn formal rules to verify their systems. The cardinal rule of writing is "Know your audience." In our opinion, the best use cases are semi-formal, with just enough structure to be reasonably precise and unambiguous in the way they communicate important concepts (see **PreciseAndReadable** [p. 138]). Yet they should be simple enough so that a stakeholder who is familiar with the problem domain can read and understand it. Rigid formality does not help this cause.

Good use case models tend to use the *includes* and *extends* relationships judiciously. Models that overuse the *extends* relationship tend to use extensions to describe implementation details, frequently describing alternatives on a user interface. We have seen models in which a use case has dozens of extension use cases, with extensions on extensions. Many readers would quickly throw such work back at the writer, or worse, simply ignore it.

Furthermore, writers frequently use these relationships to create director-style use cases, in which including or extending use cases specify the details of each step. The consequence of this technique is that the model usually represents the developer's point of view, causing the readers to lose sight of the important actor goal in the details.

We have identified three patterns that help use case writers understand these relationships.

- **CommonSubBehavior** (p. 176) states that you should consider creating an *includes* relationship between use cases when two or more use cases share a common set of actions. The purpose is to consolidate common behavior and simplify your model by reducing redundancy.

- **InterruptsAsExtensions** (p. 182) recommends that you consider an extension use case when an alternative interrupts a number of steps in a scenario. This technique helps simplify the model by consolidating the related interrupting actions in one use case, rather than dispersing them across several alternative courses of action.

- **PromotedAlternative** (p. 190) suggests that you may also want to use extensions when you have some important alternatives to emphasize. In this case, you can "promote" these alternatives into an extension use case so that they stand out. You should use this technique sparingly, so that you don't conflict with the guidelines described in **InterruptsAsExtensions** or **RedistributeTheWealth** (p. 204).

We haven't yet seen many good models utilizing the UML generalization relationship to create a pattern for guiding its use. However, our colleague Dan Rawsthorne has provided us with a pattern called **CapturedAbstraction** (p. 198), that suggests an appropriate use for generalization. This pattern suggests you create an abstract use case when you have multiple use cases with the same goal and it is inappropriate to **MergeDroplets** (p. 209).

Supercharger plant workers buffing delicate airplane engine parts

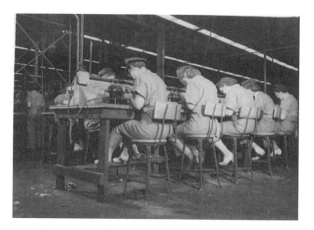

7.1 CommonSubBehavior

You are writing use case descriptions as **ScenarioPlusFragments** (p. 125).

> Writing the same steps for different use cases is wasteful and makes it more difficult to see common subprocesses within a use case model.

Maurice Wilkes once gave a lecture on his role in the development of EDSAC, the first stored-program computer. Unlike ENIAC, which was programmed from a hardware plugboard, EDSAC actually stored its instructions in the same memory that was used to store data, an approach that is the basis for all modern-day computers. Programs were fed into EDSAC, using paper tape.

The EDSAC team quickly noticed that while all of their programs solved different problems, they frequently employed the same sets of instructions. Punching paper tape for EDSAC was a labor-intensive and tedious activity, and people found that repunching the same instructions over and over again was even more tedious, error prone, and a waste of time.

Someone finally took the initiative and began cutting out the common sets of instructions from the paper tapes and storing them in little 35-millimeter film canisters. Then when someone wanted to write a program that used that sequence of instructions, the programmer could retrieve the paper tape, attach it with Scotch tape to the program, and then feed the paper tape into EDSAC. It made programming EDSAC much easier and less error prone.

Rewriting common steps is redundant and increases the risk of inconsistencies or inaccuracies in the model. Different processes may have common steps. For example, buying and selling stock are two distinct activities, yet each requires a valuation of the stock being traded. Similarly, paying property taxes on a house, selling a house, and buying a house are all different activities that require an assessment of the house's value. The steps for stock valuation can be rewritten for both the purchase and sale of stock, but redundancy is never a good thing to have in a model. First, it is simply a waste of time writing and reading the same steps over and over again for each process.

Second, redundancy can lead to inconsistencies in the model, if the commonly used steps must be changed. A frequent source of errors in requirements models results from the need to change a repeated behavior and forgetting to change every instance of that common behavior. For example, let's say the rules for assessing the value of a property change. We change the steps in the *Purchase Property* use case, but we forget to change the steps in the *Pay Tax* use case. We run the risk of building a system that is inconsistent in the way that it assesses property values because we have created inconsistent environments.

Partitioning individual use cases tends to scatter important behavior and makes them harder to understand. "One-stop shopping" is a useful requirements writing principle. Simply, people reading the requirements should be able to get all the information they need from one document or from one section of a document. They should not have to jump between different sections to understand the requirement.

A classic example of violating this principle is the famous *The Joy of Cooking* cookbook that mothers traditionally give to their sons when they leave home. *The Joy of Cooking* is probably one of the most complete, self-contained cookbooks written. It is also difficult to use, because each recipe forces you to jump back and forth between different sections of the book to discover how to make the white sauce, how to braise the beef, how to blanch the beans, and so on.

The greatest benefit of the use case is that it tells a story that provides the context for understanding requirements. Forcing a reader to jump between different use cases risks losing this benefit.

Misunderstanding the includes *relationship leads to its misuse.* Programmers are trained to break up large blocks of program logic into more manageable subroutines. But when they apply this technique to use cases, they often include more detail in the "called" use cases than in the callers, effectively turning the high-level use cases into transaction centers that simply call a number of lower level use cases to perform their tasks.

Again, the problem becomes the high probability that the use case will be too formal and the all-important story context may be lost. Many use case books encourage this practice by creating contrived examples in an effort to demonstrate *includes* relationships.

In addition, programmers are trained to prefer formality to informality, and UML tends to encourage an excessive level of formalism in use case models. Relationships between use cases such as *includes, extends,* and generalization have well-defined formal definitions in UML. Unfortunately, there is a great deal of uncertainty about how these formal concepts translate to useful concepts in the everyday world of requirements.

Therefore:

> Express shared courses of action with lower-level *included* use cases.

Ideally, create *includes* relationships between use cases when two or more use cases share a common set of steps. Extract the common steps and place them into their own use case.

Avoid using *includes* simply as a mechanism for partitioning a long, complex use case into smaller ones, even though that might seem more manageable. A long, complex use case is often a symptom of one or more of the following problems.

- The scope of the use case is too large (identify each **CompleteSingleGoal** [p. 118]) and **RedistributeTheWealth** [p. 204]).
- The steps in the use case are written at too low a level of detail for the goal of the use case or are written at different levels of detail (create **LeveledSteps** [p. 153]).
- Nonfunctional requirements such as user-interface details have crept into the use case (put them into **Adornments** [p. 133]).

Examples

Wings Over the World and *Includes*

A problem found in many use case sets is the "director" use case—that is, a use case that depends on several *included* use cases. See Figure 7.1 and Use Case 7.1, for example.

Use Case 7.1   Use Case Horror: Director-style *Book Flight* Use Case That Incorrectly Applies the *Includes* Relationship

Book Flight

Level: User Goal

1. The use case begins when the agent selects Set Travel Itinerary. Call *Capture Flight Information* to get the travel itinerary.
2. The agent chooses Select Flight. Call *Reserve Flight Segments* to reserve a flight segment.
3. The agent chooses Book Flight. Call *Obtain Payment Information* to get payment choice.
4. Call *Issue Ticket* to print ticket.

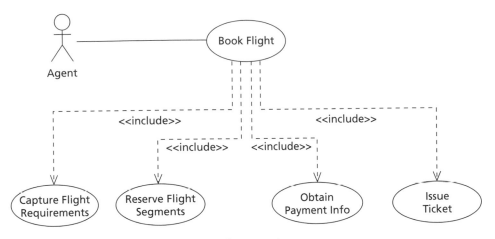

Figure 7.1 *Misuse of* includes *to create a director-style use case*

The problem is that the *included* use cases in this case are trivial. They are too simple and small to justify their existence as entire use cases. The *included* use cases are, to use a visual metaphor, *droplets*. The repair for droplets is to **MergeDroplets** (p. 209).

Instead, use **EverUnfoldingStory** (p. 102), as shown in Figure 7.2 and Use Case 7.2

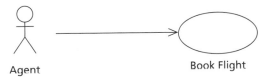

Figure 7.2 Book Flight *use case*

Use Case 7.2 The Revised *Book Flight* Use Case

Book Flight

Level: User Goal
1. The use case begins when the agent specifies a travel itinerary.
2. The system searches a set of appropriate flights and presents them to the agent.
3. The agent selects the flight.

4. The system verifies that space is available on the flight and reserves the seats on the flight.
5. The agent finalizes the booking by supplying payment information.
6. The system books the seats and issues the ticket.

The appropriate application of *include* is to eliminate redundancy that would otherwise make the set of use cases difficult to understand. If two or more use cases have a set of steps in common, then rather than rewriting those steps, we can collect them into a common use case, as illustrated in Figure 7.3.

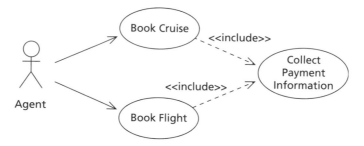

Figure 7.3 *Using* include *to consolidate CommonSubBehavior*

Here, both *Book Cruise* and *Book Flight* use *Collect Payment Information*. No matter what kind of trip we are booking, we always collect payment the same way, so why write the same thing twice?

♦ **CommonSubBehavior and UML, by Dan Rawsthorne**

The *includes* relationship is fairly simple and useful. It is often used to graphically depict an **EverUnfoldingStory** (p. 102) as well as **CommonSubBehavior,** as shown in Figure 7.3. There is one major restriction on an *includes* relationship, according to the UML: *included* behavior is *always* executed; it is never part of an extension or alternate scenario. In practice, this means that after you extract the **CommonSubBehavior** into its own use case and you edit the text to show where it's invoked, there are two ways to draw the diagram: (1) with an *includes* relationship if the common behavior is in the main success scenario, or (2) with an *extends* relationship if the common behavior is in an alternate or extension scenario. While this makes no difference in the written version of the use cases, the different relationships on the diagram show that the common behavior is either required or optional. Note that this means that the same common behavior can be *included* in one use case and *extended* another.

As you can see, the *includes* relationship is a stereotype of a dependency (dashed arrow shown in Figure 7.3). If your tool will not allow you to draw this, use either an aggregation or an *includes* stereotype of an association—don't use a generalization arrow. I know that the initial *uses* relationship was a stereotype of a generalization, but this was just wrong, wrong, wrong. There is no way that the *includes* relationship can logically be rationalized as a stereotype of a generalization. So, use either the notation shown in Figure 7.3 or the "diamond-tipped" lines shown in Figure 7.4. Do *not* use the arrows shown in Figure 7.5.

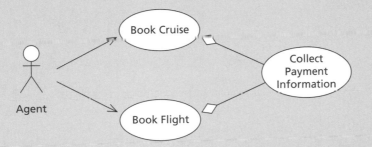

Figure 7.4 *An alternative approach to drawing an* includes *relationship if your drawing tool does not support the UML* includes *relationship.*

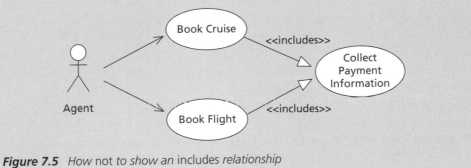

Figure 7.5 *How* not *to show an* includes *relationship*

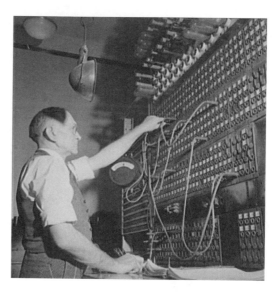

Telegraph switchboard of the Pennsylvania Railroad in Union Station, Chicago, Illinois

7.2 *InterruptsAsExtensions*

You are writing a use case description as a **ScenarioPlusFragments** (p. 125).

> An alternative that affects more than one step in a scenario can scatter related details throughout a use case, causing the reader to become confused or lose track of important information.

It seems that a lot of human resources departments go out of their way to make hiring temporary or contract employees difficult. Most firms have a conventional process they follow when they hire a new employee. Usually new hires simply fill out a personal data form, then complete some kind of tax-withholding form, sign up for company benefits, assign their intellectual property rights to the company, and finally specify where they want their pay deposited.

The human resources department seems to enjoy taking this paper-shuffling process to new heights of complexity for contract employees. Just like regular employees, contract employees usually have to fill out most of the same forms, but they may have to do some or all of the steps differently. For example, contractors may not be eligible for company benefits, or may be required to invoice the company to receive pay. They may have to negotiate the transfer of intellectual property rights. So, when hiring a new contractor, the human resources department may go through each of its normal steps for hiring, but then modify some of the steps or require additional work.

Multiple diversions or alternatives that interrupt several steps in a scenario can cause the readers to lose track of the path that they are trying to follow, and can indicate problems with the basic scenario itself. The recommended approach for coping with an alternative course of action is to write the alternative as a fragment off the main success scenario (**ScenarioPlusFragments**). This technique works well for most alternatives because they are usually a simple diversion from a step in either the main success scenario or a step in a fragment. In either case, once the diversion is completed, the scenario resumes from the point where the diversion took place.

However, what happens when the alternative requires repeated diversions on more than one step in the use case? You can write a diversion for each step, but then it is easy for readers to lose track of the alternative thread that ties these related diversions together.

Creating extension use cases tends to scatter important behavior and makes them harder to understand. "One stop shopping" is an important requirements writing principle. Simply, a person reading the requirements should be able to get all of the information they need from one document or from one section of a document. They should not have to jump between different sections to understand the requirement or its context.

A major benefit of *use* cases is that they tell a story that provides the context for understanding requirements. Forcing a reader to jump between different use cases runs the risk of negating this benefit.

Misunderstanding the extends *relationships leads to its misuse.* If you ask five use case experts, "What does the *extends* relationship mean?" you will get ten different answers. *Extends* has historically been likened to an inheritance relationship between use cases, and most programmers are trained to interpret inheritance as a specialization. Recently however, the UML revision task force decided to change the formal definition of *extends* from an inheritance relationship to that of a dependency. While this change is interesting to those concerned about the formal structure of the UML, it has made life very difficult for many analysts. In many ways, the formal definition is irrelevant in real life.

In addition, as we've said, programmers are trained to prefer formality to informality, and UML tends to encourage an excessive level of formalism in use case models. Relationships between use cases such as *includes, extends,* and generalization have well-defined formal definitions in UML. Unfortunately, there is a great deal of uncertainty about how to apply these formal concepts pragmatically in the everyday world of requirements.

Therefore:

> Create an extension use case when an alternative course of action interrupts a number of steps in a scenario.

This is an obscure situation and does not occur all that often. If you discover that you are frequently applying this pattern then you should re-evaluate your use cases. It may be the case that you do not have a **CompleteSingleGoal** (p. 118), or you do not have **LeveledSteps** (p. 153).

Create an extension use case by extracting all of the steps that are associated with the thread of the alternatives and placing them in an extension use case. For each statement in the extension use case, specify which statement in the original or base use case is being interrupted. This approach has two benefits.

+ The thread of an interrupting alternative is kept together, and therefore the reader can see the context of the alternative (one-stop-shopping principle).

+ The original or base use case is not cluttered with interrupting alternatives.

Examples

Wings Over the World and Extensions

Use Case 7.3 describes how a flight is booked. (See Figure 7.6.) The main success scenario is relatively straightforward, with the agent using the system to build up a travel itinerary for a client, and then to reserve it. However, there are extensions to many of the steps in the main success scenario if the client is a frequent flier, because frequent fliers get privileges and services that are not available to conventional clients.

Agent   Book Flight

Figure 7.6 *The* Book Flight *use case*

Use Case 7.3   Use Case Horror: Confusing Frequent Flier Alternatives for *Book Flight*

Book Flight
1. The use case begins when the agent specifies a travel itinerary for a client.
2. The system searches a set of appropriate flights and presents them to the agent.
3. The agent Selects a Flight.
4. The system verifies that space is available on the flight and reserves a seat on the flight.

5. The agent finalizes the booking by supplying payment information.
6. The system books the seats and issues the ticket.

Alternatives

2a: Client is a frequent flier:

   2a1. The system retrieves the client's profile and displays the flights sorted by the client's airline preference.

4a: Client is a frequent flier:

   4a1. The system offers premium seats for the client.

4b: Seat is not available in ticket category:

   4b1. The system informs the agent that no seats are available in the client's chosen price category.

   4b2. The agent specifies another price preference.

4c: Seat is not available (flight fully booked):

   4c1. The system informs agent that no seats are available at all.

   4c2. The agent specifies another set of departure time preferences.

4d: Client is a frequent flier and seats are not available:

   4d1. The agent puts the client on a priority wait list for the seats.

5a: Client is a frequent flier:

   5a1. The system verifies that client has upgrade coupons in his or her account.

   5a2. The system wait-lists the client for an upgrade on the flight.

In this example, it is all too easy for the use case reader (and sometimes even the use case author) to forget that all of the individual frequent flier alternatives listed in the use case's alternatives section represent the thread of an ongoing alternative course of action.

We can clarify this situation by using an extension use case that collects all of the frequent flier alternatives together, as shown in Use Case 7.4 and Figure 7.7.

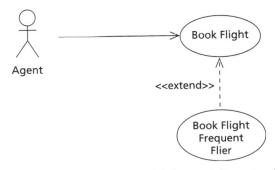

Figure 7.7 *The* Book Flight *use case diagram with frequent flier extension*

Now all alternative courses of action associated with the frequent flier are collected together into one *extends* use case.

Use Case 7.4   Extension Use Case: *Book Flight for Frequent Flier*

Book Flight for Frequent Flier

Extends *Book Flight*

2a1. The system retrieves the client's profile and displays the flights sorted by the client's airline preference.

4a1. The system offers premium seats for the client.

5a1. The system verifies that the client has upgrade coupons in his account.

5a2. The system wait-lists the client for an upgrade on the flight.

Alternatives

4d: Client is a frequent flier and seats are not available:

4d1. The agent puts the client on a priority wait list for the seats.

The extension use case keeps all the steps in the frequent flier alternatives together, making it easier to follow the frequent flier thread alternatives. It is less likely now that the reader (and even the use case author) will lose the thread of the alternatives within the other alternatives.

◆ **InterruptsAsExtensions and UML, by Dan Rawsthorne**

According to the UML, this use of the *extends* relationship is legal and proper. However, some people just don't get it because this approach seems complicated to them. All it is doing is saying, "This use case does what that one does, with the following additions . . ." To some people, this sounds like one use case inheriting from another, and in some sense it is. In fact, it can be viewed as a legitimate specialization because the **VerbPhraseName** (p. 122) of the "child" use case indicates that it is more than the parent, rather than just an add-on. So, if it makes more sense to you or those that need to understand your models, just give in and use a specialization relationship, like the one shown in Figure 7.8.

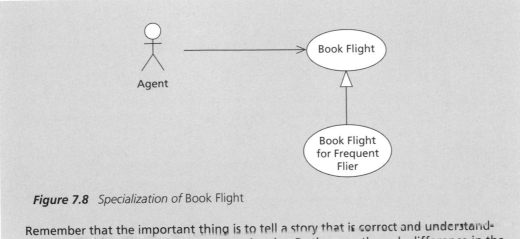

Figure 7.8 *Specialization of* Book Flight

Remember that the important thing is to tell a story that is correct and understandable, not to blindly follow some semantic rules. By the way, the only difference in the textual representation of this specialized use case is to replace the line "Extends *Book Flight*" in the first line with "Specializes *Book Flight*."

Extensions and UML Extension Points

Extension use cases are not independent of their base use case and must reference statements in the base use case. For example, the extension use case *Book Flight for Frequent Flier* directly references statements in the base use case *Book Flight*. Each of the alternatives and statements in *Book Flight for Frequent Flier* are direct references to a statement numbering of *Book Flight*. If *Book Flight* is updated and the statement numbering changes, then we will have to relabel and renumber the statements in *Book Flight for Frequent Flier* as well. The UML extension point feature helps mitigate this problem by providing extension points for the extension use case. (See Figure 7.9.) Technically, an extension point is a point at which additional behavior may be inserted. These extension points are like symbolic labels, and they help make the extension use case more independent of the internal structure of the base use case. Use Cases 7.5 and 7.6 illustrate the details.

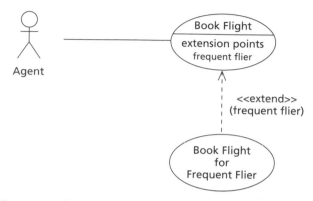

Figure 7.9 UML use case diagram featuring an extension point

Use Case 7.5   The *Book Flight* Use Case with Extension Points

Book Flight

1. The use case begins when the agent specifies a travel itinerary for a client.
2. The system searches a set of appropriate flights and presents them to the agent.
    (frequent flier a)
3. The agent chooses Select Flight.
4. The system verifies that space is available on the flight and reserves a seat on the flight.
    (frequent flier b)
5. The agent finalizes the booking by supplying payment information.
    (frequent flier c)
6. The system books the seats and issues the ticket.

Alternatives

4a: Seat is not available in ticket category:
>   4a1. The system informs the agent that no seats are available in the client's chosen price category.
>   4a2. The agent specifies another price preference.

4b: Seat is not available (flight fully booked):
>   4b1. The system informs the agent that no seats are available at all.
>   4b2. The agent specifies another set of departure time preferences.
>   *(frequent flier d)*

Use Case 7.6 *Book Flight for Frequent Flier* Extension Use Case Referencing Extension Points

Book Flight for Frequent Flier

Extends *Book Flight*

frequent flier a

1. The system retrieves the client's profile and displays the flights sorted by the client's airline preference.

frequent flier b

1. The system offers premium seats for the client.

frequent flier c

1. The system verifies that the client has upgrade coupons in his account.
2. The system wait-lists the client for an upgrade on the flight.

Alternatives

Seats are not available:

frequent flier d

1. The agent puts the client on a priority wait list for the seats.

*Couple on graduation day,
University of Nebraska, Lincoln*

7.3 PromotedAlternative

You are writing use case descriptions as **ScenarioPlusFragments** (p. 125).

> Long or complex alternatives can dominate a use case, and appear to be more important than they really are just because they are so prominent.

Normally, the military strictly adheres to a formal, well-defined process for promoting officers. Candidates must meet all of the qualifications for their particular rank, must have served the required amount of time, and must have a spotless service record. But in wartime, especially during urgent situations, commanders will promote someone, be it an experienced enlisted man or a junior officer, to fill a critical need. They refer to these special cases as "battlefield promotions."

Sometimes, an alternative scenario stands out. It suddenly becomes important, because it fills an important hole in the system. When it does, it makes sense to elevate it to be a use case.

Complex or long alternatives clutter a use case and can obscure other alternatives. A use case can become difficult to write and even more difficult to follow when the alternative is too long or complex, especially when it contains several alternatives itself. Use cases are supposed to be easy to read and understand, not complicated engineering documents.

Some problems are very complex, and they require complex use cases to describe them adequately. Hard technical problems don't simplify themselves just because we want to simplify our use cases. Some systems can be very complicated and hard to understand. Yet these are the kinds of systems that we need to describe especially well, so that everyone working on them will have a clear understanding of how the system is supposed to behave in all reasonable situations.

Partitioning individual use cases tends to scatter important behavior and makes them harder to understand. One of the biggest benefits of using use cases is that they tell stories that provide a context for understanding requirements. Forcing readers to jump between different use cases risks negating this benefit, because it violates the one-stop-shopping principle. We believe that people should be able to get all of the information they need about a requirement from one place, without having to refer to several documents to understand it.

Therefore:

> Consider moving complex alternatives that overly dominate a use case into a separate use case.

An alternative course of action should never dominate a use case. After all, it's supposed to be an alternative and represents a less common behavior than the main success scenario. The best way for handling alternative courses of action is to write them as fragments based on a main success scenario (**ScenarioPlusFragments**). But sometimes there are alternatives which may require a long, complex series of steps (such as control break processing and boundary conditions). Under these circumstances, you may consider extracting the alternative from its base use case and creating a separate use case for it.

You need to exercise caution when using this pattern to justify the creation of an extending use case, because complex alternatives may indicate that the use case is too detailed or too large (see **EverUnfoldingStory** [p. 102], **LeveledSteps** [p. 153], **CompleteSingleGoal** [p. 118], and **RedistributeTheWealth** [p. 204]). If this is not the case, then promoting the alternative to its own use case is a reasonable course of action.

Examples

Wings Over the World

All of us who have to fly frequently in those small things the airlines pass off as seats appreciate seat upgrades. Use Case 7.7 shows when a seat upgrade may be requested at the time of booking.

Use Case 7.7   Use Case Horror: The *Upgrade Seat* Alternative Dominates the *Book Flight* Use Case

Book Flight
  1. The use case begins when the agent specifies a travel itinerary for a client.
  2. The system searches a set of appropriate flights and presents them to the agent.
  3. The agent selects a flight.
  4. The system verifies that space is available on the flight and reserves a seat on the flight.

5. The agent finalizes the booking by supplying payment information.
6. The system books the seats and issues the ticket.

Alternatives

4a: Client is eligible for seat upgrade:

    4a1. The agent requests an upgrade for the client.

    4a2. The system verifies that there are seats available for upgrade on the selected flight.

    4a3. The system verifies that client has sufficient upgrade coupons for upgrade.

    4a4. The system changes ticket class to "upgraded."

    4a   **Alternatives**

      4a2a: No seats available for upgrade:

          4a2a1. Agent places client on wait list for upgrades.

          4a2a2. Continue with regular ticket booking at step 4.

      4a3a: Client has insufficient upgrade coupons:

          4a3a1. Agent buys additional upgrade coupons for client.

4b: Seat is not available in ticket category:

    4b1. The system informs the agent that no seats are available in the client's chosen price category.

    4b2. The agent specifies another price preference.

4c: Seat is not available (flight fully booked):

    4c1. The system informs the agent that no seats are available at all.

    4c2. The agent specifies another set of departure time preferences.

Notice how the *Seat Upgrade* alternative obscures the other alternatives, and dominates the use case. According to **PromotedAlternative**, *Seat Upgrade* is clearly a candidate for a separate use case, and making it such is fairly straightforward. But how to reference it from the original use case is another matter altogether. Two competing schools of thought exist: one using *includes* and one using *extends*. As we mentioned at the start of this chapter, the question has perplexed both beginning and experienced use case writers. Our recommended approach is to promote the alternative as an included use case. This makes the main use case much simpler to follow, as you can see in Use Case 7.8, 7.9 and Figure 7.10.

Use Case 7.8 *Book Flight* after *Upgrade Seat* Alternative Has Been Promoted via *Includes*

Book Flight

1. The use case begins when the agent specifies a travel itinerary for a client.
2. The system searches a set of appropriate flights and presents them to the agent.

3. The agent chooses Select Flight.
4. The system verifies that space is available on the flight and reserves a seat on the flight.
5. The agent finalizes the booking by supplying payment information.
6. The system books the seats and issues the ticket.

Alternatives

4a: Client is eligible for seat upgrade:

   4a1. The agent *Upgrades Seat* for the client, if possible.

4b: Seat is not available in ticket category:

   4b1. The system informs the agent that no seats are available in the client's chosen price category.

   4b2. The agent specifies another price preference.

4c: Seat is not available (flight fully booked):

   4c1. The system informs the agent that no seats are available at all.

   4c2. The agent specifies another set of departure time preferences.

Use Case 7.9 *Upgrade Seat* as a Separate Use Case

Upgrade Seat

1. The agent requests an upgrade for the client.
2. The system verifies that there are seats available for upgrade on the selected flight.
3. The system verifies that the client has sufficient upgrade coupons for an upgrade.
4. The system changes ticket class to "upgraded."

Alternatives

2a: No seats available for upgrade:

   2a1. Agent places client on wait list for upgrades.

3a: Client has insufficient upgrade coupons:

   3a1. Agent buys additional upgrade coupons for client.

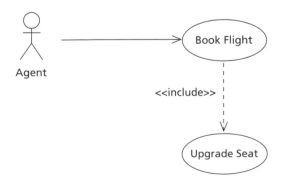

Figure 7.10 *Diagramming the* includes *relationship between use cases*

Using *Extends*

Some use case writers prefer to promote a complex alternative, as shown in Use Case 7.10 and Figure 7.11.

Use Case 7.10   *Book Flight* after *Upgrade Seat* Alternative Has Been Promoted via *Extends*

Book Flight

1. The use case begins when the agent specifies a travel itinerary for a client.
2. The system searches a set of appropriate flights and presents them to the agent.
3. The agent chooses Select Flight.
4. The system verifies that space is available on the flight and reserves a seat on the flight.
5. The agent finalizes the booking by supplying payment information.
6. The system books the seats and issues the ticket.

Alternatives

4a: Seat is not available in ticket category:

    4a1.   The system informs the agent that no seats are available in the client's chosen price category.

    4a2.   The agent specifies another price preference.

4b: Seat is not available (flight fully booked):

    4b1:   The system informs agent that no seats are available at all.

    4b2:   The agent specifies another set of departure time preferences.

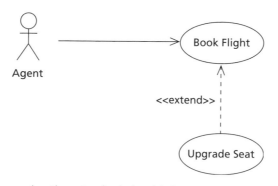

Figure 7.11   *Diagramming the* extend *relationship between use cases*

The difference in using *extends* to promote an alternative is that the base use case—*Book Flight*—does not reference the extending use case (contrast with using *include* for promotion in Use Case 7.8). Instead, the extending use case directly references the base use case as shown in Use Case 7.11.

Use Case 7.11   *Upgrade Seat* as an Extending Use Case

Upgrade Seat

Extends *Book Flight*

4c1: The agent requests an upgrade for the client.

4c2: The system verifies that there are seats available for upgrade on the selected flight.

4c3: The system verifies that the client has sufficient upgrade coupons for the upgrade.

4c4: The system changes ticket class to "upgraded."

Alternatives

4c2a: No seats available for upgrade:

> 4c2a1: Agent places client on wait list for upgrades.

> 4c2a2: Continue with regular ticket booking in *Book Flight* step 4.

4c3a: Client has insufficient upgrade coupons:

> 4c3a1: Agent buys additional upgrade coupons for client.

◆ **PromotedAlternative and UML, by Dan Rawsthorne**

In my mind, this is a classic use of an *extends* relationship, and what I believe the UML developers had in mind: that an *extending* use case is one that modifies the behavior of the base use case in alternative and exceptional scenarios. The way I see it, the main difference between *includes* and *extends* relationships (besides the direction of the arrows) is that an *included* use case is always executed, while an *extending* use case is executed only when some condition is met.

In Use Case 7.11, we see that the additional use case is referenced explicitly in the base use case (Use Case 7.8). This need not be so. Note that in Figure 7.12, we have also included the *extending* use case *Provide Special Meal*, which indicates that a client may also request and receive a special meal (perhaps the client is a vegetarian) as an extension to *Book Flight*. What the diagram tells us is that *Provide Special Meal* and *Upgrade Seat* are two options that can be added onto *Book Flight*, if the conditions are right.

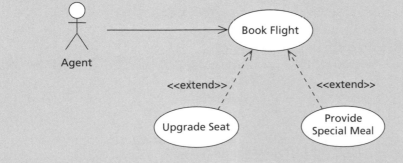

Figure 7.12 *Showing* Special Meal *as an extension of* Book Flight

Note that the extending use case has an **VerbPhraseName** (p. 122) that represents the additional functionality by itself rather than the totality of the extended use case and the additional functionality. This makes it possible for an extending use case to extend more than one base use case, which is an option that is explicitly mentioned in the UML. In fact, it could also be included in another use case if it was part of that use case's main success scenario. For example, the *Upgrade Seat* use case could conceivably extend a *Book Train* use case, as well.

Therefore, unlike the case in **InterruptsAsExtensions** (p. 182), it is inappropriate for this relationship to be represented by a specialization, whether stereotyped or not. So, if your tool will not allow an *extends* relationship, use a stereotyped association, or even an aggregation, but not a generalization—unless you change the name appropriately to represent the complete goal.

7.4 *Trade-offs and Collaborations*

These guidelines improve the organization of the **ScenarioPlusFragments** (p. 125) by helping us either to reduce complexity or to eliminate redundancy in our use cases. But these benefits can be expensive, because adding extension use cases can break up the flow of the story, making it harder for the reader to find and follow additional use cases. Therefore, you need to weigh the benefit of reduced complexity against the benefits of better readability when deciding whether to create specialized use cases.

These patterns govern the extraction of information from a use case under different circumstances. **CommonSubBehavior** (p. 176) recommends that you extract behavior only when it is common to several use cases, to reduce redundancy and potential inconsistencies. **InterruptsAsExtensions** (p. 182) and **PromotedAlternative** (p. 190) focus solely on alternative courses within a scenario. **InterruptsAsExtensions** describes creating extending use cases when an alternative affects multiple steps within a scenario, so that the alternative course is easier to follow. Sometimes, though, alternatives can be so complex, or contain so much important information, that it makes sense to create a new use case by using **PromotedAlternative**, so that the alternative doesn't overshadow the base use case.

The question is "When should you use these constructs?" The answer is to do so judiciously, and only when their use adds some demonstrable value to your use cases. Properly used, they can greatly improve the quality and even readability of a set of use cases. The danger is that they are quite easy to abuse, and can cause more problems than they solve. For that reason, you're better off avoiding them when their use is questionable; apply them only when you can show some benefit from doing so. As a general rule, "If in doubt, don't use them."

These patterns apply to only a few situations that deal specifically with alternative courses and repetitive behavior. You are likely to find other problems with your use cases, such as excessive complexity, which require you to reorganize them significantly. That subject is the topic of the next chapter.

Before we move on to the next chapter, we would like to offer a supplemental relationship pattern covering UML's generalization construct, contributed by our colleague, Dan Rawsthorne.

Sailors looking at painting entitled "Sailors Beware," Fine Arts Building, San Diego, California

7.5 CapturedAbstraction—A Pattern for Applying UML Generalization, by Dan Rawsthorne

You are writing use case descriptions as **ScenarioPlusFragments** (p. 125).

> Trying to document two or more distinct alternatives, neither of which is dominant, is very difficult and confusing in a single use case.

In Europe, business travelers are as likely to take trains as planes for business trips. For example, to travel from Frankfurt to Munich by train takes approximately four hours door to door, while it takes three hours by plane. The plane costs slightly more.

Sometimes there is more than one dominant scenario for a single use case. Each scenario could be its own use case, but they all fill the same hole in the system, meeting the same goals for the same actors. When this happens, it makes sense to create an abstract use case that documents the actors and goals, put each dominant scenario in its own use case, and have them inherit from the abstract one.

Complex or long alternatives clutter a use case and can obscure other alternatives. A use case can become difficult to write and even more difficult to follow when the alternatives are too long or complex, and cannot be easily written as a main scenario plus fragments. Use cases are supposed to be easy to read and understand, not complicated engineering documents.

Some problems are very complex, and have several distinct solutions. Keeping the solutions in separate use cases makes writing them easier, but it sacrifices the traceability to the problem. Yet this traceability is important, so that everyone working on the system will understand how the system is supposed to behave in all reasonable situations.

Having many individual use cases tends to scatter important behavior and makes the behavior harder to understand. Again, one of the biggest benefits of using use cases is that they tell stories that provide a context for understanding requirements. Forcing readers to jump between different use cases to understand solutions risks negating this benefit, because it violates the one-stop-shopping principle. We believe that people should be able to get all of the information they need about a requirement from one place, without having to explore several documents to understand it.

Therefore:

> Consider creating a generalized abstract use case. Put each distinct variant scenario that specializes the abstraction in its own, specialized use case.

A use case is defined by its goal. When more than one use case has the same goal, there is the possibility of confusion. Logically, in this situation you have multiple use cases that collectively contain a number of scenarios of the same use case. The first option would be to combine the use cases using **MergeDroplets** (p. 209), but this can't be done if the individual scenarios are complex. The second choice would be to document the dominant scenario in the main use case, and have the secondary ones as extending use cases, using **InterruptsAsExtensions** (p. 182) or **Promoted-Alternatives** (p. 190). You should consider using an abstraction only if there is no dominant alternative.

You need to exercise caution when using this pattern to justify the creation of an abstract use case, because complex alternatives may indicate that the use case is too detailed or too large (see **EverUnfoldingStory** [p. 102], **LeveledSteps** [p. 153], and **CompleteSingleGoal** [p. 118]). If this is not the case, then putting each distinct alternative in its own use case that specializes an abstract use case is a reasonable course of action.

Examples

Wings Over the World

Assume that retinal scanners are being installed in order to identify agents who want to use the system. If it is also possible to login to the system in the usual way (via name and password), then we are in a situation where an abstraction named *Validate Agent* may be appropriate, as shown in Figure 7.13. (Note that italics indicate abstraction in the UML.)

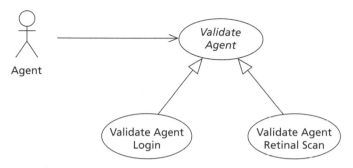

Figure 7.13   *UML generalization relationship*

Note that there is a natural tension between this pattern and **TechnologyNeutral** (p. 167), as these abstractions are often used to eliminate technology variations that lie in the specializations. In fact, it could be argued that this example is just such a thing. However, sometimes discussion of technology is necessary, because it is part of the problem domain and not the solution domain. A general rule is that mentioning technology is permissible if it is an intrinsic part of the goal, but not when it is part of the solution documented in the alternatives.

♦ **CapturedAbstraction and UML**

This technique is often used graphically when eliciting requirements using **Breadth-BeforeDepth** (p. 48). It should be used sparingly, and pains must be taken to assure that both the abstraction and the specializations are at the same structural level. When relying on this pattern, make sure to use the abstraction when you use the **EverUnfoldingStory** (p. 102); that is, refer to *Validate Agent* rather than either *Validate Agent with Login* or *Validate Agent with Retinal Scan.*

Chapter 8

Editing Existing Use Cases

◆ **Well, It Sounded Like a Good Idea at the Time**

You are sitting with Sitra in one of those tiny closets that Wings Over the World calls a conference room. Sitra has been working with Yitka developing the requirements for creating new client accounts. Things seem to have been going well, until Yitka literally tore a strip off of poor Sitra's use cases. Now Sitra has asked you to help her revise them.

Sitra: When I started working with Yitka on the new client account feature, I built this little UI prototype and walked her through each of the forms. She was happy enough about that, but when I wrote up the use cases she just threw them back at me saying, "These are like little pieces of a puzzle. There is no story here." I don't think anyone can make that woman happy.

You pick up the use cases from the table and quickly glance at their names: Open Account, Fill in Client Personal Details, Fill in Client Travel Preferences, Save Client Account.

You: This looks like you created a use case for each one of the user-interface forms that the user fills out to create a new client account.

Sitra: That's exactly what I did. I thought that would be a good way of doing things because I could show someone the user-interface form, and then the use case that drives it. I thought a use case was a terrific way to deal with all the different errors someone could get if they filled the form in wrong.

You: Okay, a lot of people run into this problem. Usually, filling in a single user-interface form does not represent a **CompleteSingleGoal** (p. 118) for the user. This use case here, *Open Account,* it really has no value unless I go on to also *Fill in Client Personal Details, Fill in Client Travel Preferences,* and then *Save Client Account.* None of these use cases really stands on its own, and none of them have enough context in them to make it easy for a reviewer to understand.

Sitra: So what should I do?

You: There is nothing wrong with having an ongoing dialog with the actor, and nothing wrong with having a few forms pop up for a use case. This is very good in fact, because the use case provides the context for the forms. Think of each of these use cases that you have written as a fragment, or droplet if you like, of the real use case that has a useful goal. Call that new merged use case *Create New Client.* We have a guideline called **MergeDroplets** (p. 209) that applies to situations like this.

You notice that Sitra is quickly counting up the steps for the new use case.

Sitra: There'll be almost twenty steps in the main success scenario if we merge all of these use cases together.

You: Yes, so it means we may have to edit the new use case. The odds are that most of the steps are low-level ones, so if they are still relevant, then we may **RedistributeTheWealth** (p. 204) by moving them to lower level use cases.

Analysis is a process of discovery, with many false starts and dead ends. What seemed like a good idea at the time may later become redundant or obsolete. Inevitably, some of your use cases will become out of date and fail to describe properly the system you are building. None of this is surprising, for two reasons. First, requirements specification is not a precise science. The requirements underpinning the system are themselves highly arbitrary and subject to continual change because writing use cases is frequently a revealing process. Ideas that made sense when you started writing your use cases may no longer seem reasonable as you discover more about the underlying system. Second, use cases that span multiple development cycles are likely to fall behind as the system matures and evolves in unforeseen directions. Consequently, your use cases may fail to keep up as your understanding of the system evolves.

Use cases can degrade in several ways. They might contain outdated information left over from the initial attempts at describing the system. Or, they might partition the system in a manner that no longer supports the vision or business case for the system. Concepts that once represented a useful sequence of events may now illuminate only a fragment of some isolated behavior.

Conversely, some use cases may be too big or may encompass too much functionality, describing too many actions.

You have several options available for correcting these problems. You may decide that it wasn't **QuittingTime** (p. 68) after all, and you need to enhance or even write more use cases. On the other hand, you may find that your use cases are reasonably complete, and you just need to spend some time reorganizing them to improve them. Obsolete use cases are the easiest to handle, as you can simply **CleanHouse** (p. 213) by discarding them.

In his book *Refactoring,* which deals with refactoring object-oriented software, Martin Fowler (1999) refers to signs that software may require refactoring as "bad smells." One of the bad smells we think that you should always be sniffing about for in a use case is excessive length. The main success scenario of a good use case is usually between three and nine steps. A main success scenario containing more than nine steps may indicate that the use case either has multiple goals or includes lower level details. In either case, you should **RedistributeTheWealth** (p. 204), equitably partitioning the larger use case into smaller cohesive ones.

Another bad smell can result from use cases that fail to address a **Complete-SingleGoal** (p. 118) and therefore deliver only a fragment of a **UserValuedTransaction** (p. 95) to the primary actor. This bad smell frequently results from either CRUD-style use cases or systems in which the authors have created a use case for each user interface form (Lilly 1999).

This section describes three patterns for removing bad smells from existing use cases. **RedistributeTheWealth** involves separating the independent portions of an overly complex use case into simpler ones that can stand alone. **MergeDroplets** (p. 209) describes the opposite action of combining fragmented use cases into more complete ones. Neither of these actions is arbitrary but involves applying some rules so that the resulting use cases are both cohesive and singular in purpose. Last, **Clean-House** recommends eliminating those use cases that do not provide value or help us see how the actor can achieve a goal.

Children waiting in line for soup given out each night by the city mission, Dubuque, Iowa

8.1 *RedistributeTheWealth*

You are discovering the **UserValued-Transactions** (p. 95) for the system.

> An excessively long use case is unwieldy and hard to use, causing users to become distracted and lose focus.

During the 60s and 70s, many corporations merged into conglomerates that operated in various unrelated lines of business. For example, Canadian Pacific Ltd. operated railways, passenger airlines, and shipping lines, and developed real estate. The multinational oil company Exxon even started a computer division. The business diversity of the conglomerate was seen as a way to protect the interests of shareholders from downturns in a specific market sector. The principle behind these conglomerates boiled down to the prudent proverb "Don't put all your eggs in one basket."

The trouble was that the conglomerates' share prices and earnings tended to lag behind those of more narrowly focused corporations. The usual source of the problem was the difficulty corporate managers had in creating a single unifying vision for the company to embrace across all of its diversified divisions. Eventually, in the 90s, most of the conglomerates broke themselves up into separately traded corporations. In most cases, the value of the shareholder assets increased.

The use case's goal must be clear to the stakeholders. The ideal use case is clear, precise, and unambiguous because it forms an implicit contract (perhaps even a legal one) between the developers and the stakeholders. The use cases must paint a clear picture of the system, demonstrating how everyday users will normally use it in language that they can understand.

It is expensive to add new use cases. New use cases don't appear by magic; they often require the efforts of several people following a specific process. Someone must spend time sifting through requirements or talking to customers to understand a feature's basic characteristics, and then they must exhaustively identify all plausible error conditions and alternative behaviors. One or more persons need to organize this information and write the text, while others must review it. Additional use cases mean additional development work, because developers must implement the new feature. All of these efforts take time and cost money, so it makes sense to write only those use cases that provide measurable value.

Excessive detail can make use cases too hard to read and understand. Each use case should address only one goal and clearly describe how the system helps an actor reach that goal (**CompleteSingleGoal** [p. 118]). If a use case attempts to go beyond this scope, then the readers and even the writers can easily lose sight of the important parts of the story line in the tangents and various plot twists. Use cases that describe behavior beyond their prime objective cloud the boundaries between use cases, duplicating or even contradicting them, making the system even murkier and harder to understand.

Therefore:

> Move a long, unwieldy passage or an overly complex extension to its own use case.

An effective use case will address a **CompleteSingleGoal**. Be especially wary of long use cases. Although size by itself may not be a problem, a long main success scenario (say, over nine steps) may be a "bad smell" indicating that the use case addresses more than one goal. When you discover that a use case has multiple goals, divide it into separate use cases, one for each goal. How you reorganize depends on the level of those goals and their relationship to other use cases.

Relocate fragments to other use cases. If the stories for these extra goals are fragments of behavior that belong in another use case, then incorporate them into that use case. **MergeDroplets** (p. 209) by folding these fragments into the appropriate use case, providing that you can do so without violating the other use case's **CompleteSingleGoal**.

Create a new use case. If the extra stories describe behavior that both stands alone and fulfills an actor's goal, then create a new use case for that behavior. This approach requires more than just moving the extra pieces to another document and calling it a use case, because the result must meet all of the criteria for a use case (**CompleteSingleGoal**, with a **VerbPhraseName** [p. 122]). It also involves making the new use case complete by extracting related information from the original use case, as well as identifying new alternative scenarios. If the resulting use case(s) are closely coupled, then this may indicate potential relationships between the use cases (**PromotedAlternative** [p. 190], **InterruptsAsExtentions** [p. 182], or **CommonSub-Behavior** [p. 176]).

Create a new lower level use case. If there are extra story steps that describe lower level behavior, then level the use case steps (**LeveledSteps** [p. 153]) by creating a lower level use case with its own **CompleteSingleGoal**. Relocate the lower level steps to the new use case (**EverUnfoldingStory** [p. 102]), and reference the lower level use case from the original (this is the *includes* relation).

Relocate superfluous fragments to the supplementary specifications. If super-fluous story fragments were included to help clarify the use case description, then save them as **Adornments** (p. 133).

Examples

Call Processing

Consider Use Case 8.1, which provides a simplified description of making a phone call from the viewpoint of the service provider.

Use Case 8.1   Use Case Horror: The *Process Normal Call* Use Case with Multiple Goals

---

Make a Phone Call

Primary Actors: Caller—Person making the call
                     Called—Person being called

Secondary Actor: Switching Network—Equipment handling calls between tele-phones

Level: User Goal

Main Success Scenario

1.   Caller takes the phone "off-hook."
2.   Caller dials number.
3.   Switching Network translates the digits, connects Caller to Called's phone, and sends ring signal.
4.   Called answers the phone (goes off-hook) and talks to Caller.
5.   Called and Caller hang up.
6.   Switching Network logs billing information about the call. If this is the Caller's first call of the day, it initializes a daily usage report entry in the customer's file.

> If this is a local call, then it logs it in the service provider's log as well. If it is long distance, then it records an entry in the appropriate long distance provider's log.
>
> 7. Switching Network tears down the connection and frees all of components that the call required.
> 8. The use case ends once the Switching Network frees all of its components used in the call.

While its length is acceptable, this use case violates **CompleteSingleGoal** (p. 118) because it describes two separate behaviors: making a phone call and billing the user. Once you detect this situation, your options include creating a new use case, creating a new sub–use case, or even including the extra information as **Adornments** (p. 133). In this case, *Log Billing Information* appears to fulfill a lower level goal and so a sub–use case is appropriate (**EverUnfoldingStory** [p. 102]). To **Redistribute-TheWealth**, you should:

1. Extract the bill logging information from the use case, and create a new sub–use case with it. See Use Case 8.2.
2. Modify step 6 in the *Process Normal Call* use case to refer to this new sub–use case, as in Use Case 8.3.

Use Case 8.2   RedistributeTheWealth by Creating the *Log Billing Information* Sub–Use Case

Log Billing Information
Primary Actor: Caller—Person making the call
Supporting Actor: Switching Network—Equipment handling calls between telephones
Level: User Goal
Main Success Scenario
1. Switching Network logs billing information about the call. If this is the Caller's first call of the day, it initializes a daily usage report entry in the customer's file. If this is a local call, then it logs it in the service provider's log as well. If it is long distance, then it records an entry in the appropriate long distance provider's log.

Use Case 8.3   RedistributeTheWealth in *Process Normal Call* to Give a Use Case a CompleteSingleGoal

Process Normal Call
Primary Actors: Caller—Person making the call
Called—Person being called

Supporting Actors: Switching Network—Equipment handling calls between telephones

Level: User Goal

Main Success Scenario

1. Caller takes the phone "off-hook."
2. Caller dials number.
3. Switching Network translates the digits, connects Caller to Called's phone, and sends ring signal.
4. Called answers the phone (goes off-hook) and talks to Caller.
5. Called and Caller hang up.
6. Switching Network *Logs Billing Information.*
7. Switching Network tears down the connection and frees all components that the call required.
8. The use case ends once the Switching Network frees all of its components used in the call.

A quilting party in an Alvin, Wisconsin, home

8.2 MergeDroplets

You are discovering the **UserValuedTransactions** (p. 95) for the system.

> Use cases that describe tiny or isolated fragments of behavior don't convey enough information to help readers understand how the system delivers **UserValuedTransactions**.

Many of us enjoy playing with picture puzzles. There is a wonderful challenge in trying to merge hundreds, sometimes thousands, of little picture fragments into a single complete picture. Imagine sitting at the kitchen table with thousands of puzzle pieces scattered across its top. You carefully compare a fragment of sky to the picture on the box and try to position it roughly where you think it should be. Slowly, bigger pieces of the puzzle come together. Soon you will have larger fragments of sky, ground, and the castle on the hill. Some serious puzzle aficionados refuse even to look at the picture on the box; instead, they turn all the pieces over and solve the puzzle only by merging pieces without help from matching colors or images.

Use cases are not puzzles. A use case represents a **CompleteSingleGoal** (p. 118); a reader should not have to hunt down and mentally merge several use cases to see the complete picture.

Partial use cases are incomplete and fail to tell the whole story. An individual use case should present a "complete usage of value" to the actor. Fragments of use cases or partial use cases will cause readers to lose sight of system goals and overlook valuable features. To understand a single and complete behavior, readers are forced either to find other use cases, if they can find them, or to attempt to fill in the gaps themselves. Often, readers end up missing important features or adding unnecessary ones.

It is best to localize information whenever possible. Distributing the thread of a story throughout a set of use cases makes it very difficult for the readers to follow the narrative. Localizing information about a feature to a use case helps readers understand the primary actor's goal and the context surrounding the functional requirements.

Developers often implement systems on a per-use-case basis. If you distribute actions across multiple use cases, then you increase the likelihood that your developers will miss some features, or that multiple teams will be unknowingly working on the same features, wasting valuable development time and potentially delaying the project.

It is best to minimize the number of use cases. Every use case you must implement adds to the cost of the project, requiring you to manage, design, write, review, and test more code. Each additional feature adds an element of risk to the product, so you want to implement as few use cases as necessary when building a system, especially when time to market is an important factor.

Smaller use cases are easier to understand and use. Ideally, you want to write short, concise use cases that tell the readers everything that they need to know about a system, nothing more and nothing less. Each of your use cases should adequately describe how the system helps the actor meet one goal (**CompleteSingleGoal** [p. 118]), without unnecessary or technical details (**TechnologyNeutral** [p. 167]). Otherwise, you run the risk of overwhelming your readers.

Therefore:

> Merge related tiny use cases or use case fragments into the use cases that relate to the same goal.

Merging use cases requires more effort than simply throwing several steps together and calling the results a use case, because the final product must still contain the patterns for a good use case. The best approach is to carefully edit the pieces together into a cohesive unit that describes a **CompleteSingleGoal**. If the resulting use cases are too large or too detailed, then refine their steps to keep **ActorIntent-Accomplished** (p. 158), or level them to make them more understandable (**LeveledSteps** [p. 153]), **EverUnfoldingStory** [p. 102]). It is quite likely that you will also have to sift through the alternative courses, removing some and adding others.

How you reorganize partial use cases depends on their presumed goal and their relationships to other use cases.

Merge fragments to create a new use case. If several partial use cases describe behaviors that are related to the same goal, then merge them. Merging partial use cases especially makes sense when they must run in a specific order, because serial use cases are prone to repeat information. The resulting use case must still meet all of the criteria for a use case **CompleteSingleGoal**.

Merge fragments into existing use cases. If a use case describes behavior that belongs in another use case, then incorporate it into that use case. As with **RedistributeThe-Wealth** (p. 204), you should combine them only when you can do so without violating the resulting use case's integrity and still provide a **CompleteSingleGoal**.

Examples

Call Processing

Let's look at making a phone call again. It can be tempting to break down a use case into smaller, serialized use cases, with each describing a distinct functional action, as the simplified example in Use Case 8.4 shows.

Use Case 8.4 Use Case Horror: A Set of Small Use Cases for Placing a Telephone Call

Primary Actors: Caller—Person making the call

Called—Person receiving the call

Supporting Actors: Switching Network—Equipment handling calls between telephones

Level: User Goal

Use Case 1: *Place Call*

Preconditions: Caller's and Called's phones are on-hook.

Success Guarantee: System has collected all of Caller's dialed digits.

Main Course:

1.   The use case begins when Caller takes phone "off-hook."
2.   Switching Network sends dial tone.
3.   Caller dials call.
4.   Switching Network translates digits.
5.   Switching Network connects call to Called's phone.
6.   Switching network sends ring signal to Called's phone.
7.   Switching Network sends ring signal to Caller's receiver, and the use case terminates.

Use Case 2: *Talk on the Phone*

Preconditions: Use Case *Place Call* has sent ring signal to Called's phone.

Success Guarantee: Users have finished call.

Main Course:

1.   The use case begins when Called's phone rings.
2.   Called answers phone, taking phone "off-hook."
3.   Switching Network completes connecting Caller and Called.
4.   Called and Caller talk.
5.   Called and Caller hang up, and the use case terminates.

Use Case 3: *Terminate Call*

Preconditions: Call is connected via *Talk on the Phone*.

Success Guarantee: Switching Network has broken down call, and all companies are in the same state they were before call.

Main Course:

1.   The use case begins when Caller and Called hang up.
2.   The Switching Network frees all of the components that the call required.
3.   The Switching Network *Logs Billing Information,* and the use case terminates.

This level of proceduralization is great for writing code, but not use cases. These use cases are incomplete because they describe only part of the call, and all but the first use case depend upon the completion of other use cases. Also, each of these use cases met a subgoal of our main goal, which is making a phone call. These factors indicate that we should merge these use cases.

A better way to write this use case is shown in Use Case 8.5.

Use Case 8.5 Droplet Use Cases Merged into a New Use Case

Make a Phone Call

Primary Actors: Caller—Person making the call

Called—Person receiving the call

Supporting Actors: Switching Network—Equipment handling calls between telephones

Level: User Goal

Preconditions: Caller's and Called's phones are on-hook.

Success Guarantee: Switching Network has broken down call, and all components are in the same state they were before call.

Main Course:

1.   The use case begins when Caller takes phone "off-hook."
2.   Switching Network sends dial tone.
3.   Caller dials call.
4.   Switching Network translates digits.
5.   Switching Network connects call to Called's phone.
6.   Switching Network sends ring signal to Called's phone and to Caller's receiver (so that they can hear it ringing).
7.   Called answers phone and talks to Caller.
8.   Called and Caller hang up.
9.   The Switching Network breaks down the connection, *Logs Billing Information,* and the use case terminates.

This use case is much easier for the readers to follow, because it contains all of the information necessary to place, make, and conclude a phone call. The reader doesn't have to sift through several use cases to find the necessary information about this behavior; it is all there, and in order.

Also notice that in this example at least, the total number of steps required to express the behavior drops once the use cases are combined. The combined use case contains as much information as the three partial use cases, but it doesn't need to repeat the setup data or provide information to help the readers connect the separate smaller use cases.

House adjoining a junk pile, Milwaukee, Wisconsin

8.3 CleanHouse

You are discovering the **UserValuedTransactions** (p. 95) for the system.

> Use cases that don't contribute value to the whole are distracting and can lead the audience down the wrong path.

Our culture is one of acquisition. Closets, basements, and attics throughout North America attest to our ability to accumulate possessions, most of them long forgotten. Our garages are so full we can't park our cars in them. We spend countless hours cleaning and rearranging things, trying to find better ways of storing these belongings so that they aren't in our way, even to the point of renting expensive storage units so we can accumulate even more. Incredibly, we spend more dollars and hours boxing up these items and transporting them across the country when we move, so that we can clutter up our new garages, closets, basements, and attics. Much of this stuff we will never use again, but we keep it anyway, because "it might come in handy someday." But do we really want polyester to come back into fashion? Ironically, people usually feel much better after they finally throw things away, and wonder why they didn't do it years earlier.

Similarly, unnecessary use cases become nothing but clutter, distracting the readers from the system's main purpose. Worse, they can waste a lot of time and energy working on something that no one wants or needs.

Cleaning up old use cases consumes time and intellectual energy. You can't modify or discard active use cases without understanding them or their value to your system. New ones are usually fresh and relatively easy to understand, but old ones often require work. Relearning takes time, and the older your use cases, the longer it will take, because you will likely need to review your entire collection before you can accurately make any changes or decide that you no longer need some of them.

Unused use cases clutter up the workspace and waste intellectual energy. Every use case you create requires some effort to maintain and adds to the cost of a project. The more use cases you have, the harder it is for the readers to keep them straight. A collection of use cases should contain only members that describe meaningful interactions between the various actors and the system. Meaningless features don't add any value to the system; rather, they only create unnecessary work for everyone using them. Unnecessary use cases can become legacy items that no one understands yet everyone is afraid to remove because they might be valuable (see the Lava Flow Pattern in Brown et al., 1998), and they remain as a fixture for the life of the system.

Removing a use case avoids a huge amount of development work and conserves intellectual energy. Every use case that you have to implement requires more time, increases your costs, and adds an element of risk to your project. You want to implement only as many use cases as necessary. Every use case that you can eliminate right from the start reduces your overhead significantly.

The consequence of leaving unnecessary use cases in your collection is that someone might try to implement them, wasting valuable development time on something you don't need, and delaying your time to market. This possibility is more likely in large development organizations, where the writers and developers are separated by organizational boundaries and don't communicate much.

Therefore:

> **Remove those use cases that do not add value to your system or that are no longer in your active list.**

Remove these use cases from your collection as soon as you determine that they no longer contribute value (**UserValuedTransactions** [p. 95]). You may save any of them you feel are useful as **Adornments** (p. 133), but discontinue writing them immediately. A general rule for determining whether to discard a use case is "When in doubt, throw it out." Don't worry if you throw out what later turns out to be a valuable use case. If it is valuable, then you can always bring it back into your collection later.

Weigh the implementation cost of your use cases against their perceived value, and remove those use cases whose goals are too small compared to their development cost. Some use cases cost the project more than they will ever contribute to it. Consider removing these use cases and saving some money. The chances are good that you will never implement them anyway, as you will be maintaining and enhancing more important features.

Examples

Hospital Claim

Consider the following four use cases for paying medical insurance claims for a physician's services:

Use Case 1: *Pay Hospitalization Claim*
Use Case 2: *Pay Outpatient Claim*
Use Case 3: *Pay House Call Claim*
Use Case 4: *Pay Office Visit Claim*

Each of these potential use cases describes separate and distinct situations, each having their own subtleties, expenses, and forms. But doctors rarely make house calls anymore, so Use Case 3 is impractical. It doesn't belong in the collection because it doesn't contribute any value to the system, even though it might contain interesting information that the other ones don't. It might make a good **Adornment** (p. 133), though, if it offered useful information.

CleanHouse addresses a real problem common to many professions beyond software development. For example, we identified several patterns while writing this book that we eventually decided not to use. Several of them were quite good; unfortunately, they became less valuable as work progressed, so we discarded them. It wasn't easy, and we had several spirited discussions about some of the patterns, but we eventually felt that the book would be much better without them.

8.4 Trade-offs and Collaborations

Writing quality use cases can be a complicated process, made even more so by the volatile nature of the underlying requirements. Goals change, and what once represented quality use cases may now be incomplete fragments of behavior or large chunks that address too many issues. We may even have written some use cases that are no longer needed. In short, and often through no fault of our own, some of our use cases fail to meet the standard of a **CompleteSingleGoal** (p. 118).

The patterns in this chapter are helper patterns for **CompleteSingleGoal**, and provide guidance for editing existing use cases to meet this standard. Each relies on **CompleteSingleGoal**, which states that a use case should completely address one and only one goal at its level, as the standard for determining what belongs in a specific use case. We can use this principle in two ways: determining whether something belongs in a particular use case and, if not, where it belongs. These editing patterns cover three situations:

1. Breaking up excessively large use cases and reducing them to a manageable size (**RedistributeTheWealth** [p. 204])
2. Combining incomplete use case fragments into new or existing use cases (**MergeDroplets** [p. 209])
3. Eliminating unnecessary use cases (**CleanHouse** [p. 213])

More important, they tell us how to accomplish these actions, and what to do with the leftover pieces. Breaking up excessively large use cases involves identifying and removing information that does not pertain to the use case's goal. We don't necessarily want to get rid of this information; we usually want to redistribute it, either by moving it into a new use case or combining it into an existing one. Combining fragments into cohesive units makes it easier for readers to understand specific tasks without having to find their own path through the entire system to understand a specific function. Localizing closely related behavior in one use case also reduces the risk that some of the less informed readers might miss some detail that is buried in another, seemingly unrelated use case. Last, eliminating unnecessary use cases makes everyone's lives easier, by reducing the size and number of use cases to maintain and eliminating work for the implementers.

We may also decide that some fragments or even whole use cases no longer fit into the scheme of things, yet they contain some information we wish to preserve. We can always treat those cases as **Adornments**, and save this information without directly including them in our use cases.

One final note: Editing use cases can be rather involved, requiring that you understand both the system and most of the use cases in your collection before you start. This knowledge helps you identify the out-of-place pieces, as well as determine where they belong. Otherwise, you are likely to miss many of the subtleties contained in the system and make things even worse. If you don't have this experience, take some time to acquaint yourself with all of the use cases you are editing, so that you may understand them better before you begin.

References

Adolph, W. S., 1996. "Cash Cow in the Tarpit: The Reengineering of a Legacy System." *IEEE Software,* May.

———. 2000. "Lost in Chaos: A Chronology of a Failure." *Software Development Magazine,* January.

Alexander, Christopher. 1979. *The Timeless Way of Building.* New York: Oxford University Press.

———. 1977. *A Pattern Language.* New York: Oxford University Press.

Berard, Edward V. 1998. *Be Careful with Use Cases.*

Boehm, Barry W. 1981. *Software Engineering Economics.* Englewood Cliffs, N.J.: Prentice-Hall.

Brooks, Frederick P., Jr. 1995. *The Mythical Man Month Anniversary Edition: Essays on Software Engineering.* Reading, Mass: Addison-Wesley.

———. 1987. "No Silver Bullet: Essence and Accidents of Software Engineering." *IEEE Computer,* Vol. 20, No. 4, April.

Brown, W. J., et al. 1998. *Anti-Patterns, Refactoring Software, Architectures, and Projects in Crisis.* New York: John Wiley & Sons.

Cockburn, Alistair. 1998. *Surviving Object-Oriented Projects.* Reading: Addison-Wesley.

———. 2001. *Writing Effective Use Cases.* Boston: Addison-Wesley.

———. 2002. *Agile Software Development.* Boston: Addison-Wesley.

Constantine, Larry, and Lucy Lockwood. 1999. *Software for Use.* Reading: Addison-Wesley.

Coplien, Jim. 1996. "Software Patterns." *SIGS Management Briefings,* p. 7.

———. 1998. Lecture to the Phoenix Patterns Group, Phoenix, Ariz.

Fowler, Martin. 1999. *Refactoring.* Reading, Mass.: Addison-Wesley.

Gabriel, Richard. 1996. *Patterns of Software.* New York: Oxford University Press, p. 56.

Gamma, E., et al. 1995. *Design Patterns: Elements of Reusable Object-Oriented Software.* Reading, Mass.: Addison-Wesley.

Graham, Ian. 1997. Remarks at Andy Pol's OOPSLA Workshop. Atlanta.

Jacobson, I., et al. 1992. *Object-Oriented Software Engineering: A Use Case Driven Approach.* Reading, Mass.: Addison-Wesley.

———. 1995. *The Object Advantage: Business Process Reengineering with Object Technology.* ACM Press.

Kraus, Andy. 1996. "Use Case Blue." *Object Magazine,* May, pp. 63–65.

Larman, C. 2002. *Applying UML and Patterns: An Introduction to Object-Oriented Analysis and Design and the Unified Process,* 2nd Edition. Prentice-Hall.

Lilly, Susan. 1999. "Use Case Pitfalls: Top 10 Problems from Real Projects Using Use Cases." Proceedings of the TOOLS USA '99, IEEE Computer Society.

Marx, Arthur. 1972. *Son of Groucho.* New York: McKay.

Riel, A. J. 1996. *Object-Oriented Design Heuristics.* Reading, Mass.: Addison-Wesley.

Rising, Linda. 1998. *The Patterns Handbook: Techniques, Strategies and Applications.* Cambridge: Cambridge University Press.

———. 2000. *The Pattern Almanac.* Boston, Mass.: Addison-Wesley.

Photo Credits

p. xxii. Photograph by Christine Bramble, 2000. © Christine Bramble. Used by permission.

Chapter 2

p. 31. Photograph by Andreas Feininger, 1942, Library of Congress, Prints & Photographs Division, FSA-OWI Collection (LC-USE6-D-008461).

p. 35. Photograph by Marjory Collins, 1942, Library of Congress, Prints & Photographs Division, FSA-OWI Collection (LC-USW3-011149-D).

p. 39. Photograph by Russell Lee, 1939, Library of Congress, Prints & Photographs Division, FSA-OWI Collection (LC-USF33-012380-M5).

Chapter 3

p. 48. Photograph by John Vachon, 1941, Library of Congress, Prints & Photographs Division, FSA-OWI Collection (LC-USF346-063960-D).

p. 52. Photograph by John Vachon, 1940, Library of Congress, Prints & Photographs Division, FSA-OWI Collection (LC-USF33-T01-001878-M2).

p. 58. Photograph by Theodor Horydczak, circa 1920–1950, Library of Congress, Prints & Photographs Division, Horydczak Collection (LC-H823-2414-027).

p. 64. Photographer unknown, circa 1935–1945, Library of Congress, Prints & Photographs Division, FSA-OWI Collection (LC-USW3-036569-D).

p. 68. Photograph by Arthur S. Siegel, 1943, Library of Congress, Prints & Photographs Division, FSA-OWI Collection (LC-USW3-023528-D).

p. 73. Photograph by Theodor Horydczak, circa 1920–1950, Library of Congress, Prints & Photographs Division, Horydczak Collection (LC-H814-0083-B).

Chapter 4

p. 80. Photograph by Jack Delano, 1941, Library of Congress, Prints & Photographs Division, FSA-OWI Collection (LC-USF33-021285-M4).

p. 86. Photograph by Don Olson, 1976. © Don Olson 1976. Used by permission.

p. 90. Photograph by Theodor Horydczak, circa 1920–1950, Library of Congress, Prints & Photographs Division, Horydczak Collection (LC-H814-1903-001).

p. 95. Photograph by Marion Post Wolcott, 1941, Library of Congress, Prints & Photographs Division, FSA-OWI Collection (LC-USF34-057426-E).

p. 102. Photograph by John Collier, 1941, Library of Congress, Prints & Photographs Division, FSA-OWI Collection (LC-USF34-080802-D).

Chapter 5

p. 118. Photographer unknown, circa 1935–1945, Library of Congress, Prints & Photographs Division, FSA-OWI Collection (LC-USW3-036912-E).

p. 122. Photograph by Russell Lee, 1938, Library of Congress, Prints & Photographs Division, FSA-OWI Collection (LC-USF33-011638-M2).

p. 125. Photograph by Theodor Horydczak, circa 1920–1950, Library of Congress, Prints & Photographs Division, Horydczak Collection (LC-H814-T-2241-185).

p. 129. Photographer unknown, circa 1935–1945, Library of Congress, Prints & Photographs Division, FSA-OWI Collection (LC-USW3-010594-E).

p. 133. Photograph by John Collier, 1941, Library of Congress, Prints & Photographs Division, FSA-OWI Collection (LC-USF34-080356-D).

p. 138. Photograph by Arthur Rothstein, 1942, Library of Congress, Prints & Photographs Division, FSA-OWI Collection (LC-USW3-004482-D).

Chapter 6

p. 148. Photograph by Fred Driscoll, 1943, Library of Congress, Prints & Photographs Division, FSA-OWI Collection (LC-USW3-038405-D).

p. 153. Photographer unknown, circa 1890–1899, Library of Congress, Prints & Photographs Division, Detroit Publishing Company Photograph Collection (LC-D4-11307).

p. 158. Photograph by Marjory Collins, 1942, Library of Congress, Prints & Photographs Division, FSA-OWI Collection (LC-USW3-010932-D).

p. 162. Photograph by Arthur S. Siegel, 1942, Library of Congress, Prints & Photographs Division, FSA-OWI Collection (LC-USW3-008475-C).

p. 167. Photograph by Arthur S. Siegel, 1943, Library of Congress, Prints & Photographs Division, FSA-OWI Collection (LC-USW3-024443-D).

Chapter 7

p. 176. Photograph by Ann Rosener, 1942, Library of Congress, Prints & Photographs Division, FSA-OWI Collection (LC-USE6-D-007007).

p. 182. Photograph by Jack Delano, 1943, Library of Congress, Prints & Photographs Division, FSA-OWI Collection (LC-USW3-015566-E).

p. 190. Photograph by John Vachon, 1942, Library of Congress, Prints & Photographs Division, FSA-OWI Collection (LC-USW3-002986-D).

p. 198. Photograph by Russell Lee, 1941, Library of Congress, Prints & Photographs Division, FSA-OWI Collection (LC-USF34-039293-D).

Chapter 8

p. 204. Photograph by John Vachon, 1940, Library of Congress, Prints & Photographs Division, FSA-OWI Collection (LC-USF34-060600-D DLC).

p. 209. Photograph by Russell Lee, 1937, Library of Congress, Prints & Photographs Division, FSA-OWI Collection (LC-USF34-010885-D).

p. 213. Photograph by Carl Mydans, 1936, Library of Congress, Prints & Photographs Division, FSA-OWI Collection (LC-USF34-006011-D).

Index

Note: Pattern names are in **bold**; use case names are in *italic*.

A

Abstraction
    and goals of steps, 153
    use cases written as different levels of, 103
Abstract use cases, 108, 109
Access ATM description, with technology-
      specific steps, 161
Access ATM use case, improved Technology-
      Neutral, 161
Access e-mail use case, 131–132
Accuracy
    of requirements, 139
    verifying, 65
Active verbs, 159
ActorIntentAccomplished, xiv, 5, 23, 103, 127,
      147, 154, 158–161, 163, 210
    examples, 159–161
    improving *Withdraw Cash* description with,
      160
    and purpose, 171
    Withdraw Cash description without, 159–
      160
Actor-less ATM example, 159–161
Actor lists
    and briefs, 56
    for Pharmacy System, 93
    for revised Pharmacy System, 94
    for Wings Over the World (sample), 55
Actors, 1, 23, 24, 51, 54, 78, 79, 89, 114, 117
    and accomplishments of value, 118–119
    and context diagrams, 88
    duration of goals for, 119
    identifying, 90
    naming, 92
    naming use cases and goals of, 123
    in pharmacy example, 92–94
    stakeholder's competing visions about, 81
Adolph, Steve, xix
Adornments, 4, 22, 42, 117, 121, 127, 133–137,
      142, 146, 147, 155, 163, 169, 178, 206,
      207, 214, 215, 216
    examples, 135–137
    and use cases, 22
    Wings Over the World with, 135–137
Agile Software Development, xix
Agile Software Development Ecologies, xix
Agile Software Development Series, xviii
Alexander, Christopher, xvi, 6, 7, 8, 9, 10
Alexandrian form, 10, 16
Alternative courses of actions
    coping with, 183
    handling, 191
Ambiguity, 68–69, 70, 141, 174
    and imprecision, 141
    reducing, 159
    removing, 81
    in scenario, 171
Analysis, 202
Anchor points, 12, 17, 96
Apollo Saturn V spacecraft, 38
ARJIS. *See* Automated Regional Justice Infor-
      mation System
Armstrong, Neil, 80
ATM JAD system example, 150–152

Audience. *See also* Customers; Users
    amount of information needed by, 61
    knowing, 175
    and names of use cases, 122
    and readability of use cases, 138
Auto insurance claim handling, 128
Automated railway signaling, 84
Automated Railway Signaling System, vision
    statement for, 84
Automated Regional Justice Information
    System, 33

B
BalancedTeam, 20, 30, 32, 39–42, 43, 92
Balanced use cases, 69
Batch job distribution, example, 60
Best practices, and pattern form, xiv
Blob, The (film), 86
Book Flight for Frequent Flier, 187
Book Flight for Frequent Flier extension use
    case, 186
    referencing extension points, 189
Book Flight use case
    after *Upgrade Seat* alternative promoted via
        extends, 194
    after *Upgrade Seat* alternative promoted via
        includes, 192
    brief for, 56
    with business rules, 135
    confusing frequent flier alternatives for, 184
    with extension points, 188
    with incorrectly applied includes relation-
        ship, 178
    more detailed version of, 107
    revised, 179–180
    shortening with **EverUnfoldingStory**, 106
    thirty-page use case horror, 105
Boundaries, different points of view about,
    86–87
Boundary conditions, 191
Brainstorming, 33
Bramble, Paul, xix
Branch-and-join process, 33
BreadthBeforeDepth, 20, 47, 48–51, 52, 53, 55,
    68, 71, 98, 140, 200
    and alternative conditions, 131

    examples, 51
    and order for use case writing process, 51
    QuittingTime facilitated by, 72
    SpiralDevelopment interacts with, 54, 76
    and stopping points in use case, 127
    and UML, 51
    and use case diagrams, 89
Bridges of Madison County, The (film), 90
Briefs, 55
    and actor lists, 56
    for *Reserve Flight* and *Book Flight,* 56
"Brittle" requirements set, 4
Brooks, Frederick, 1, 51, 84
Builders, and expansion of system scope, 81
Business purchasing, 61–63
Business rules, 127, 134, 136, 147, 149
    Book Flight with, 135
    Change Seat adorned with, 135–136
    specifiers, 2
Business-value check, 66
Buy something (casual version) use case, 61

C
Call processing examples, 206–208, 211–212
Canadian Pacific Ltd, 204
Candidate use cases, identifying, 50
CapturedAbstraction, 51, 175, 198–200
    and UML, 198
Change Seat use case
    adorned with business rules, 135–136
    business rules in, 152
    informal version of, 140
    review of, 121
"Chaos" reports, xiii
ChiliPLoP conferences, xix
"Choose your own adventure" story
    differences between use case and, 126
    and writing use cases, 125
Claim Insurance use case
    not making sufficient forward progress, 165
    revised to make forward progress, 166
CleanHouse, 21, 50, 54, 202, 203, 213–215
    examples, 215
ClearCastOfCharacters, 11, 13, 15, 48, 79,
    90–94, 118
    and **EverUnfoldingStory**, 113

examples, 92–94
and services identification, 97
and use case sets, 22
and **VisibleBoundary**, 87
and vision, 82
Clear vision, lack of, 80
Cockburn, Alistair, xiv, xv, xix, 7, 27, 104
Code bloat, 149
Common steps, rewriting, 176
CommonSubBehavior, 23, 51, 121, 174, 176–
  181, 196, 206
examples, 178–181
and includes relationship, 174, 180
and UML, 180–181
Communication
common forms and facilitation of, 59
strengthening channels of, 81
Complete group, defining, 66
CompleteSingleGoal, xiv, 8, 15, 97, 117, 118–
  121, 122, 125, 127, 138, 139, 142, 143,
  154, 159, 184, 191, 199, 203, 205, 206,
  207, 209, 210
and addressing more than one goal, 120
examples, 121
factors to consider with, 142
and goals associated with use cases, 5, 14,
  103, 117
helper patterns for, 215
and individual use cases, 22
for *Process Normal Call* use case, 207–208
and scope of use case, 178
and structuring of use cases, 4
use cases as representative of, 209
Complexity
controlling, 119
incremental, 126
reducing, 196
Complex use cases, 178, 190
Computer-Aided Software Engineering (CASE)
  tools, for generating use case diagrams,
  xviii
Concrete details, 167
Conditions, 148
Connery, Sean, 90
Consensus, 57
Constantine, Larry, 43

Content, reviews of, 64
Context
and patterns, 15
in **UserValuedTransactions** pattern sample,
  11
Context diagrams, for Wings Over the World,
  88–89
Control break processing, 191
Core competencies, 69, 71
Corporate vision, and technology vision, 83
Create, Read, Update, and Delete, 12, 78, 80, 96
Create Customer use case, and mortgage origi-
  nation system, 100
CRUD. *See* Create, Read, Update, and Delete
Cruddy mortgage origination system, 100
Crystal Clear, xix
Customers. *See also* Audience; Users
final authority on product and, 36
movie-making and consultation with, 38
soliciting input from, 37
and use case development process, 36, 37,
  43

D
Data
formats, 136
specifiers, 2
validation rules, 134
Davis, Wade, 73
Day at the Races, A (film), 38
Deadlines, 53
Delays, expense of, 53
Delete Customer use case, and mortgage
  origination system, 100
Dependency, 183
Deployment diagram, 87
*Design Patterns: Elements of Reusable Object
  Oriented Software* (Gamma), 6–7, 8, 9
Details
addition of, by developers, 138
handling, 49
DetectableConditions, 23, 127, 136, 148–152,
  171
examples, 150–152
and scenarios, 147
and variations, 131

Developers
    and detectable conditions, 149
    errors handled by, 130
    and use case readability, 138
Development organizations, and end user
    representation, 35
Development patterns, 19
Development team, 66
Diagrams, and **SpiralDevelopment**, 57
Dictionaries, iterative writing and, 57
Diminishing returns, avoiding law of, 54
Director-style *Book Flight* use case, with incor-
    rectly applied includes relationship, 178
Diversions
    creating, 162
    with insufficient forward progress, 165
    multiple, 182
    repeated, 183
    in scenarios, 163
Diversity
    and **BalancedTeams**, 32
    lack of, 41–42
Documentation group, and use cases, 37
Domain experts, 37, 40
Dr. Strangelove (film), 90
Droplets, repairing, 180
Droplet use cases, merging into new use cases,
    212

E
Eastwood, Clint, 90
Editing, 19, 21
Editing existing use cases, 201–216
    CleanHouse, 213–215
    MergeDroplets, 209–212
    RedistributeTheWealth, 204–208
    trade-offs and collaborations, 215–216
EDSAC, 176
e-mail access example, 131–132
Encyclopedias, iterative writing and, 57
Engage Art use case, 109–110
Engage Diversity use case, 110–111
ENIAC, 176
Errors
    developers and handling of, 130
    in requirements models, 177
    and reviews, 64, 65

Estimates, 2
EverUnfoldingStory, xvi, 14, 15, 79, 97, 100,
    102–113, 118, 154, 159, 179, 191, 199,
    200, 206, 207, 210
    and *Book Flight* use case, 112
    and Centre A: The Museum for Contempo-
      rary Asian Art, 109–111
    examples, 104–110
    and goals, 120
    good use cases in context of, 113
    and includes relationship, 180
    and LeveledSteps, 171
    shortening *Book Flight* with, 106
    systems described as, 113
    and UML models, 111
    and use case sets, 22
Examples
    actor-less ATM, 159–161
    ATM JAD system, 152–154
    auto insurance claim handling, 128
    automated railway signaling, 84
    batch job distribution, 60
    call processing, 206–208, 211–212
    Cruddy mortgage origination system, 100
    e-mail access, 131–132
    File Accident Claim: tied to technology,
      169–171
    hospital claim, 215
    insurance claims, 123–124, 165–166
    mobile dispatching, 85
    Museum for Contemporary Asian Art, 92,
      109–110
    for patterns, 18
    pharmacy receptionist, 92–94
    purchasing for a business, 61–63
    vision statement for Wings Over the World,
      82–83
    Wings Over the World, 54–57, 104–109,
      199
    Wings Over the World: diversionary
      scenario, 163–164
    Wings Over the World: precise but
      unreadable, 140–141
    Wings Over the World: readable but
      imprecise, 139–140
    Wings Over the World and avoiding form-
      focus, 98–99

Wings Over the World and extensions, 184–186

Wings Over the World and includes, 178–180

Wings Over the World and User-Valued Transactions, 98–99

Wings Over the World (continued), 66, 71–72, 75

Wings Over the World goals, 121

Wings Over the World seat upgrade alternative, 191–193

Wings Over the World with **Adornments**, 135–136

Exception processing, 130

ExhaustiveAlternatives, 5, 8, 50, 59, 117, 127, 129–132, 142, 148, 150

examples, 131–132

and use cases, 22

Expandability, and high-quality system, 83

Expert users, 40

Extends relationship, 23, 108, 173, 175, 180, 186, 196

and alternatives, 194

formal definitions in UML for, 178

includes relationship *versus*, 174

interpretations for, 109

misunderstanding, 183

PromotedAlternative and UML, 195

Extends use cases, 183, 184, 185, 195, 199

Book Flight after *Upgrade Seat* alternative promoted via, 194

Book Flight for Frequent Flier, 186

and UML extension points, 187–189

Upgrade Seat as, 195

Extension points, *Book Flight* use case with, 188

Extensions, 24

Wings Over the World and, 182–184

External interface protocols, 134

Exxon, 202

F

Feature creep, 65

File Accident Claim use case
technology-dependent, 169–170
technology-neutral, 170

Find Flight, lower level use case for, 105–106

Forces affecting problem, and patterns, 16–17

Formality, 59, 175, 177, 183

Formal specifications, 141

Formats, choosing for use cases, 59

Form-focus, Wings Over the World and avoidance of, 99–100

Forms-based use case set, 99

ForwardProgress, 23, 127, 147, 154, 159, 161, 162–166

examples, 163–164

and steps in scenario, 171

Fowler, Martin, 202

Fragmented use cases, 121

Fragments, 24, 127

combining of, into cohesive units, 215

merging into existing use cases, 210

relocating to other use cases, 205

Frequent flier alternatives, confusing for *Book Flight,* 184–185

Functional requirements, nonbehavioral information and, 134

G

Gabriel, Richard, 9

Generalization relationships, 174, 200
formal definitions in UML for, 178

Generalizations, 173, 181, 196

Generalizes relationship, 23

Get Paid for Car Accident use case, 128

Goal fragments, use cases written around, 121

Goal level, and actor list, 55

Goals
actor, 119
good characteristics of, 120
improper, 118
project, 80–81
and **SharedClearVision**, 96
and subgoals, 25
of use cases, 117
use cases written around, 97

Gold plating, preventing, 84

Gold Rush (Cockburn), 7

Graham, Ian, 13, 95

Grammatical errors, 65

Granularity, 142

Graphical user interface, 169
Group dynamics, 20
GUI. *See* Graphical user interface

H
"Happy day" scenario, 24
High-level use cases, 55, 108. *See also* Briefs
Hospital claim example, 215

I
If statements, 126
Implementation details, 91, 167
Improving Software Organizations, xix
Included use case, 195
Includes relationship, 23, 108, 111, 112, 173,
    175, 181, 195, 206
  and alternatives, 192
  Book Flight after *Upgrade Seat* alternative
    promoted via, 192
  extends relationship *versus*, 174
  formal definitions in UML for, 178
  interpretations for, 109
  misunderstanding, 177
  restriction on, 180
  Wings Over the World and, 178–180
Incremental complexity, 126
Inheritance relationships, 183
Internal stakeholders, and use case develop-
    ment process, 36, 37
InterruptsAsExtensions, 23, 51, 175, 182–189,
    196, 199, 206
  examples, 184–186
  and extension use cases, 175
  and UML, 186–187
Invalid actors, identifying, 88
Iterative approach, 76
Iterative development, and SpiralDevelopment,
    54
Iterative life cycle, xiii

J
Jacobson, Ivar, xiii, 1, 2, 23, 110
JAD. *See* Joint Application Development
Jargon, 39
Java, 167
Job flow engine, 37–38

Joint Application Development, 150
Joy of Cooking, The, 177

K
Kennedy, John F., 80
"Know your audience" rule, 175
Kraus, Andy, 33
Kubrick, Stanley, 90

L
Large groups
  facilitating: no design without representa-
    tion, 33
  and frequent checkpoints, 33
Large steps, 153
Large teams, problems with, 32
Large use cases, 119, 153
  breaking up, 216
Larman, Craig, 2
20,000 Leagues Under the Sea (Disney film),
    158
LeveledSteps, 4, 23, 127, 153–157, 162, 163,
    165, 167, 171, 172, 178, 184, 191, 199,
    206, 210
  examples, 154–157
  revised *Purchase Goods* use case with, 155
  scenarios with, 147
  steps of scenario written as, 158
Log Billing Information sub-use case,
    RedistributeTheWealth by creating, 207
Lower level included use cases, shared courses
    of action expressed with, 178
Lower level use cases
  creating, 206
  referencing from higher level use cases,
    110

M
Main success scenario, 203
Make a Phone Call use case, 212
Manifesto for Agile Software Development, xix
Marx Brothers, 38
McQueen, Steve, 86
MergeDroplets, 21, 50, 54, 175, 179, 198, 202,
    203, 205, 209–212, 216
  examples, 211–212

Metaphoric story
  and patterns, 16
  in **UserValuedTransactions** pattern sample,
    11–13
MGM, 38
Miscommunication, cost of, 159
Mission of organization, 81
Mistakes, 70
Mobile Dispatching System, vision statement
    for, 85
Model formality, 69
Movie-making, and customer consultation,
    38
MultipleForms, 20, 47, 50, 58–63, 75
  batch job distribution, 60
  examples, 60–63
  purchasing for a business, 61–63
Museum for Contemporary Asian Art
    (Centre A)
  and **EverUnfoldingStory**, 109–111
  use case model for, 111
Museum for Contemporary Asian Art
    (Vancouver, Canada), 92

N
Names and naming
  goal-based, 123
  of patterns, 14–15
  of primary actor goal, 120
  in **UserValuedTransactions** pattern sample,
    11
  value of, 122
NASA, 38, 80
National Software Quality Experiment (2000),
    xiii
Network Administrator
  Provision a Cross-Connect (Engineering-
    Centric Version), 41
  Provision a Cross-Connect (User-Friendly
    Version), 42
Network Element
  Provision a Cross-Connect (Engineering-
    Centric Version), 41
  Provision a Cross-Connect (User-Friendly
    Version), 42
Night at the Opera, A (film), 38

Normal Call use case, processing with multiple
    goals, 206
Nouns/noun phrases, for actors, 92

O
Object Constraint Language, 141
Object-oriented software, refactoring, 202
Object-oriented software development, use
    cases as element of, 2
OCL. *See* Object Constraint Language
"One-stop-shopping" rule, 177, 183, 199
On-line store
  long and tedious use case for, 154–155
  use case mixing large and small steps for,
    156
  use case with excessively large steps for, 155
OOPSLA 98 (Vancouver, Canada), xix
"Outer" reviews, purpose of, 66
Outlines, 49–50
Outsourcing, 72
Overlapping responsibilities, discovering, 91
Overspecification, 68, 69
Overstaffing, 32
Overviews, early, 49

P
Parallelism, 49
Partial use cases, 209
ParticipatingAudience, 20, 30, 32, 35–38, 40,
    43, 65, 76, 82, 139
  examples, 37–38
Passive voice, 160
  Withdraw Cash Description written in,
    160–161
Pattern Almanac, The (Rising), xix
Pattern Handbook, The (Rising), xix
Pattern Language, A (Alexander), 10
Pattern language heritage, xix
Pattern language organization, 19–23
  development patterns, 19
  editing, 21
  process, 20
  relationships, 23
  scenarios and steps, 22–23
  structural patterns, 21
  team, 20

Pattern language organization, (*cont.*)
  use cases, 22
  use case sets, 21–22
Pattern languages
  Alexander's work on, 6–7
  use of, 9–10
Patterns, xiv
  description of, 6–8
  development, 19
  for evaluating use cases, xiv
  structural, 19, 21
  use case set, 78
Patterns of Software (Gabriel), 9
Pay Tax use case, 177
Performance information, 127
Pharmacy receptionist example, 92–94
Pictures, in patterns, 15
Placeholders, 50
Pols, Andy, xix
Porting a system, 167
Post-conditions, 56
PreciseAndReadable, 20, 22, 59, 117, 120, 127,
    134, 138–141, 142, 158, 159, 167, 175
  examples, 140–141
Precision, 65, 139. *See also* Accuracy
Preconditions, 56
Preconditions sections, of use cases, 75
Problem statement
  and patterns, 16
  in **UserValuedTransactions** pattern sample,
    11
Process, 19, 45–76
  BreadthBeforeDepth, 48–51
  MultipleForms, 58–63
  and quality use cases, 20
  QuittingTime, 68–72
  SpiralDevelopment, 52–57
  trade-offs and collaborations, 75–76
  TwoTierReview, 64–67
  WritersLicense, 73–75
Process Normal Call use case, **Redistribute-
    TheWealth** in, to give use case a
    CompleteSingleGoal, 207
Process patterns, xvi
Productivity, improving, 49
Programmers, and reviews, 66

Project priorities, incremental approach based
    on, 50
Projects
  differing needs of, 58
  slippage in, 74
PromotedAlternative, 23, 51, 127, 174,
    190–196, 199, 206
  examples, 191–196
  and extensions, 175
  and UML, 195–196
  Engineering-Centric Version, 41
  User-Friendly Version, 42
Proxy (pseudo actor), 106
Purchase Goods use case
  with excessively large steps, 155
  revised, 155–157
  revised, with leveled steps, 155
  with unleveled steps, 154
Purchase Property use case, 177
Purchasing for a business, 61–63

Q
Quality assurance group, and use cases, 37
Queues, 44
QuittingTime, 20, 47, 50, 54, 66, 68–72, 73–74,
    76, 140, 202
  examples, 71–72
  use cases passing test for, 74

R
Railway signaling, automated, 84
RAPIER
  failure codes, 152
  reservation system, 145–146
Ratliff, Rick, xix, 48, 167
Rawsthorne, Dan, xx, 51, 57, 89, 111–113, 175,
    186–187, 195–196, 198–200
Readability, verifying, 65
Reading, and consistent writing style, 73
Receive Customer use case, 93
  with actor's role defined as Receptionist, 94
RedistributeTheWealth, 21, 50, 175, 191, 202,
    203, 204–208, 210, 216
  by creating *Log Billing Information* sub-use
    case, 207
  examples, 206–208

in *Process Normal Call,* to give a use case a **CompleteSingleGoal**, 207
and scope of use case, 178
Redundancy
  eliminating, 180, 196
  and inconsistencies in model, 177
Redundant behavior, 90
Refactoring (Fowler), 202
Register for Courses (Use Case with Extensions), 24–25
Relationships, and use cases, 23. *See also* Extends relationship; Includes relationship
Release schedules, 2
Reliability, and high-quality system, 83
Representative democracy, 64
Request Upgrade use case
  with forward progress, 164
  with steps diverting forward, 164
Requirements
  high cost of mistakes, 53
  improving definition of, xiii
  source of errors in models, 177
  specifications, 68, 202
  volatility of, 53
Requirements gathering, 53
  as process of discovery, 49
  prolonging, 69
Reserve Flight, brief for, 56
Reserve Flight Segments use case, 112–113, 145–146, 152
Reuse, and large use cases, 119
Reviewers, 33
Reviewing, 149
Reviews, 37, 64–66
  effective, 64
  two types of, 65
Rising, Linda, xix, 9
Risk factors, delaying discovery of, 52
Robust design, and variations, 130

S
Scalability, and high-quality system, 83
ScenarioPlusFragments, 50, 117, 120, 125–128, 133, 142, 153, 163, 171, 176, 182, 183, 190, 191, 196, 198

and goals in use cases, 22
  examples, 128
  use cases written as, 129
  and variations, 131
Scenarios, 19, 22–23, 117, 147
  balanced, 171
  clear steps in, 162
  mixing levels of detail in, 153
  number of steps in, 154
  organizing steps in, 171
Scope creep, and poorly defined boundaries, 87
Screen designs, 127
Sellers, Peter, 90
Sentence fragments, 5
Sequential life cycle, xiii
Serpent and the Rainbow, The (film), 73
Services, sets of, 92
SharedClearVision, xv, 11, 12, 15, 17, 31, 48, 80–85, 90, 95
  and **EverUnfoldingStory**, 113
  examples, 82–85
  lack of, 82
  and services identification, 97
  and system goals, 96
  and use case sets, 21
  of use case writers, 78
  and user identification, 92
  VisibleBoundary and limits/support of, 86
Slippage, 74
Small steps, 153
Small use cases, 119, 153, 210
SmallWritingTeam, 20, 30, 31–34, 35, 38, 39, 40, 43, 65
  and audience participation, 38
  examples, 33–34
  vision created by, 82
Software for Use (Constantine and Lockwood), 37, 43
Software patterns, benefits of, 123
Solution
  of pattern, 18
  in **UserValuedTransactions** pattern sample, 13–14
Specialization relationships, 186

Spelling errors, 65
SpiralDevelopment, 20, 47, 50, 52–57, 64, 96
    BreadthBeforeDepth coupled with, 76
    examples, 54–57
    and regular assessments of use cases, 66
    and roles of actors, 92
    and system boundary, 87
    and UML models, 57
    and use case diagrams, 89
Stacks, 44
Stakeholders, 119
    competing visions of, 81
    and good specifications, 141
    input of, 119
    and overspecification, 69
    and system boundaries, 86
    and use case goals, 204
    and use case readability, 138
    use cases understood by, 173
    and useful systems, 90
    vested interest in use cases by, 65
Standish Group, xiii
Star Trek (television series), 162
Statement of purpose, 81
Step patterns, 147
Steps, 22–23
    behavior put into, 162
    clear and succinct, 162
    conditions met by, 171
    excessively small and large, 153
    organizing in scenarios, 171
    Purchase Goods use case with excessively large, 155
    and repeated diversions, 182
    writing, 158
Stockholder meetings, 35
Stories
    good, 145–147
    quality, 147
    variations, 126
Structural patterns, 2–3, 19, 21
Style guides, 74
Subfunction goals, 25
Subfunction Level, of use case, 104
Subgoals, 25

Subject matter experts
    narrow focus of, 91
    and small use cases, 120
Subsets, of briefs, 56, 57
Sub-use cases, 207
Success scenarios
    alternatives to, 125
    identifying, 127
SuD. *See* System under discussion
Summary goals, 25
Summary Level, of use case, 104
Supplementary specifications, superfluous fragments relocated to, 206
Surface and Dive technique, 56
Surviving Object-Oriented Projects, xix
System-focused use cases, 121
Systems
    deficient, 95
    and detectable conditions, 148
    useful, 90–91
System's scope, documenting interactions outside of, 89
System under discussion, 24, 25

T
Tablature (guitar), 138
TBDs. *See* To Be Determined issues
Teams, 20, 29–44
    and BalancedTeam, 39–42
    composition of, 30
    developers and end users on, 40
    and differing amounts of formality, 58–59
    organization of, 19, 30
    and ParticipatingAudience, 35–38
    size of, and use case quality, 30
    SmallWritingTeams, 31–34
    trade-offs and collaborations, 43–44
    and well-written use cases, 26–27
Technical errors, 65
Technological details, and increased costs in reading/writing use cases, 168
Technology, volatility of, 168
Technology details, in use cases, 152
TechnologyNeutral, 4, 23, 133, 134–135, 140, 161, 167–171, 200, 210
    and *Access ATM* use case, 161

examples, 169–171
and scenarios/steps, 147
and steps, 154
Technology vision, and corporate vision, 83
Telephone calls, set of small use cases for placing, 211
Templates, 50, 58, 59, 74, 127
Terminators, in context diagrams, 88
Testers, 2
Time pressures, 80, 91
Titles, for use cases, 117
TL1 code, 42
To Be Determined issues, 134
Traceability, 198
Trace relationship, 111–112
Trainers, 37
Trust, 72
TwoTierReview, 8, 20, 33, 37, 47, 54, 64–67, 73, 76
examples, 66–67

U
UML. *See* Unified Modeling Language
UML extension points, and extension use cases, 187–189
UML models
and **EverUnfoldingStory**, 111
and **SpiralDevelopment**, 57
and **VisibleBoundary**, 89
Unbalanced teams, 30
Unified Modeling Language, xvii–xviii, 173, 174, 175, 178
and **BreadthBeforeDepth**, 51
and **CaptureTheAlternative**, 197
and **CommonSubBehavior**, 180–181
deployment diagram in, 88
and **InterruptsAsExtensions**, 186–187
and **PromotedAlternative**, 195–196
Unleveled steps, *Purchase Goods* use case with, 154
Update Customer use case, and mortgage origination system, 100
Upgrade Seat, as extending use case, 195
Upgrade Seat alternative
Book Flight after promotion of, via extends, 194

Book Flight use case after promotion of, via includes, 192
dominates *Book Flight* use case, 191–192
as separate use case, 193
U.S. Department of Defense, xiii
Usability, formality favored over, 174
"Use Case Blue" (Kraus), 33
Use case development process, 53
customers and internal stakeholders involved with, 36
customers involved in, 43
Use case diagrams, styles for, xviii
Use case forms, standard, 59
Use case horrors
Access ATM description with technology-specific steps, 161
Book Flight with business rules, 135
Claim Insurance not making sufficient forward progress, 165
confusing frequent flier alternatives for *Book Flight,* 184–185
Director-style *Book Flight* use case with incorrectly applied includes relationship, 178–179
Get Paid for Car Accident, 128
mixing large and small steps in use case, 156
naming horrors, 123–124
Process Normal Call use case with multiple goals, 206–207
Provision a Cross-Connect (Engineering-Centric Version), 40
Purchase Goods use case with excessively large steps, 155
Purchase Goods use case with unleveled steps, 154
Register for Course, 3
Request Upgrade with steps diverting **ForwardProgress**, 164
set of small use cases for placing telephone call, 211
supplementary requirements anchored by, 136–137
technology-dependent *File Accident Claim* use case, 169
thirty-page *Book Flight* use case, 105

Use case horrors (*cont.*)
　　Withdraw Cash description without
　　　ActorIntentAccomplished, 159
　　Withdraw Cash description written in
　　　passive voice, 160
Use case models, 142
　　formalism in, 183
　　UML and formalism in, 178
Use case names, good, 124
Use case pattern form
　　context, 11, 15
　　description of, 10–18
　　examples, 11, 18
　　forces affecting the problem, 11, 16–17
　　metaphoric story, 11, 16
　　names, 10, 14–15
　　pictures, 10, 15
　　problem statement, 11, 16
　　solution, 11, 18
　　stepping through sample pattern, 11–14
Use case pattern languages, reasons for, 5–6
Use case relationships, 19, 173–200
　　CapturedAbstraction, 198–200
　　CommonSubBehavior, 176–181
　　InterruptsAsExtensions, 182–189
　　PromotedAlternative, 190–196
　　trade-offs and collaborations, 196–197
Use cases, xiii, xvi, 19, 22, 115–143. *See also*
　　　Editing existing use cases; Examples
　　adorning, 117
　　Adornments, 133–137
　　alternatives and cluttering of, 190
　　alternatives for, 129
　　balanced, 68, 171
　　brief tutorial on writing, 23–27
　　Buy something (Casual Version), 61
　　Buy something (Fully Dressed Version),
　　　61–63
　　capturing alternatives/failures handled in,
　　　131
　　and changes, 96
　　cleaning up and removing, 213–215
　　clear, succinct steps in, 162
　　complete, 70
　　CompleteSingleGoal, 118–121
　　complex, 190

complex alternatives and cluttering of, 198
complicated and imprecise, 138
correct, precise and readable, 26–27
creating lower level, 206
creating new, 205
crisscrossing structure revealed with, 126
developing in iterative, breadth-first
　　manner, 53
different detail levels in, 102
effective, 149
example of poorly written, 3
excessive detail in, 205
ExhaustiveAlternatives, 129–132
expense of adding, 205
extension-handling behavior for, 54
fragmented, 121
goal levels, 104
groups with vested interest in set of, 35–36
high-level, 55
high-quality, 75–76
large, 119, 153
levels of, 102–103
localizing closely related behavior into, 216
localizing information about features in, 209
long, 204
main scenario for well-written, 5–6
merging, 210
minimizing number of, 210
necessary information in, 95
nonfunctional requirements in, 133, 134
organizing, 113
outlines for, 50
overviews of, 49, 50
partial, 209
partitioning, 177, 190
patterns for evaluation of, xv
PreciseAndReadable, 138–141
preconditions sections of, 75
purpose of, 74, 133–134
quality, 158, 215
readability of, 138, 139
readable and comprehensible, 117
reasons for using, 1–2
relocating fragments to, 205
reviewing, 64–66
ScenarioPlusFragments, 125–128

selecting format for, 59
signs of quality in, 78
small, 119, 153, 210
stability of, 96
stopping development of, 70
story lines in, 117
and style issues, 73
technology details in, 152
and telling of good stories, 2–5
trade-offs and collaborations, 142–143
unnecessary, 51
and value-added services, 96
value to business shown by, 103
VerbPhraseName, 122–124
for workstation monitor server, 60–61
and "writer's license," 74
writing in technology-neutral manner, 168
Use case sets, 19, 21–22, 77–114
ClearCastOfCharacters, 90–94
and context diagrams, 88
EverUnfoldingStory, 102–113
forms-based, 99
organization in, 103
SharedClearVision, 80–85
trade-offs and collaborations, 113–114
UserValuedTransactions, 95–101
VisibleBoundary, 86–89
Use case structure, levels of, 21
Use case template, additional fields in, 134
Useful services, identifying, 96
User Goal Level, of use case, 104
User interface designers, 2
User-interface details, 3, 134
User-interface navigation, 136
User-interface sketches, 134
Users. *See also* Audience; Customers
services tied to, 91
and useful systems, 90
UserValuedTransactions, 8, 15, 16, 17, 25, 50,
79, 95–101, 102, 116, 131, 142, 168, 203,
209, 213, 214
and *Book Flight* use case, 108
and **EverUnfoldingStory**, 114
examples, 98–101
stepping through, 11–14
and system analysis, 92

and use case sets, 22
and vision, 82
for Wings Over the World, 98–99

V
Value-added services, 12, 96
Variations
capturing, 131
having information about, 130–131
identifying, 130
Vehicle Control Center (VCC), 84
VerbPhraseName, 7, 22, 51, 122–124, 186, 196,
206
for each use case, 50
examples, 123–124
for primary actor goal, 120
for use cases, 117, 142
Verbs, 159
Verne, Jules, 158
Vietnam War, 118
VisibleBoundary, 86–89
and **EverUnfoldingStory**, 113
examples, 88–89
and project's vision and scope, 79, 82
and system scope, 92
and UML models, 89
and use case sets, 21
Vision
changes to, 82
consistency in, 82
of stakeholders, 81
Vision statements
for Automated Railway Signaling System, 84
items included in, 81–82
for Mobile Dispatching System, 85
for Wings Over the World, 83, 98

W
Walters, Rusty, 3
"Waterfall" life cycle, xiii, 53
Web site, use cases discussion at, 27
Whiteboard drawings, 51
Wilkes, Maurice, 176
Wings Over the World, xvi, xvii, 18, 152
actor list (sample) for, 55
with **Adornments**, 135–137

Wings Over the World (*cont.*)
    and avoiding form-focus, 99–100
    briefs for *Reserve Flight* and *Book Flight,* 56
    context diagrams for, 88–89
    discussion with chief architect at, 115–116
    and editing existing use cases, 201–202
    examples, 54–57, 66–67, 71–72, 75,
       191–195, 199–200
    and extensions, 184–187
    and goals, 121
    initial conversation with CIO of, 45–46
    precise but unreadable example, 141
    readable but imprecise example, 140
    red-eye flight to, 77–78
    and *Reserve Flight Segment* use case,
       145–146
    and **UserValuedTransactions**, 98–99
    vision statement for, 83, 98
    winning contract for, 29
Withdraw Cash
    description without **ActorIntent-**
      Accomplished, 159–160
    description written in passive voice, 160
    improving description with **ActorIntent-**
      Accomplished, 160
    use case, 151
Workstation monitor server, use case for,
    60
WritersLicense, 20, 47, 70, 73–75, 76
    examples, 75
Writing, 149
    consistent style of, 73
    at different levels, 103
    and "know your audience" rule, 139
    quality use cases, 158
    reviews of, 64
    steps, 159
    in technology-neutral manner, 168
Writing Effective Use Cases (Cockburn), xiv, xv,
    xix, 3, 25–26, 27, 61, 104

X
XML, 44
XP, 71

The Agile Software Development Series

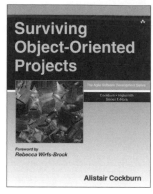

0201498340

0201702258

0201758202

0201699699

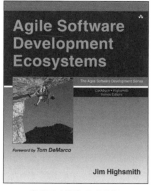

0201760436

0201721848

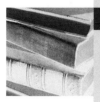

Development Patterns

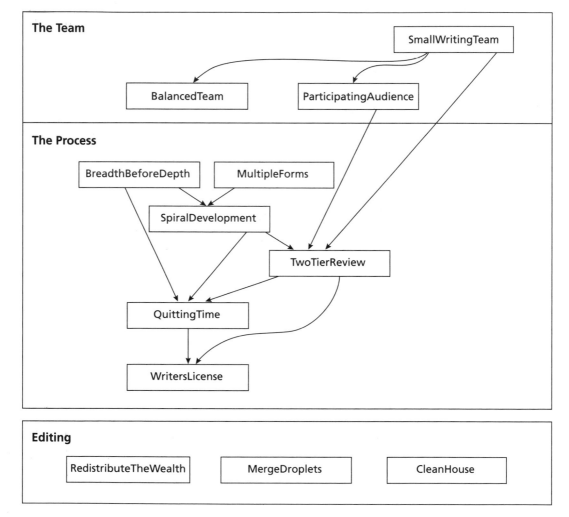